William A. Reed

THE FOUR SIDES

The transformation of a coach and the legacy of a principal

NEBRASKA PRINTING CENTER

Layout and Design by Jesse Hodges, Nebraska Printing Center

The University of Central High School

The name was for play but the feeling was for real

The 3Side West

Photo by Bryan Bell

Central after dark, gazing from the windows of Joslyn Art Museum

Established on a State Capitol Site 1870

Dick Holland

He was smart enough to be among the first to invest with Warren Buffett in a little venture called Berkshire Hathaway. Now his investments are in people. If you've never met a great man here's your chance. Dick Holland is a man of great wealth but it has nothing to do with money. He is rich in character, attitude and personality. Never have I seen a man with so much care about so many that have so little. That four letter word, c-a-r-e defines his greatness and from that derives his legacy. I will always treasure the days I spent with him and I will always take pride in him being the first person ever to read this book.

-William A. Reed

~ Foreword ~

This is a fascinating book written by a successful high school football coach. It is not a recitation of his successes on the field, but a memorial to his growth as an individual in his relationship with Central High's principal, Dr. G.E. Moller. It is captivating reading and leaves you wanting to hear more details. I began to read it about 3:00 p.m. in the afternoon and finished about 7:30 p.m. because I couldn't put it down (I am a Central grad). But let all who read it try to picture how ideas conflict between two persons both of whom want the very best for their students. It is a tribute to read in this recitation of how William grew as a person.

-Richard D. Holland.... Central High Class of 1939

William A. Reed: The Four Sides
Copyright © 2015

Printed and Published by Nebraska Printing Center
2145 North Cotner Blvd., Lincoln, Nebraska 68505

Cover photo property of Brad Williams Photography

The Omaha Central night picture; created by Bryan Bell with all rights to William A. Reed

All quotes marked "WRO"; sole original property of William A. Reed and governed by censored usage

Contract Computer Services

All pictures marked OB; indicates derived from the Central OBooks and protected by the Central High School Foundation

All blueprints, renderings and landscaping photos; property of the Omaha Public Schools

"The Letter"; property of Doctor G.E. Moller, Omaha, Nebraska

Baton Rouge, Louisiana pictures property of Revolutions 21's Blog For The People

Resources and Information

Special thanks to:

- Omaha Central High School Foundation

- Brad Williams Photography

- Paul Bryant-President at Leadership Institution for Urban Education

- Robyn G. Hubbard–Central High Foundation

- Jim Wigton-Omaha Central High Historian

- The Omaha Public Schools

- Bryan Bell-Bell Photography

- Dr. Jerry Bartee-Associate Superintendent OPS

- Mr. Dan Daly-former Omaha Central English Department Head

- Scott Stewart-Nebraska Printing

- Steve Marantz-Author

- The Central High OBooks 1904-1990

Acknowledgements

• When I first decided to write this book I sat down with one of my closest friends, **Dr. Jerry Bartee**, Associate Superintendent of the Omaha Public Schools. At the time I wasn't sure if I should write it or not. When I asked his opinion his words were passionately strong; "absolutely, go for it!" Later he would help me in everything I needed, giving me a great inspiration that spelled out, "you can do it!" Thanks Jerry.

• To all the **family and friends** who have encouraged and supported the writing of this book, I thank you. Without you, all of you, its completion would not have been possible.

• Special and personal thanks to **Dick Holland** whose initial advice and continued praise and opinions motivated me to finish this book with pride and confidence.

• Thanks to **Linda Santo**, who offered her support from day one. Your transcriptions, content, advice and preliminary editing helped get the book off on the right foot. Thanks for being there all the times you could.

• As I started the book I made a call to **Steve Marantz**, author of the Omaha Central book, The Rhythm Boys. Steve helped me with order and set-up and some very pertinent advice, like getting an interview with Doc Moller would be crucial to the process!

• Omaha Central just might boast the strongest high school alumni foundation in the midwest and I can't thank **Dr. Keith Bigsby** and Executive Director **Michelle Roberts** enough for their support and offer of access to the foundation's historic bank of facts and resources. Special thanks to **Dan Daly** for lending me his inherent knowledge of Central years past.

• Outside of my home, my daughter's home has been grand central station for this book...no pun intended! **Kalisha Reed** has transcribed, edited, tracked down resources and advice, provided room, board and utilities, not to mention the use of her computer and all else that I've ever needed. She has given great time and effort to this book and I thank her from the top of my heart.

• When I received a call in Belize it signaled my need to come home. That single call eight years before was the root of this writing. I'd like to thank **Carol Heinke McBride** for the call and for subsequently typing the hand written letter that is the main character in this book. Also, thanks for personally mailing it to Doc, retrieving it eight years later and all the help you've given since then.

• Because I lack the greatest grammar skills, it is a Godsend to have an English teacher in the family. **Marcie Reed Muhammad**, thank you for all the suggestions on grammar, sentence structuring and recommendations on content. Thanks for always being on the other end of the phone when I needed questions answered on the fly.

• When you write a book, it's nice to have someone willing to print it. **Scott Stewart** is a good person and I'd like to thank him and his company, Nebraska Printing Center for their tireless support.

• Finally I received so much support from my good friend, WOWT-6 TV Sportscaster, **Dave Webber**. Dave was so supportive throughout the year so I just had to send him a very heartfelt Christmas card. He called me two days after Christmas sobbing somberly. He said, "William I got your card and it made me cry man"... I was touched and started tearing up myself. I said, "Dave you know how I feel, you don't have to cry. He said, "No, it isn't that. When I was opening it I got a paper cut and it's hurting like hell man!" With that we both burst into laughter! I handed Dave a copy of this book one Sunday morning, while sitting in the Marilyn Monroe booth at Shirley's Diner in Millard Nebraska. He turned a few pages and said, how do you do it, then looked at me and laughed. When he laughed it made me laugh! So I'd like to thank my good friend Dave Webber for always helping me and so many others... simply to laugh!

Mr. Thomas Lee Harvey

This book is written with remembrance of a great educator. Thomas Lee Harvey was the former Associate Superintendent of the Omaha Public Schools and my brother-in- law. He is the man most responsible for bringing me to Nebraska and then helping me to stay. He was a doer and a giver and he will be sorely missed. May the skies of Houston, Texas forever warm your soul. Thanks for everything... love you man.

In Loving Memory

THE FOUR SIDES
~ Table of Contents ~

Prologue

Back in Washington D.C. on the register of historic places is a site in Nebraska with coordinates 41° 15' 38" (north), 95° 56' 37" (west). During the time between 1900 and 1912 a German born architect by the name of John Latenser Sr. designed a masterpiece within this corridor that has withstood the movement of time. It started with an existing structure, Mr. Latenser then created a new structure adjacent to its front. Later he would add two more buildings adjacent to its right side (south) and the backside (west). In the 12th year of his project he created a building adjacent to the left side (north), bonding the new buildings, east to west. Now the four distinct buildings were all connected and fully incased the original one. Once the four sides were completed the original building was torn down leaving an empty space inside. This empty space eventually evolved into a courtyard that connected each of John Latenser's four masterpiece structures.

The project, completed in 1912, remains since one of the oldest and most prestigious creations in the state of Nebraska. It was built to serve mankind in a particular and prideful manner. Its original intent was to help society. More than 100 years later it is still fulfilling that goal. The creation has produced many rare treasures in the form of people. These human treasures have since multiplied and helped to change the world. Yet, even within all its wonders of such a bountiful history and glorious reputation, the structure has forever remained open to any who seek to better themselves. Its name is Omaha Central High School!

This four sided, historic place was created on a plot of land once chosen to represent a state. Over the years each building eventually declared its own independence, yet remained recognized as a part of the whole. Later, they would come to be referred to as sides. Specifically in the order of their creation and direction; the 1side (east), the 2side (south), the 3side (west) and the 4side (north). Together, these four sides have been framed by four cohesive embodiments; Unity, Strength, Purpose and Determination. This fusion of quality and excellence has since shaped and molded some of the great people of our time; doctors, lawyers, educators, actors, athletes, billionaire philanthropist, business people, Nobel Prize winners, war heroes and a host of other select prodigies.

"Since 1870, the consistent pattern of production within these four buildings has led to a tradition and reputation that pays homage to the great American educational process. Through the years Omaha Central High has served as a connected series of unbiased vehicles, offering vast opportunities for advanced possibilities down the road to success." (W.R.O.)

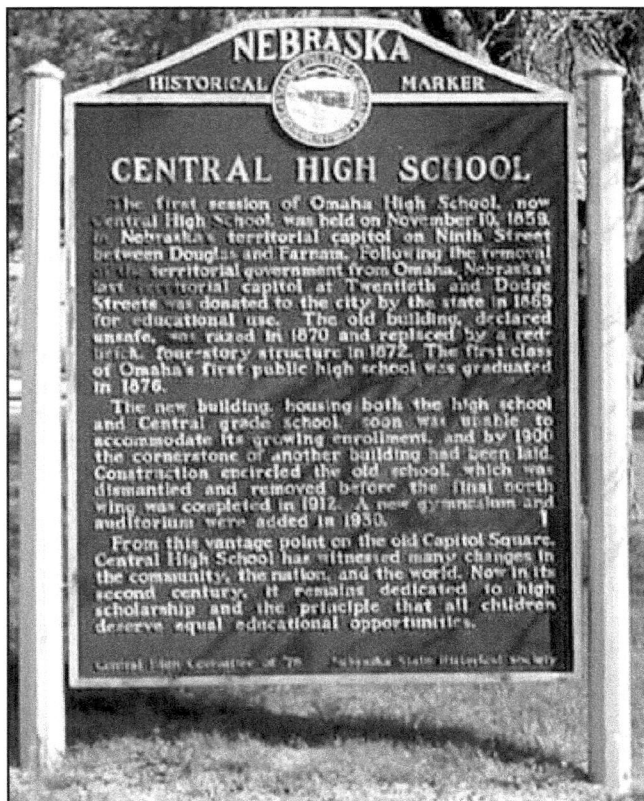

Preface

This is a story that began in 1979 around and through the confines of Omaha Central High School, amidst adversity, demands and sometimes heated rhetoric. It then began again near the quaint little Cedar Hills Golf Course with an embrace of sincerity, respect and tearful acknowledgement. There is four sides to the building where it all happened, four sides to my life, and four sides to the story that I am about to tell.

They say that there is a gift in sharing, and this book is written to share with you a heartfelt letter. A letter that poured out one crisp cold November day in 2003. It is written from me to Dr. G.E. Moller and it speaks of appreciation, acceptance and overdue gratitude. The letter praises a life, honors a life and helped one also. It praises the life and enthusiastic greatness of one Ben Hofmeister, it honors the life of a dedicated leader, Dr. Gaylord E. Moller, and it helped the life of a once lost coach, just by writing it.

What is this letter? Why was it written to Doc? Why was it written by me and how was it inspired by Ben? The answers to these questions are hidden deep within four distinct walls inside a complex menagerie that spans nearly a quarter century. They are deeply rooted answers discovered inside a letter, Doc, me and Ben. Four distinct stories, told from four exclusive perspectives, all traced back to an origin that formulated within the parameters of Omaha Central High School. One story began in a housing project inside the jaws of 1950's Louisiana; while the other was weaving through the plains of western Nebraska. A chance encounter in Omaha, Nebraska would bring them together, until a puzzling request for transfer would cut them apart. Separated for nearly a decade, one would vacate an educational kingdom after 32 years, while the other created his own inside the world of golf. There they would find each other again at the dawn of a new century. It was the year 2000, the new millennium came with much joy but by the third month it also brought much sorrow, grief and unspeakable pain. A pain that would send one to explore the paradise of the Caribbean, while the other retired to grandpa land. They were disconnected again, before finally permanently bonding forever at a peaceful plot of Evergreen land called H-West.

There must have been a reason that our paths obviously crossed.
I think God's plan was that we needed to learn something from one another.

In 1979, as a teacher/coach in the Omaha, Nebraska Public School system, I was transferred to Omaha Central High School. That transfer would eventually bring me face to face with one Doctor G.E. Moller. Though I would find great success in the coaching box, he would demand that my triumphs be in all other facets of life as well. He would dog me through the years, briefly leaving me with an impression of wrongful persecution. I only found out later that his was a push for perfection and an expectation that I become someone better than I had ever been before. By the time I fully understood his motives I was far removed from the hallways of Central High. However, after a time, through painful losses and chance encounters we would eventually meet again. There, on a dark and dreary day on the front end of a Nebraska November, I would acknowledge his influence and the impact he had made by writing him a letter. Those two pages would spell out an invisible pattern of the things he had taught me and the indelible mark he forever left on my life.

From the beginning he taught me how to thrive at living.
In the end I taught him how to survive after dying. (W.R.O.)

A Toast to Doc

~For Doc~
So here's to all the students, that turned into Central grads
Here's to the futures that made them moms and dads.
Here's to the teachers, who taught them all so much
Here's to the school that keeps us all in touch.
Here's to the laughter, Here's to the tears
Here's to the principal and 27 years.
A letter of thanks for saving a life
Words to praise man & wife.
It's a book about you
and me back then,
and about golf
Jackson
And
Ben.
Enjoy!
William William William

A journey to a bridge called better and a tribute to the man who helped me cross it

"We were as different as night and day. I was black from the Louisiana projects. He was white from many places, including the Nebraska plains. We would meet in 1979 as coach and principal and settle our differences in the hallways of Nebraska's most productive high school. It was a battle of wills...
THANK GOD HE WON!

The

1One Side

"In the Beginning"

The 1Side was the first of the new four-sided structure and was completed in 1901. It was molded onto the front of the original building and faced east towards 20th Street.

The
Awesome
Omaha Central

Under the big top, the life and times within the four sides

It was the year 1912 in Omaha, Nebraska. At the time the school at 124 North 20th Street was named Omaha High School. Within the school there was a commercial department that was big enough to make it two high schools in one. But now a brand new building had been built, by John Latenser. After the completion of the new building the board of education decided to separate the two. The commercial department was moved to a new location and upon moving was renamed the Omaha High School of Commerce. The main school kept the name of Omaha High. With the two schools both having Omaha High in their title the word "central" was added to identify the one housed in the new building. Thus, the name Omaha Central High School was born.

In 1923 the Omaha High School of Commerce found its own home, at 30th & Cuming Street and took on a completely new name. That new name was Omaha Technical High School. The Tech High building, though still standing, has since become the public school's administrative headquarters, while the old Omaha High, that became Omaha Central, has remained constant in its original stature. Unique, prestigious and tradition rich, it is still Nebraska's finest high school!

Chapter 1

COMING TO
OMAHA CENTRAL
My journey to the eagle's nest

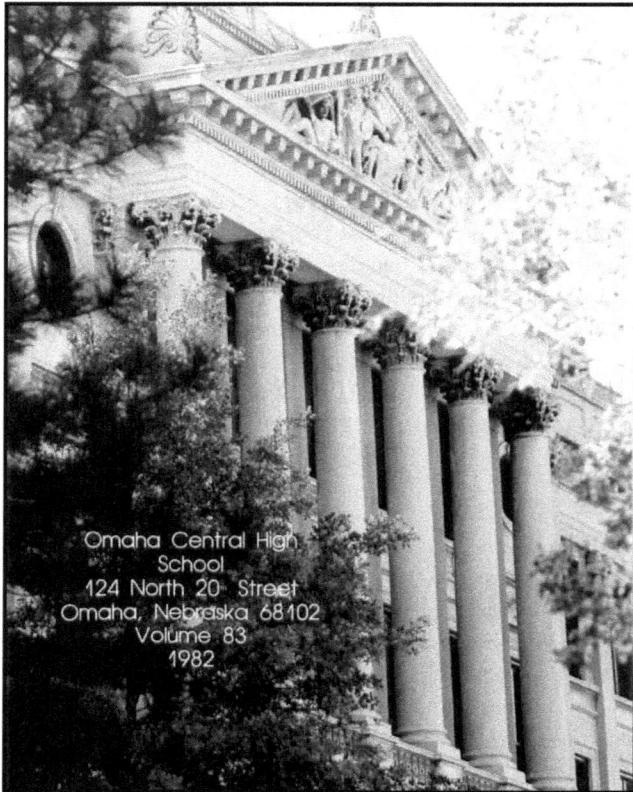

OB

A Migration from the South

There has never been a school like Omaha Central. There has never been a principal like Gaylord Moller. There has never been a coach like William Reed and there was never a time like the 1980's when all came together. It was the perfect storm, a tale worthy of telling. It is a story about truth, because the truth is the easiest thing to remember, and the truth shall set us free!

Henry Fonda, Peter Kiewit, Dick Holland, Jack Lewis, Buffet and Buffet, Sayers and Sayers, Fous, Offutt, Station, Heeger, Zorinsky, Green and the list goes on and on. It's no secret that some of the great names in our nation's history hail from Omaha Central High School. I think it's safe to say that if you polled anyone from the group of more than 100 staff members of Omaha Central during the 1980's, I'm sure you would find nearly 100% would not be surprised that a book was being written about the days behind the walls of this great school. Neither would they be surprised that Dr. Gaylord Moller was its main character, since he is the longest tenured principal in the school's history (27 years), dating back to its first principal in 1870. No, neither of these scenarios would be alarming, but if you took a poll of that same group as to which staff member from that time would be writing such a book, William Reed would be last on every single list! In fact, that truth is what places this unlikely story into legitimate reality. This brings me to an old saying that reads; ***Sometimes the people who no one imagines anything of, does things that no one can imagine.***

There is a good chance that throughout the 1980's Doc Moller disciplined no teacher more so than he did me, and I resented that discipline from day one. From the beginning, Doc and I were like oil and water, two substances that don't mix well. He was like water, with its ingested intent to sustain life. While I, like oil was recommended for change every 3,000 miles. From the start, I tugged and scratched to break his grip on my life at Central. Now, I search my brain every day trying to remember some of the great lessons he taught me. It took a long time for me to ***get it***, but you have to know Doc to learn from him. Once I understood, I realized that what he tried to do for my life was more than helping a teacher, it was akin to developing a man. That development started in 1979 in a downtown high school in Omaha Nebraska that had begun changing lives like ours way back in the 1800's.

The school made history in 1901 with the creation of an innovative new building which by 1912 was multiplied times four. Through the years Omaha Central became known for its trail blazing exploits. For instance, back in the 1920's radio was just hitting its stride and just like today, Central High School was right in step. Would you believe that the school on the hill created its own radio station and was broadcasting in a 100 mile radius? KFCZ radio was one of the first of its kind on the airwaves. At one point it challenged even the largest of the midwest stations back then, including the famed Woodmen Of The World backed, WOAW. Just think, even back in the roaring twenties Central High was on the cutting edge of progress and its voice was heard a hundred miles away. A radio station, in a high school, in the 1920's? Now that's awesome! But Central has always been out front and continues to be into the twenty-first century.

My journey to Omaha Central was a long and winding road and just as improbable as a high school with a 100 mile radius radio frequency in the 1920's. It began in Monroe, Louisiana and ended nine years later upon my arrival at 124 North 20th street in Omaha Nebraska. It was a journey like many had taken before me. One that offered a new kind of hope and opportunity that may never have been possible from whence we came. All I knew about Omaha, Nebraska before I came was that it was the place where Dorothy and the wizard were headed when last I saw them leaving Oz! Yes, Omaha was a mystery, but it had to be better than where I was. In fact, in the year that I left Louisiana bound for Omaha, there was only one state in America still holding to "*labeling blood*" yes, the one I was leaving! Of all the foolish and degrading bigotries that surrounded me in the Jim Crow South, none bothered me more than the practice of labeling blood. So, when I saw a road leading out of town, out of state and out of the south, the only word that

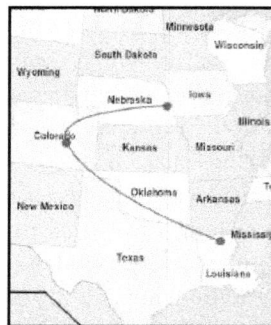

4

mattered to me was "out", regardless of where it carried me.

From 1965 to around 1975 there seemed to be a strong push by the Omaha Public Schools to add to its list of black educators. One of the best places to maximize their efforts were the fertile grounds of the historic all black colleges in the south. Right around that time there were many who had grown up in the throngs of a slow changing south, who couldn't wait to leave their native states. It was during this span of about ten years that the changing seasons told the birds of winter to fly south and many young, black, would be educators passed them as they headed north. The difference was that the birds would return in the spring while the educators would build permanent nests in their new places up north and become visitors to the old southern states they once called home. That migration would bring me and several others like me to the city of Omaha. It would be the beginning of the journey that would eventually take me to the man and school that would change my life's path forever.

I recalled back then that most of us, particularly the males came with backgrounds and people skills that were highly suited for coaching. I think because back in the south one of the few things a black person could be widely respected for by all manner of people was athletic ability. To a certain degree at certain times that respect even over rode those ridiculous rules of non-engagement that separated us based on race. This knowledge of athletic achievement in exchange for respect was derived through upbringings and we all came with ambitions that suited our prior existence.

The truth was, that any one of us from that migration, particularly the males, would have been totally satisfied with becoming a head high school coach in a system like the Omaha Public Schools. However, opportunities of securing administrative positions, which offered more control and more money was a lure that changed the goals of just about everyone. These opportunities became very real, when a just and fair system began filling positions with deserving men and women of color. For me it was a time of unimaginable change and I was awed by what I was witnessing. It would be hard to comprehend today, but before my arrival in Omaha I had never seen a situation where black and white individuals worked equally side by side within an educational setting. Nor had I ever witnessed or heard about a white teacher teaching black students or vice versa. This was a strange new place and I could hardly believe the interactivity between the races. This was all foreign to me but man was it refreshing to see. When it all hit me I realized that the sixties had just ended and down in Louisiana I had been openly classified as a *minority* all my life. That classification had always made me seem small but in Nebraska, the word took on a different meaning. *Here minorities are the people that didn't care for the beloved Cornhusker football team.* What a deal! I loved my new home state and I jumped quickly into the majority society for the first time in my life. And though I didn't know what the hell it meant, it wasn't long before I was shouting from the roof tops "GO BIG RED!"

I grew up in a city and state during the 1960's where I had never truly met one white person in my life, not one! I recall my maiden voyage to Nebraska, I had changed planes in Denver, Colorado and was the only black person on board as we headed to Omaha. I wondered, "am I headed to the right place?" I only had six dollars to my name but there were five northeast Louisiana friends that I had grown up with, all waiting to help in my transition, and they all worked in the Omaha Public School System. When the plane finally landed and my luggage wound its way around the carousel at Eppley Air Field it hit me. I had survived the 60's, escaped from Louisiana at the onset of the 70's, and surfaced in Nebraska. Once I settled into my new state and new life I ran into another white that I had never met... "SNOW". I had come to Nebraska on a mild August day, but by the first week of October there were six inches of snow on the ground. It was 1970 and one can only imagine my awkwardness, because where I'd come from they didn't even show snow on the TV weather maps! I felt nothing could ever send me back down south, but those four days toward the end of the first week of October almost did.

When the snow subsided, I burst into my new life and hit the ground running. After spending one year at Omaha Tech Junior High School, I was assigned to the Benson High "feeder" school, Monroe Junior High. there I spent four years, three as head football coach. At Monroe I met the best of people and reached a pinnacle of success that accelerated my life and bolstered my confidence. We lost only one football game during all the years I coached there. It was a feat that may seem small to some, but for me and where I'd come from, it was the greatest accomplishment I could have ever imagined. I actually felt important for the very first time in my 26 year old life. So small were my ambitions at the time, that I was prepared to make Monroe Jr. High School my last job in life. I'd made plans and dedicated myself to retiring as a math teacher and head football coach of the Junior Mustangs. You could say that I was content.

However, in 1976 in anticipation of one of those unprecedented opportunities previously mentioned, I received a message. I was told that Roger Sorensen (Benson High's head football coach) was retiring at the end of the next school year. While that rumor was swirling, someone got the bright idea that I should be a high school coach. There was an unwritten rule at the time, one that suggested that you could not be hired for a high profile position at the high school level unless you were teaching in a high school at the time of your application. In 1970 Nebraska, head high school football coaches particularly in Class A (Nebraska's largest class) were considered high profile. I truly was happy where I was, I loved Monroe Jr. High and didn't really need anything more. Yet, somewhere ego came into play and I was coaxed into transferring to Benson High School for the 1976-77 school year.

From its inception, on through the 1950's and into the '60's Benson had been a bustling suburb of Omaha and nearly one hundred percent white. It was rich in pride and bursting with tradition. However, from the mid seventies to the mid eighties it became more diverse by the minute. I thought, here's a great place of the past, that I can enjoy in the present and become a glowing part of its future. This was the kind of bait a hungry human could not resist and I swallowed it all, hook, line and sinker! My only regret was that in the midst of all this grandeur that I was about to embellish, I had to first become a "Bunny". Not a little white or brown bunny. No, I was about to become a big green and white Benson Bunny. It was the mascot of all mascots, I think the only one of its kind. A bunny??? The mere thought of

7

becoming one was like taking Castor Oil back in the south. It was a little hard to swallow but it sure made you feel better once you took it. This was that way, hard to swallow the bunny part, but the opportunity, great kids and supportive parents made it all worthwhile. Of course the references were all in good fun. In reality I was all in. If I had to turn into a rabbit to become a head football coach, then hand me my green and white bunny suit. I was willing to hop!

The Benson High Rejection

It was the beginning of the 1976-1977 school year. I had gone to bed a gold and green Monroe Mustang and woke up kicking and screaming, transformed entirely into a green and white Benson Bunny! But it was like home there, the parents of the student athletes at Benson during that time were like family to me. Most of the athletes were products of my undefeated football teams I'd trained at Monroe. In fact Benson's senior athletes were mostly comprised of players from my first team at Monroe; the juniors were my second year players and the sophomores my third. So popular was I among the students at Benson that year, that even as a first year teacher, I ran away with the 1977 "Teacher of the Year" award. However before that honor, the previous semester I had turned in my application to become the next head football coach at Benson High School. Unfortunately for me, in that selective process the students didn't have a vote.

To me, it seemed becoming the head football coach at Benson was a no-brainer. For the most part these were all my kids from Monroe. They and their parents knew me and I knew them. Indeed it was a new time for

Benson High School and I thought for sure that I was the man for the times. The school was now occupied by a new diverse group of a rare new blend of students that signaled change was on the horizon. It was the kind of mixture that not everyone of that day could manage, but I felt I knew the secret. Victor Jordan, Tony Franks, Craig Willis - these were some of the best 9th graders of that year and they along with many others were following Peter Cotton Tail..."hopping down the bunny trail". With all this in mind, when the Benson High School head football coaching job came open in the fall of 1976, for the '77-'78 school year, I immediately went to pick out my new green and white coaching outfits. In my mind I was not only a good candidate for the job, I felt I was "THE" candidate for it! I was so ready and could hardly wait for the formality of the announcement. It would be one of those perfect fits for both coach and school!

Unfortunately the Benson administration didn't see it that way. "Not quite ready" in their words, "a bit too young," they said of my 28 years; "not quite enough high school experience" of my one year teacher/assistant coach at the high school level. That last entry I was told was the fatal blow and the main reason given for my rejection. I can still feel my heart beat from that morning, when I pulled the letter from my mailbox marked "Omaha Public Schools Personnel Department." *"Thank you for your interest and application concerning the vacant position of head football coach at Benson High School. The position has been filled. You will be notified in the future if any similar positions become available."* And with that Dan Carruthers had been named the new head football coach at Benson High School. I just stood there in that little mailbox area, not moving for a long while. Frozen in time, lost in disappointment.

I admit it, at the time I wasn't too keen on the process of bagging a high profile job. There were some factors I did not consider. Still, I was somewhat dazed and confused since it had been suggested by personnel that I transfer for the specific reason of becoming the new coach. I really felt wronged in the aftermath. It was a huge letdown, this was a dream job and I was crushed not to get it. Yet, through it all I stayed on as assistant to the new coach. I think because I'd gone out and bought all of those green and white bunny clothes.

But mostly I stayed based on the word of a particular public school administrative official, Dr. Ron Anderson, Associate Superintendent and head of the Omaha Public School's Personnel Department.

During his time behind the desk Dr. Anderson was one of those tough school officials that seemed to exude an aura of power. I had often heard in loose gossip that some people didn't particularly care for him. I don't know what their issues were but with me he had always been firm, strong, direct and to the point. Clearly his best attributes were fairness and honesty! He was a man that you could take at his word, for better or for worse.

The man always made me feel important no matter the circumstance and he never ever lied to me! I was lost, hurt and traumatically disappointed after the rejection at Benson, all the while contemplating leaving the system. I probably would have, had I not been summoned to his office a few days after the letdown. He looked me in the eye that day and promised that a head football coaching job would be open within the next few years. He acknowledged my disappointment and apologized for things not coming together in my bid at Benson. He went on to say that I would be at the head of the list to receive one of the next football head coaching positions, if I just stuck it out.

From day one, Dr. Anderson had always proven to be a man of extreme character and integrity. He had never failed to follow through on his word, so I had no reason to doubt him this time either. True to his word, two years later I was back in his office and he said, "We have two football openings and I'm almost certain you can have one of them, either Omaha Tech or Omaha Central." This was music to my ears because before falling in love with the Benson community I had been dreaming about returning to Tech High since my departure from the junior high there in 1972. This would be a new dream come true!

When he presented those choices it was 1978, just before Christmas break. I said, "I can tell you now I'd like to apply for the Tech position," to which Dr. Anderson replied, "Well, why don't you consider Central." I replied, "No, no thanks, I'd rather go to Tech." Dr. Anderson then almost insisted, saying "Bill, I think you ought to try Central." Again I said, "I'll stick with Tech, and if I can't get that I'll just be content to wait." At that point, with an "I'm the boss" expression he said, "Okay, I'm putting you down for Central, get this application back to personnel by the end of the week."

I felt he was really being a bossy bully, but I held my thoughts. Reluctantly complying with his strong demand I asked, "If this doesn't come through will I still have the opportunity to apply for the Tech job?" He closed the conversation without looking up from the papers he was signing…"Good day Mr. Reed," he said, as if my question meant nothing. Of course at the time he knew something that I didn't. Like maybe *"TECH HIGH WOULD BE CLOSED FOREVER WITHIN THE NEXT TWO YEARS AND BE TRANSFORMED INTO THE PUUBLIC SCHOOL'S ADMINISTRATION BUILDING!"* Wow, Dr. Anderson was always good to me. I was fortunate to follow his demand and will always be grateful.

The Central High Job

I thought the Central job had come to me by way of some rational electoral vote or perhaps through the careful choosing of a well constructed selection committee. Neither was true. Instead I would find that in fact my being chosen had come personally from Doctor G.E. Moller and his belief that it was time for Central High to try something different. He chose me as that difference then demanded that I be a difference maker.

Not knowing at the time what Dr. Anderson knew, when I turned in my official application for the Omaha Central head football coaching job I was very uncomfortable with it. I had heard so much about Central and just didn't feel that I fit there at all. Based on the rumors I'd heard, Omaha Central High just wasn't the place for a black head football coach in 1979. From the prejudicial attitudes of the teachers, to the rich spoiled, sadistic students they taught, I was warned that it just wasn't the place to be. Yes, believe it or not a lot of that kind of negative rhetoric reverberated throughout the system. The rumors also included the arrogant, dictator like principal and the horrible athletic facilities. And then there was that terrible, intimidating smoke stack.

I'd never seen the building up close or inside, but ooooh... how I loathed that smoke stack! Like the beast that guards the castle or the moat that circles its walls, that big chimney hovered atop the hill like a twenty-four hour sentry and for no apparent reason it just bothered me. I was a regular visitor downtown in the 1970's, consistently frequenting the nearby Nebraska Furniture Mart. This meant I saw the stack often. In fact it was usually all I saw of Central High on my visits downtown. Throughout my early years in Omaha, I came to identify the school by that awful, out of place looking smoke stack!

Along with that imposing big brick chimney, I had heard all manner of stories surrounding Central, including their second-rate athletic facilities and low level respect for sports. One lady told me that they practiced volleyball without a net,

OB

The two and three sides of Omaha Central High School 1977

a man said wrestling took place in a study hall, without mats! And though the basketball team had won the state championship four years earlier, I was told the court they practiced on was only 75% regulation size. On top of all that, they said the gym was up on the fourth floor in the cafeteria. Which was true, but during another time... like the year 1929. I'd heard there were no fields, not even a walking track. Added to all that, it was said that they cared so little about football that they made the team practice some twenty miles away.

So really, who would want to coach at Central? Of course this all turned out to be ridiculous fabrications; I mean, even Chicken Little was more accurate than some of the nonsense I'd heard. Yet, the rumors were out there and they certainly had me worried. However, despite the worries, I heeded Dr. Anderson's demands and applied for the head football coaching job at Omaha Central. My application was in, however my feelings were anything but. Though I had applied for the job, I felt it was under duress and it was okay if I didn't get it. I was almost hoping I wouldn't. In fact, I purposely tried to sabotage the interviews, consistently talking like some black militant from the 1960's during the entire process. But despite my negative posture, upon my return from Christmas break there it was; the next chapter of my life, just lying there in my mailbox like any other letter.

We are pleased to inform you that your placement as a member of the professional staff of the Omaha Public Schools for the 1979-80 school year is:

School	Assignment	Principal
Central	Math/ Head Football	Gaylord Moller

We hope the designation of your placement at this time will afford an opportunity for preplanning and to become acquainted with fellow staff members. Please contact the principal to discuss your specific teaching assignment.

I can't explain my feelings that day. Because I had never felt anything like it before and I've yet to feel anything like it since. There I was, standing shocked, at that same mailbox area that had broken my heart two years before. I didn't know whether to scream in joy or mumble in sadness. None of the Benson administrators had bothered to tell me what was coming. It was the zaniest, craziest, most unimaginable matchup one could digest... Coach Reed was going to Omaha Central High School! An assignment that would connect him to one Gaylord E. Moller for the next eleven years and a lifetime that followed. As one of the Central haters and rumor experts put it that day, "They gave you the job?!?! Now we know for sure that they don't care anything about football!"

Maybe they didn't care and maybe like some said, it was the evil empire. Regardless, four months later I found myself cruising toward downtown Omaha, driving to Central High, headed into the next eleven years of my life.

Chapter 2

MEETING DOC MOLLER
The emperor of the evil empire

OB

14

Myths and Legends

When I first walked onto the school yard at 124 North 20th Street in Omaha Nebraska in 1979, Central High had just been added to The National Register of Historic Places. Upon my arrival I could see immediately that this was more than just your average school building. In reality it was actually four buildings, all connected by a courtyard that offered access to each of them. I was quickly amazed by its uniqueness and that amazement would happen over and over again every time I walked through the doors of the school with the four sides. I had been named the Omaha Central head football coach more than four months earlier. However, I had yet to meet its mythical leader, Doctor G.E. Moller. It wasn't by accident that I hadn't met him. I had delayed the encounter for as long as I could. It was one of those, he didn't call me and I surely wasn't going to call him. But now the school year had ended and my official duties as a Benson Bunny were over. It was time to move on to a new school and it all had to begin with meeting the principal.

The scene was downtown Omaha, Nebraska and the stage was set. The organized educational circus that is Omaha Central High School was a live show, with live people playing out their parts every day, with no possibilities for do-overs! It was now clear that I was no longer a Benson Bunny, it was time to soar with the Eagles. It was life under the big top and for me there was no doubt, it was the greatest show on earth! Its ringmaster was a mythical scholastic general named Gaylord E. Moller and he presided over every event under the tent.

I had heard the tale before I met him that he had gone fishing with a teacher at a lake somewhere in Nebraska and while hooking a large fish he'd fallen in. The story goes that he couldn't swim and the teacher had to jump in to save him. When safely back in the boat the teacher turned to Doc and said, "Please don't tell anyone I saved you!", to which Doc replied, "Okay, if you promise not to tell them that I can't walk on water!"

Some actually thought he could, but the inference

> *Forget what you've heard, you can never know a person until you see.*
> *(W.R.C.)*

15

also suggested that some too would say, "You should have let him drown!" Of course, he couldn't walk on water he just seemed to know where all the rocks were. I think the broad separation of opinion was largely due to the fact that he was so damned good at his job and he was always so irritatingly correct. He ran Central High like it was the last educational outpost in the universe and gave the impression that we were all put there to save mankind. I learned quickly that Dr. Moller was not just for Central High School or about Central High School. When he walked into that building at 20th and Dodge Street he *was* Central High School! But enough of tall tales it was finally time to meet him for the very first time.

And What to My Wondering Eyes Did Appear?

That first visit to Central was like *opening up new presents on Christmas morning. You know what you've asked for but you're still not sure of just what you'll get!* (W.R.O.) I was reporting as the new head football coach and math teacher, all the time wondering might they have changed their minds. If they hadn't then I had come to see firsthand where I would be spending my next school year and whom I'd be working with. Again, I had never been physically close to the building, let alone inside, so I didn't know what to expect and I could tell by the reactions of my new bosses they didn't know quite what to expect either. Time would gradually teach us all, but on this day here I stood in all my glory, poised to officially meet the Central High School Administration.

Doug Morrow, Athletic Director greets me and introduces me to Al Lagreca, Assistant Principal. Another assistant, Dick Jones avoids me. I heard he was not so fond of me getting the job. Later he would become athletic director as well as a true ally and one of my closest friends at Central. Those meetings however, were just the warm-ups. Eventually I would be escorted to the real game, the office of Dr. G.E. Moller. I had never seen him before but I had heard everything about him. Most of which originated from an old football teammate named Bob Lowery and my sister-in-law Mary Dean Harvey. Mary had actually been a teacher at Central during the early 70's. They were both very candid and up front with their opinions about Doc Moller. Mary often questioned his ways and some of the administrative philosophies he embraced, yet she greatly respected him. While Bob, a self-professed, proud black man, basically despised him. I had gotten all sorts of advice on what to do with Doc Moller. Most of it was like water, it could quench your thirst but it could also drown you.

I'd pictured him as the hooded evil emperor, handing out orders to Darth Vader. However, Duane Haith, Omaha Public Schools Activities and Athletic Supervisor calmed me a bit when he said, "Don't worry about it, just do your job, you'll be fine." Dr. Don Benning, Assistant Superintendent and former Omaha Central Activities Director chuckled at all the warnings. He said "Doc Moller will be fair, whether that's positive or negative is up to you." Then there was Eugene Skinner, the original foundation of every black educator in the Omaha Public School system. He reminded me that I was the first black head football coach at a predominantly white high school in the history of the state of Nebraska. He then smiled and said, "Keep that in mind and you'll figure out the rest." I recall feeling pretty good after that.

So it was finally here, time to meet the man, the beast, Darth Vader's boss, the emperor of the evil empire! I'd been hearing about this notorious educator for years and from what I'd heard he had to be a giant of a man, tough, rugged and totally fearless! I'd heard that he was Stone Mountain, a man breaker and would soon be headed to the public school's Mount Rushmore, if there was such a thing. One guy even compared him to a fire breathing dragon that was intimidating and battle tested. I tell you I walked into his office that day with my hands clinched into fists, poised for battle, ready to face this Goliath principal. His picture had been in my head for five months and from all I'd heard he had to be at least 7 feet tall and some 300 pounds, with a menacing scowl and iron teeth.

I admit I was nervous and uneasy but I was ready for whatever was behind that office door. I put on my all business face and steadied myself for the entrance. I didn't want to show any signs of weakness to this intimidating warrior leader! When the door finally opened I felt as though I was walking into the lion's den. As I stepped inside I saw him for the first time and he stood to shake my hand. I hesitated and took a step back. I thought "WHAT, is this it?" I wondered to myself, "Shouldn't he be up there with the rest of the elves helping Santa Claus with the presents? Or maybe back at Snow White's pad with his six little brothers? Are you kidding me, what the hell???" Is this what all the warnings and fuss has been about? I thought to myself, this little squirt, he couldn't intimidate two Chihuahuas! "I ought to take his office from him!" I mean really, what could he do about it? Man, would I pay for those thoughts for the next eleven years. For the rest of my days at Central I think I faced off with Doc maybe 50 times and my record was 0-50. I got shellacked every time, never winning a single battle. However, those episodes all came later, but on that day, after meeting him during my first visit I was thinking to myself, I've stood face to face with Dr. G.E. Moller and I felt that I could squash him if I needed to. Of course, that conclusion was about as far-fetched as time travel, but my mind was back to the future and my only thoughts then were, "I got this... Omaha Central, I am here!"

That first meeting with Doc was very brief. He wasn't very talkative at all that day, just general stuff and we were out of his office in no time. I walked out like a new soldier, straight, strong and about two feet taller, all the while thinking to myself that the fire breathing dragon didn't really breathe fire, and for that matter wasn't even a dragon. I found that the emperor did not sport a hood and had no kingdom. Instead he was just a man who worked hard to get a job and that job just happened to be principal of one of the great high schools anywhere. There wasn't an evil empire here and no emperor to rule it. Instead I had discovered a downtown paradise surrounded by asphalt dreams and a tradition that predated my time.

This photo marks the first year of Omaha High School becoming Omaha Central. It is the year when all four new buildings completely encased the old one. Once the old structure inside was raised the space became a uniquely, open courtyard, offering access to all four buildings. Someone once asked me the question; if you're inside the courtyard at Central High are you inside the building or outside? Many are unsure of that answer, however, when you looked out from any of the windows to the world that surrounded them you were sure to get a vivid view of the downtown buildings that formed the neighborhood of which Omaha Central was a longstanding and significant part.

Chapter 3

A VIEW FROM THE INSIDE
Looking out from the windows of tradition

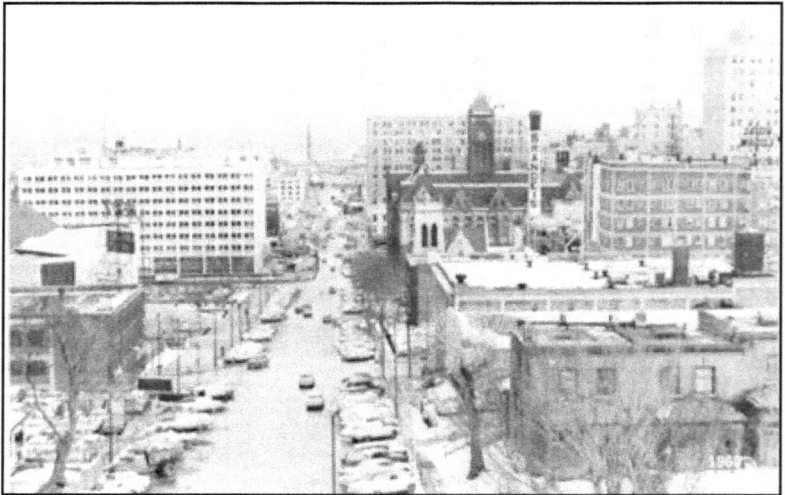

On the 1side: looking out from a third floor eastside window

OB

20

Oh, Say Can You See

It is the end of the '78-'79 school year in Omaha, Nebraska and I'm at the most curious school setting that I have ever seen. This is my first encounter inside the place and I am truly fascinated. There seems to be a merging of some sort between four separate structures, each its own wing representing a personal unique specialty. This, while seemingly bonding to one another to form a collective solid union.

The building that houses the school that is Omaha Central is a historical landmark. It sits majestically on what seems to be the highest peak in the downtown Omaha area. Despite its location, within the confines of concrete and asphalt, it sports a magnificent crew cut of sprawling green bluegrass on its eastern and southern borders. Looking from its east side **(the 1side)** you could view the famed Civic Auditorium or get a glimpse of the prestigious and tradition rich First National Bank. Keep looking and on the horizon you might even spot a boat headed up the Missouri River. If you require constant flowing action just step over to the south side **(the 2side)** where you will find Omaha's busiest street. Dodge Street allows you to see a consistent parade of Detroit's finest in every color and make imaginable. For the calm aristocrat, mosey on over to the west side **(the 3side)** and appearing less than a block away you can get a full view, up close and personal of the historical Joslyn Art Museum. You want to go to college? Then walk out the north side **(the 4side)**, head west up Davenport Street and in less than a block the Central High School campus quickly morphs into a college setting within the boundaries of Creighton University. In describing Central from within, simplistically, I concluded that it sits majestically atop downtown's highest peak and is surrounded by Omaha's most historical monuments!

The school is only four stories high, hardly the tallest building in the area. However, it dominates the scenery with its ancient and unique design. The hill it covers once cradled Nebraska's first state capitol building and is considered sacred ground in Nebraska lore. Through the times, from the inside Omaha Central has continued to be what it has always been. A purpose driven entity that develops young people into becoming great contributors to society.

Throughout time it has been said that it is the people inside that makes the school and for a long time I felt that way. However, at Central that folklore seemed to reverse itself. There, it was clear that the school and its long standing tradition made the people. Once inside, it was realized who had been there before you, and you instantly became aware of the high expectations of following them once you signed on.

The school seemed to invite you in, then demand your best. Yes, you could see the outside from an exquisite vantage point but at the same time you could feel the inside exploring your soul and challenging your being. With their great mystique the open-air of the high ceilings would seem a waste of money today, however back then they challenged us to reach them. The roomy classrooms seemed to invite the educational process in and through their windows you could see the many great things surrounding you. Stepping into the courtyard you could view the sky and take in a little sun without ever leaving the building.

From a skyward view, all of downtown Omaha was visible from the east and south side. High up from the north side you could see Interstate 480 heading for the Missouri River where it would meet with I-29 in Council Bluffs, Iowa then taking off to Des Moines, while 29 headed south to K.C. At the end of the school day a flowing march of traffic would begin to head west on Dodge Street as the suburban dwellers exit the urban job places for the green grasses of their homes.

Yes, inside the walls of the four sides of Omaha Central you could look out and see the world moving, watch things changing and see the speed of life in real time. I was about twenty minutes into my walkthrough and already I was awed by what I saw inside the structure, and my eyes were truly captivated by the surroundings that it offered sight to from within.

For more than 100 years John Latenser's artistry and imagination has continued to shine as a transformational symbol of exquisite architectural design! His foresight back in the early 1900's to fuse together four separate buildings, facing four separate directions, to create four distinct sides, is truly a work of art that has definitively withstood the movement of time.

This 1898 rendering by John Latenser, shows the majestic Omaha High in all its glory.

So consistent is the look and tradition that the students who first entered it in 1901 would still recognize it today. Proof that greatness never changes, it only gets better. This rendering became a reality in 1912. However, the statement to be made by the imposing tower didn't make the cut, as budget issues halted its creation.

Chapter 4

THE TOUR
At the turn of the century all roads of success led to Omaha High

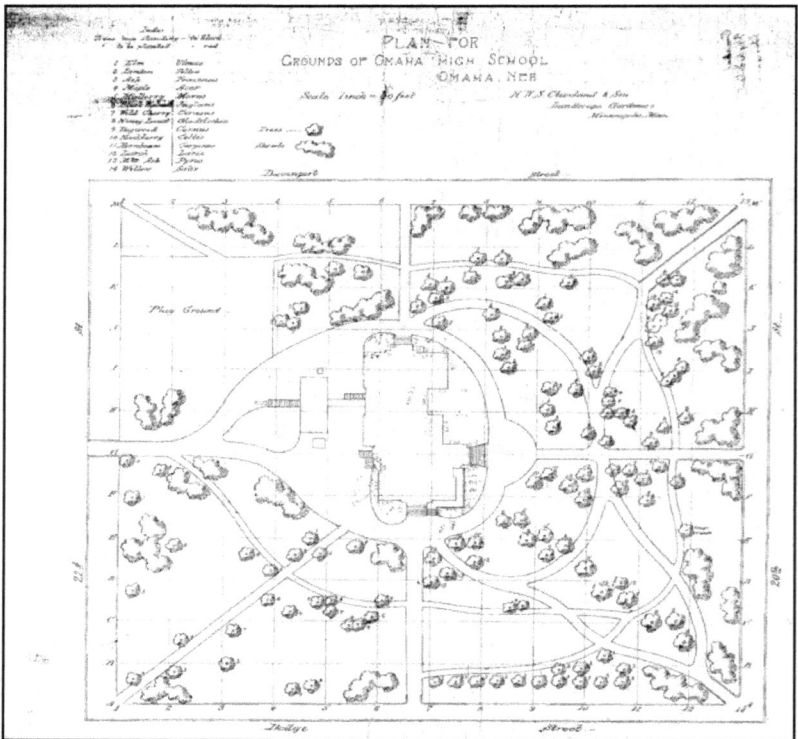

Turn of the century landscaping plan: Site of Omaha High School, original blueprint, By: John Latenser, 1898.

The Uniqueness

After viewing in awe the Central High neighborhood looking out, it was time to take my initial journey through the hallways from within. I was suddenly proud to be there and was overflowing with curiosity. In fact, I was so surprised and amazed at the uniqueness I'd encountered that it all began to feel like a dream.

Leonardo DiCaprio once starred in a very deep movie called "Inception", where the characters were able to get inside dreams and actually change things in real life. Now, walking down the hallways of Central for the very first time, that is exactly how I felt. I felt as though I was walking with all those students of high dreams and great expectations from times past. I glimpsed at the wild and daring kids of the 1920's and the depressed times of the 30's. I could hear the chant of the 1940's future soldiers, during a time on high school campuses when ROTC was spelled P-R-I-D-E! I could see the rock and roll days of the 1950's and I could feel the emotions of all the young minds during the revolutionary times of the late 60's. I was in this dream, walking it, living it and ready to add to it. When I think about it; I was in a dream, dreaming a dream and prepared to go into another dream, while I was dreaming. As I said, it was **"Inception"**- very deep!

> *Dream the dream,*
> *find the dream,*
> *live the dream.* *(w.R.o.)*

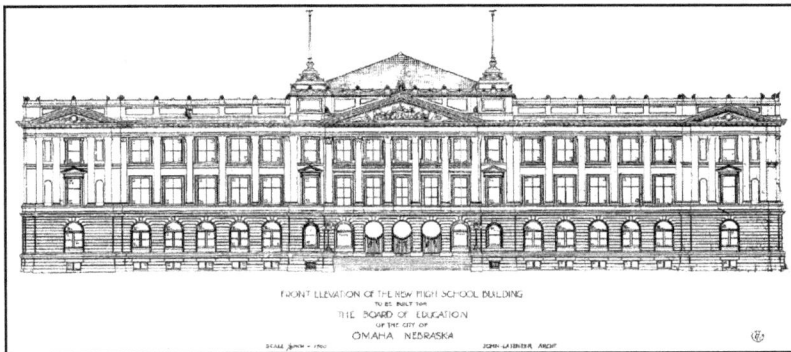

FRONT ELEVATION OF THE NEW HIGH SCHOOL BUILDING
THE BOARD OF EDUCATION
OMAHA NEBRASKA

John Latenser's Original Dream
The architectural drawing of the first of the four sides that made up Omaha High School 1900-1912

Touring the Dream of John Latenser

The definition of the word tour: *A journey of pleasure in which several different places are visited!* That definition explained perfectly my feelings when I first walked upon the hardwood floors of Omaha Central. I didn't feel anything special about it until we walked across the courtyard from the **3side** to the **1side**. We walked from indoors to outdoors and back indoors again. The courtyard was without a roof then and resembled more a plant garden with sidewalks.

The walk to classes was like a lot of things at Central, a multiple choice test. If you wanted to, you could avoid the courtyard and walk the hallways passing through each side without ever going outside at all. In fact when there was rain or snow, access to the courtyard was shut off entirely. Forcing one to make the around about walk through the hallways of each side in order to navigate the ground floor. This would be my inaugural walk through, to what I then and still believe is one of the greatest high school settings anywhere.

I started my tour from the courtyard, where I marveled at the inner-connective bond of each of the four separate buildings. When I walked into the **1side**, I was immediately intrigued by the randomness of the classroom numbers. Mr. Morrow had decided to take me all the way up to the 4th floor and we were to work our way back down. However, by the time we reached the third floor I had become confused.

> The inner sanction of greatness often reveals its true legacy.
>
> (W.R.O.)

I remember seeing room #310 on our way up and it seemed oddly misplaced! I'd just passed a few doors and all of a sudden I was at 310. I thought, what happened to 309 and where in heck was 301? I never did find either. The whole thing just didn't make sense. I recall thinking that perhaps teachers could just make up their own room numbers as they go. I felt a little apprehensive about asking why that number (310) was on that particular classroom door and why was it preceded by 349 just around the corner. I was very curious and when it was finally explained to me it all made simplistic sense.

The first number indicated the floor, while the second number showcased the side we were on and the last digit pointed to the sequential order of each door starting with 0. I thought, "this is like exploring the pyramids." You find complex routes and compartments that are really very simple but you'd have to be either an archeologist or ancient Egyptian to know the simplicity. So, where would you find room 325? **Third floor (3), two side (2), 5th door (5), room 325!** Wow, yet another Central High complexity. I thought dang, even the room number system here is a standardized achievement test!

During my stroll through the historical brick mammoth that is Central High School, the feeling of those who had been there before me seemed eerily too close to reality. You see the floors of the old building were aged hardwood. On them you could see the streaks and scuffs of decades past and they squeaked a bit as you walked. The cranky hardwood was mysterious in its own right. In that as you walked upon it the sounds it made didn't come until after you had made a step or two, leaving the impression that there were footsteps behind you. Later I was told about the ghosts of a Dean of Students and a custodian from the 1800's that still came to work every night. However, later one of the custodial staff explained that the trailing footsteps was a result of the old hardwood being pressed down and then popping back up after you walked a bit. This was good to hear but still very eerie! However, it did finally help me to understand why I couldn't shake my pursuer as I was sprinting down the hallway one night. Not that I was scared or anything, but one night after hearing what I could only recognize as footsteps

OB

Hallways after dark, creepy but friendly

I thought it was a good time to take a little sprint. The faster I ran, the faster came the sounds behind me. I didn't feel safe until I burst out of the doors on the **3side**. This weirdness was especially true at night and on weekends when the building was empty. Though the custodian's explanation sounded good I still deduced that if Mr. Custodian and Dr. Dean of Students was still hanging around they could only be on the **1side** since that was the only building in place during their time. So, not being afraid (I heard they were friendly ghosts) but more respecting their space, during my entire eleven year stint at Central, I only once walked the **1side** hallways after dark.

Continuing my initial tour I remember all the doors showing signs of majestic wear, forensic evidence of old royalty who had entered them during another time. The staircases wound up and down, coordinating so that one of them serviced the girls with restrooms on the landings and the other side serviced the boys with the same. The restrooms were without doors, I suspect for easy monitoring and making it clearly inappropriate for opposite sexes to walk the same stairs. The strategically placed restrooms were well monitored, always clean and sanitized. There was a privacy barrier of walls but they were always doorless, making it very difficult for the illegal campus puffers!

The main office sat strategically and appropriately on floor number one on the **3side**. It featured a view of the historic Joslyn Art Museum and perhaps a

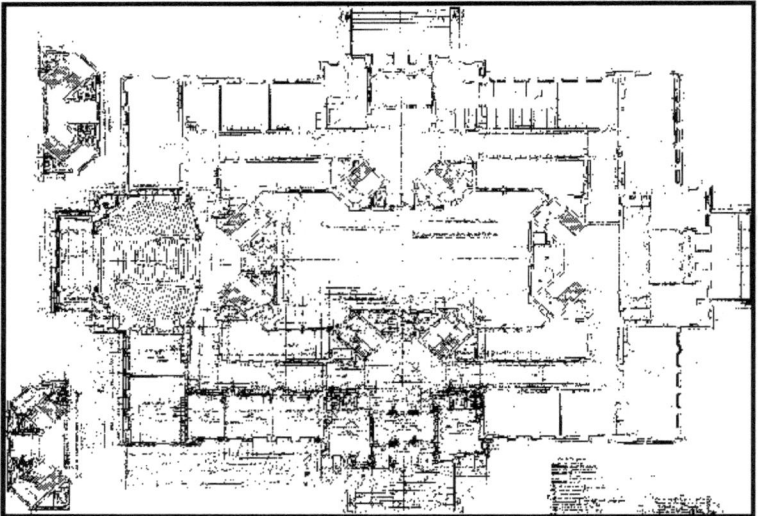

Omaha High School 1st floor original blueprint, John Latenser, 1898

glance at something that resembled an athletic field, if you looked hard enough. Take the elevator down and you find yourself in the basement. The maintenance gang's "hang out" is just across the hall as you step out. Although the room numbers down there all began with zero, it was definitely not a nothing part of the building. The Home Economics Department was there, along with America's future finest, the ROTC, led by Major McDaniel and Sergeant Middleton. These two men reminded me of a cross between Mash and Hogan's Heroes. They were light hearted and quick with a joke but very serious about their trade.

The 4th floor housed two similarly large sized cafeterias on two different

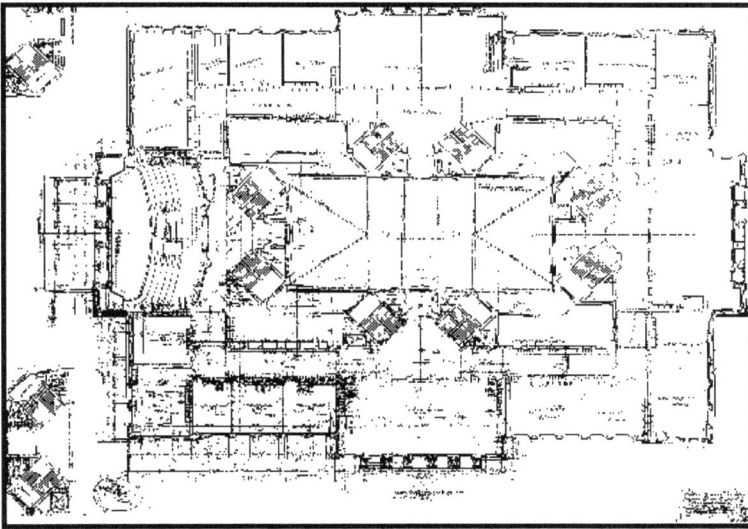

Omaha High School 2nd floor original blueprint, John Latenser, 1898

sides, the **3side** and the **4side,** with Art Classes and the Science Lab occupying the two remaining sides on the floor. From the inner rooms facing the courtyard you could look out and see the sky or look down and catch the ever crossing traffic of students and teachers moving from one side to the other. This view was lent to leisure by only teachers and department heads, as only their offices saw out to the courtyard. The auditorium was pristine, sporting a recent overhaul of new cushion comfort seats. Larry Hausman and his gang made the stage, while Pegi Stommes and her characters played on it. There was one gymnasium in place (the old gym) with one in the infant stages (the new gym). Just below the old gym we carved out a space for a weight room, thanks to Joe McMenamin, who was way ahead of the times when it came to the importance of high school weight training. Oh, and contrary to rumors, there was a football practice field on the west side. It was solid dirt and hard

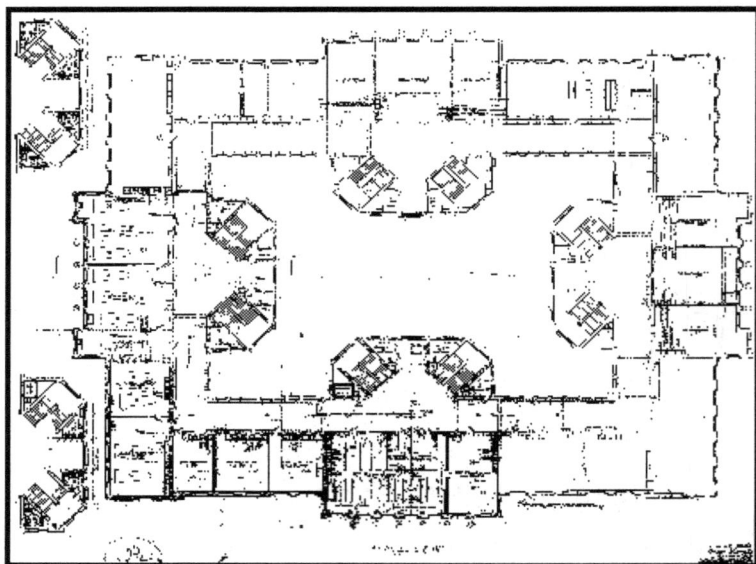

Omaha High School 3rd floor original blueprint, John Latenser, 1898

as brick but despite the naysayers, it was there. Finishing things off musically was a nostalgic band room, with a music room close by that typically housed the sounds of the famous Central A Cappella, directed by a very nice person in Bob McMeen.

As I looked around inside I could see the future and I was already surrounded by the majestic traditions of the past. Central looked like a school that had been carved out inside the ancient Greek temples, totally separate

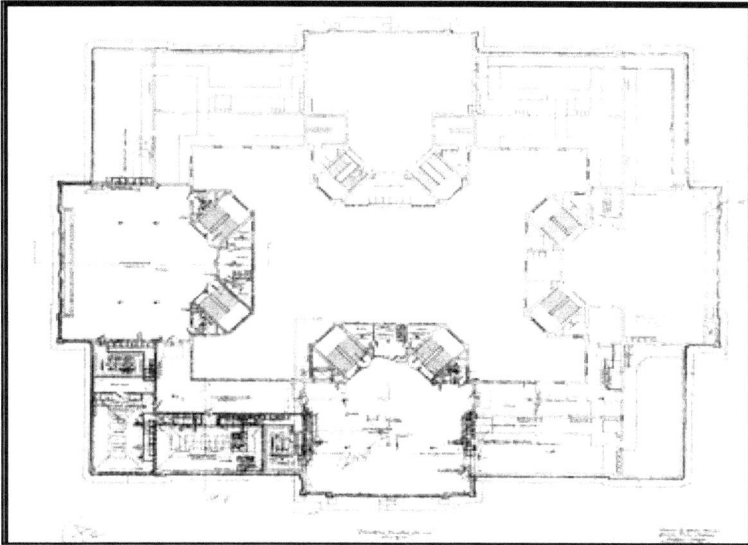

Omaha High School 4th floor original blueprint, John Latenser, 1898

from anything routine. That was my perception from within. However, when I looked out I saw a collection of exquisite buildings and views of exceptional historical sites that reminded me that it was still the 20th century. Appropriately, Omaha Central seemed to be a product of the downtown Omaha past and a major link to its journey into the future.

As I weaved my way up and down the creative staircases of John Latenser's masterpiece I landed in between on the wooden floors that form the hallways that separated them. The walls seemed recently painted but still carried with them the rustic look of years passed by.

I felt a kind of exuberance to my life and also felt as if I had become a part of a unique new club. I recall it wasn't a feeling like joining a sorority or a fraternity. It was more like moving into a new neighborhood that was of long standing tradition with high expectations placed on everyone involved. I remember the odd feeling of although no one was present one could still feel the effects of the interior surroundings. Surroundings that followed you, spoke to you, invited you, welcomed you and then warned you of the seriousness of what was to come. I could feel throughout my walk through that there was greatness inside these walls, impressive to say the least!

It was far more than I ever imagined. The walking adventure through the building now took on a brand new meaning. It became more like a discovery then just a mere tour. All of a sudden I was beyond impressed, I was delightfully overwhelmed! Each of these four sides could be its own distinct school building, but together they created a bond that qualify the quartet as something much stronger. *The four joined to become a collective embodiment of bricks and mortar, fused together to form a prominent educational environment for preparation toward higher learning.* (W.R.O.)

After two hours in splendid awe, I took a ride down the elevator to the first floor on the **3side** and with that, my exploration was over. I walked out to the courtyard, took one last panoramic view, and left the scene smitten with pride. As I cleared the west side doors that day not only did I think I belonged at Central, I felt as though I could move in and live there...and in the years that followed, sometimes I actually did.

The Omaha Central Legacy

Through the years this engaging structure has attracted thousands, consisting of some of the most talented and gifted young men and women of our time. When they leave, they carry with them a tradition that still endures, with a reputation that puts it among the finest high schools in the country.

Gale Sayers
Successful businessman and entrepreneur. NFL Hall of Famer. Most exciting runner in NFL history.

Henry Fonda
One of the greatest actors of our times. Named the sixth greatest male star of all time.

Susan T. Buffett
Singer, businessperson, activist, and philanthropist. A director of Berkshire Hathaway and one of the greatest givers ever.

WHEN THEY WERE EAGLES.......

Henry Fonda
Senior 1923

Gale Sayers
Senior 1961

Susan Thompson
Senior 1950

OB

Chapter 5

MADE IN THE CHS

The downtown school that could

Top row: Susan A. Buffett, Peter Kiewit, Ed Zorinsky, Henry Fonda, Larry Station

2nd row: Alan Heeger, Dr. Jack Lewis, Ahman Green, Susan T. Buffett, Jarvis Offutt

3rd row: Roger Sayers, Dr. Jerry Bartee, Dorothy McGuire, Kenneth Stephan, Dr. Albert B. Crum

4th row: Charlie T. Munger, Gale Sayers, James Fous, Dick Holland, Brenda Council

5th row: Lawrence Klein, Keith Jones, Wynonie Harris, Inga Swenson, Maurtice Ivy

See personal biographies of each in the final back pages of the book.

Tradition and Reputation

One can easily test the depth of a school by simply taking measure of the students it produces! (W.R.O.)

With alumni that seemed to span the globe, Omaha Central High School is known for producing some of the most talented people in American history. People with enormous brains and a rare mixture of even bigger hearts! Like a mother and daughter of fortune, using it more to help others than themselves; like a man of such bravery that an airbase was named in his honor; a Medal of Honor recipient; along with one of the great actors of our time. There's a Nobel Prize winner and athletes galore, including perhaps the greatest runner in National Football League history. Add to that the hundreds of doctors, lawyers, and educators, and you have one of the most productive public high schools in America. For over a hundred years a steady stream of excellence has flowed through the corridors within the four sides of Omaha Central, carrying with it excellence from the past, hope for the present, and innovations for the future. Whether it's the past, present or future, the schools' reputation and tradition is beyond reproach.

> *Reputation is what you earn, tradition keeps it going!* (W.R.O.)

Before the 1980's the Omaha Public Schools sported eight high schools, and CHS was the crown jewel of its fleet. Back then Omaha Central was a dream ship, the Titanic if you may, with a by-the-book captain that was wise enough to steer clear of icebergs. At a time when most downtown schools around the country were being shut down, Omaha Central not only survived, it flourished. There were times when it exceeded 2,300 students and over 100 faculty members. By the beginning of the 1980's there were still 1,863 students, not including a freshmen class. It's a known fact that negative reputations and stereotypical thoughts regarding downtown schools covered the United States from the mid-sixties through the advent of the eighties. Within those two decades that negativity ran rampant in urban schools across the country, but was nonexistent at 20th & Dodge Street in Omaha, Nebraska.

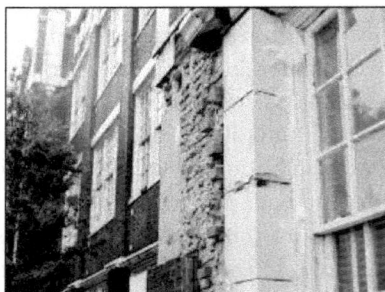

OB

None of the stereotypical diseases that hit U.S. urban schools could penetrate the four sides of Omaha Central High. It was indeed the "downtown school that could."

The photos above show the inside and outside of two schools of similar origin. Both were established in the late 1800's. At the top, downtown Omaha Central High in Omaha Nebraska and the bottom, downtown Baton Rouge High, Baton Rouge, Louisiana. Yes, students were still attending school there. This urban school neglect happened all across the country, as suburbs blossomed. Some would later be revived, as Baton Rouge High eventually was. However, through the neglect and demise of downtown urban schools, Omaha Central never missed a beat, remaining constant in its mission. Always bound for the future, while never losing its ties to the past.

Years ago I ran into an old friend whom I had grown up with in Louisiana. When we left Monroe to make our homes elsewhere, I headed north and he, to my surprise, went south. He ended up in Baton Rouge and thought me to be the crazy one as I settled into what he called "Snow Country." Fifteen years later he had a question for me, after watching Baton Rouge High disintegrate into near closure. He asked, "Why the big difference? Why did your Central flourish while ours turned to shambles?" I had a solid answer for him. I said, "*The students and faculty of today keep it going; the alumni of the past support it; its history won't let it die and the kids of tomorrow can't wait to get there!*" (W.R.O.)

Central is all about tradition, reputation, and the vast variety of people that created it all. The difference was that in our school, unlike many of that reference, safety was not an issue. We owned one of the best safety records in the state and Doc Moller was poised to keep it that way. Laws and rules were enforced to the max, sternly but fairly. Academic deficiencies? Forget about it! Omaha Central was known as the top academic college preparatory high school in the state of Nebraska. Fine arts the best, athletics even better - except for football with 18 straight losing seasons, but with my arrival that would change in a hurry!

The Unique Mystique at 124 North 20ᵗʰ Street

The structure that once occupied these grounds was the old state capitol. Now the vintage and prestigious real estate property at 124 North 20th Street is the foundation of Omaha Central High School. Indeed the land was originally chosen to embellish the most important building in the state, and the way Doc Moller demanded ones respect while they stood upon it, there was no doubt that in his mind it still did! The structure is a piece of architectural marvel, reminding one of something out of the Renaissance Era. Its exquisite design is taken for granted by the many that see it every day. However, for those who haven't seen it before, it's always a double take.

I recall picking up a friend from the airport for his first visit to Omaha.

We stopped at a downtown sporting goods store on the way in, which took us passed Central on the way out. As we approached 20th Street, moving west on Dodge, I saw his head jerk up. "What is that building?" he exclaimed. I answered "That's the Mother-ship, my friend." He asked, "What does it do?" I said, "It carries people to the future." Simply put, the building that houses the Omaha Central family is magnificent and its tradition and reputation are undeniable.

I had nightmares about the place, but then I realized that it just might be what I had been searching for all my life. Wow! Having taken in its entire splendor, I now possessed a vastly different opinion and I concluded the following - the outside view of Omaha Central is incredible, the inside magical and the mystique was genuinely captivating. Now as I'm leaving the campus walking toward Davenport Street, I took a parting look back. It seemed something was missing and I looked again. Then, as if Moses had come down to part the passageway for my coming, I saw it. Or rather, didn't see it. The smoke stack! In the beginning it had almost been enough to frighten me away. That imposing medieval symbol that had stood for half a century and one score was gone, torn down just three months after I took the job. It was as if it had been removed in respect for my arrival. Gone before I ever set foot on the campus. Was this a sign? With that fresh miracle outside, along with what I'd just seen inside, I took on a new feeling. Suddenly I was fired up. I raised my hands, pumped my fist, and shouted out loud, "Alright, let's flyyyyy!" I was indeed flying high, perhaps too much so.

Doc Moller must have heard me, because he dedicated the next eleven years to making sure that I was brought back down to earth and nailed firmly to the ground. That day, when I finally vacated the grounds at 124 North 20th Street, I thanked God and praised the awesome structure that was about to become my new life. I'd learned two important lessons that day. One, that Omaha Central was an extraordinary place and two, Doc Moller was not the evil emperor. He was simply the principal.

Later, he would ask for, and even demand perfection, something I had never considered. But that's what principals do. It would take some years for me to figure that one out, but I had time. There were about ninety days between me and my official start at Central and I was anxious to say the least. That summer of anticipation seemed to be the slowest three months ever recorded in my life. It was as if the journey of days through the calendar was made by covered wagon, they crept to the start of school. The teachers, the students, the school. I was eager to meet them all and I was literally aching to experience my first official day as a Central High Eagle!

Chapter 6

MY FIRST DAY OF SCHOOL
That unforgettable morning drive

OB

William Reed, 1979

Off To See the Wizard

"Good morning Omaha, Nebraska!!!" I remember waking up on the first Monday morning of school and feeling as though I was in the Land of Oz. That which once was black and white was all of a sudden in brilliant bright colors. You know, those Christmastime visions of sugar plums I'd heard about all my life, dancing in one's head? Well now it was happening, in late August.

There were three **firsts** going through my mind that morning. This would be my **first** official check-in at Omaha Central High and I felt like a **first** grader on his **first** day. Can you believe it? A lowly soul from the Jim Crow South was now a teacher and the head football coach at the largest and most prestigious high school in all of Nebraska.

I tell you, it was dreamland that morning. After eight years of working in the public school system in Omaha, Nebraska, I've been selected as the first black head football coach of a predominantly white high school, in the history of the state. On that day I felt as though I had just arrived in America. I was glowing with pride. This was a euphoric feeling that may not resonate in the minds of some. However, to most in this great state, it is understood that football is king, and the most universal connection to the variety of people who call it home. In fact, outside of actual religion, nothing is more sacred than our beloved Cornhuskers' football program here in Nebraska. On that day, in some strange way, I felt a part of it all.

As the new head football coach at Omaha Central High School, I was the centerpiece for new football hope at what is truly a very special place. To add to my euphoria at the time, Central had the most diverse student body state-wide. Furthermore, it was the high school that had produced the man that I thought to be the greatest running back in the history of the National Football League, The Kansas Comet, galloping Gale Sayers! At the time I could hardly believe where I was. I was just 30 years old. Everything seemed perfect. The sky was bright and there was a sweet smell in the morning breeze. I felt special and proud, it was all too surreal.

It was a nice morning, and with nervous anticipation I was too anxious to eat. I had dressed in nice slacks, a smooth polyester shirt, and a perfectly coordinated bow tie. I topped it all off with a sporty, collegiate sweater vest purchased from Joe and my friends at CrossTown Clothiers, who were huge Central fans. At the time I was living in the far north region of Omaha. I'd mapped out the best route from my residence in Colonial Acres for my drive

> The most important day in any life is the first.
> *(W.R.O.)*

that morning. The drive would take me out to State Street over to 30th and south to Craig Street. I would head east until Craig ended, trek south again, veer onto Florence Boulevard, which eventually morphed into 20th Street, finally carrying me to Davenport Street and my new job.

I pulled onto the yellow brick road about 6:55 a.m. and in a flash I was off to see the wizard! The plan had been initiated and I was en-route with my friends Marvin Gaye, The Temptations and Smokey Robinson joining me via the speakers that were attached to my personally installed 8-track tape player. The anxiousness was unlike any I had ever experienced. I could hardly wait for the clock to move because things were getting better every minute. It was a great morning to be alive. For me, a new day of life was on the horizon and the forecast was sunny and mild.

The Vega Station Wagon

I drove slowly that morning to allow a little extra time to go by to assure that the school would be at maximum capacity upon my arrival. I was feeling the time and wanted to savor each moment. I was thinking, "take your time sir, this is your day." At this point, with most of my maiden voyage complete, I was southbound on Florence Boulevard counting down the blocks to where it fades into 20th Street. I am driving into the new life, awaiting me at my new school. It's 7:10 a.m. I have teachers to meet and students to greet, what a feeling! I was into the home stretch when it hit me and I said out loud, "Mr. Reed, you're not at Benson anymore." I had been just an extra in the Broadway play there, but now this is my very own show and I'm headed to the stage for my opening act.

The show was running perfectly to script, but then the surprise. Unannounced and uninvited, there would prove to be another character in the play that morning. You see, I had the misfortune of owning a Chevy Vega station wagon, one of the worst cars ever made (according to Motor Trend Magazine back in the early 80's). Mine was, appropriately, yellow. It made good sense, considering I had never seen a lemon in any other color. This heap of a car was about to take over the starring role in the opening act of one of the great tragedies of that time.

It's late August, this is my first official day of teaching at Omaha Central High School, and OH MY GOODNESS!!! What was that awful sound??? NOOO!!! Please, say it ain't so! Three hundred sixty-five days in the year and this would be the day that the Vega chose to blow the first of three engines while in my possession. Sadly, coughing and spitting oil like it had been poisoned, the car came to a pitiful and pathetic halt. And it was officially panic time for me.

I am stranded two miles from Central, with cell phones about ten years from existence. With oil still gushing out of my smoky yellow car and time not paying attention at all to my calamity, I had to hoof it the rest of the way.

I finally made it to the lower level west side doors of my new school, but by then my grand entry was a flop. Classes had already begun and few people saw my entrance. I staggered into my first day at Central, clothes sweaty, tie crooked, shoes smoking, twenty minutes late with a broken down car excuse in tow. That explanation would certainly be a legal "get out of jail free" card on any Monopoly board in town, but at Central High, they didn't play the game during school hours. Still, despite my ragged overtime arrival I was feeling justified and completely legitimate. Whether you were legally late, understandably late, lazily late, unfortunately late or just plain "couldn't help it" late - it didn't matter. Once I was stripped of my get out of jail free card I was left with no defense. My debut that morning went up in the smoke that bellowed from the hood of my 1979 Vega and so did I. For the record, let me state that I was administratively barbecued on my first official day as a teacher at Omaha Central High School!

OB

Math department head, Miss Virginia Lee Pratt in her natural habitat, the classroom

I had no idea what I was walking into up on third floor that disastrous first day at Central. I'd only seen Doc a few times after our inaugural meeting. That was only in passing and from the back row of the in-service teacher's meetings before the start of the school year. I really hadn't experienced him yet in the "Full Metal Jacket" mode. But that mode was exactly what I found waiting for me outside my classroom door on my first morning as a Central High teacher. I think what I remember most about the encounter was walking into the space that he occupied in the doorway of my classroom. I wanted to be cool in that space, but I remember it being intensely hot.

OB

Doc Moller expecting order, finding mistakes, ready to pounce.

Chapter 7

THE ROYAL WELCOME

My inaugural first day greeting from
King Gaylord and Queen Virginia III

OB

First Day Visitors

Somehow I can feel that Dr. Moller standing outside my classroom door on this the first day of school with everything else going on is not part of a welcoming tradition. I am still holding out that I could get lucky here. I thought, "maybe he's at every new teacher's door on their first day at Central." However, within that thought reality set in and I knew that such a gesture was not possible. But I was still holding out hope that my broken down car excuse was legitimate and strong, it was my last hope. As I approached the opening to the doorway Doc Moller stood straddle legged on the threshold, completely blocking it. Now came the royal greeting to my first official minutes at Central High School. Doc's expression was chilling and his voice was dramatic as he said, **"William, you are twenty minutes late!"** I remembered thinking to myself, "is that some sort of classified information?" Okay, let me play my trump card and end all the drama, "Yes I know, my car broke down!". Boom!!! Take that! Now let me hear the apology.

The next statement from Doc spoke volumes to what my next years at Central would be like. He said, "All the teachers here came in cars William, but you're the only one that's late." Say what? What the heck? I was stunned and all of a sudden Doc took on a Rod Serling look. I'm talking "Twilight Zone", and I could hear that weird music ringing in my ears ...dddd dddd dddd dddd!!!!

I didn't know what to say or do and then, as if matters could not be worse, there seemed to be someone else standing behind the door. In that instant, matters indeed did get worse. Doc's visit was bad enough on the first day of school, but now he is flanked by Miss Virginia Lee Pratt. She was Central's queen of righteousness and my department head. As she stepped out of the shadows in her eyes I could see my whole life flash before me, and the bad part was... that I was going to live!

Miss Virginia Lee Pratt

OB

Miss Virginia Lee Pratt was the reigning head of the Central High math department. In May of 1979, Britain made room for its first female Prime Minister, Margaret Thatcher. They called her the Iron Lady. That same year I met Miss Pratt and she was as much an iron lady as Mrs. Thatcher, only she carried a slide rule. As Prime Minister, Mrs. Thatcher dealt from the right. In the Central High Math department, Miss Pratt dealt from the left, the right, the hook, jab, uppercut - you name it and she'd get after you with it.

The story goes that she had not only started at Central as a 1ˢᵗ grader, then graduated high school there, but that she graduated college there also. She then began to teach there and somewhere high upon the rafters above the 4ᵗʰ floor cafeterias she was actually born there. The legend, of course is false, but the reality was that math and Central were her life, and when you came to work in her department you had better damn well make it yours.

Every day at school and in life she was all business. She was a lethal mixture of 100-year-old smooth red wine and nitroglycerin. Aged to perfection, smooth and sweet, but drop the glass or shake it too hard and you're likely to get blown to bits. Careful and efficient, that's what you had to be at all times to survive Miss Pratt. She was a clean, keen math machine, so blessed with the knowledge that I think Einstein would have been jealous. When it came to Central, she was its guardian angel and its fire-breathing dragon all rolled into one. Someone once swore that she cut her finger and her blood dripped purple. She was petite in size but huge in her love of disciplined students, effective teachers, mathematics and Central High School. She made it known that as a member of the math department that your primary mission in life was to serve Central, through math, every day you were there.

Miss Pratt was inching toward retirement when I met her in 1979, but you'd never know it. She was sharp as a tack and as witty as they came. She carried herself in a highly sophisticated manner. She just *looked* in charge. Satire aside, she is a beautiful person through and through, but teaching and progressing students through mathematics was serious, serious business for her and she made sure that it was the business of everyone in her department as well.

> *In life not all greetings are welcomed times.*
>
> *(W.R.O.)*

Miss Pratt seemed to be made for Central, and it for her. I think in the end, the racket of the jackhammers, along with the firing of the nail guns and roaring machinery during the reconstruction years inside and out of the school building, became just too much uncontrolled chaos and noise. The constant disturbance seemed to unsettle her, and brought with it a definitive auditory reminder that change was in the air. Within a few years of my arrival, she retired with little fanfare. But that's how she liked it - simple, precise and accurately to the point. I know of no one who didn't respect her. Though she sometimes left grown men and women quaking in their boots while trying to serve Central to her level of expectation, she was always fair and supportive.

There have been many kings at Central, dating all the way back to John Kellom in 1870. But through it all there has only been one queen. Really, in 1937 Miss Pratt was crowned Miss Central at the "All Girls Party" sponsored by Student Control. That same year she was named the "Ideal Central Girl" by the senior class.

Cinderella Ball
Virginia Lee Pratt chosen Miss Central [?] at an all-school girls' party sponsored by Student Control

OB

If anyone ever figures out time travel, please jet back to 1937 Central High and tell the students there that they got it right. She was indeed as they predicted, Miss Central and for certain the "Ideal Central Girl." Later, she would not only teach class - she was class. No matter who you were, if you ever knew Miss Pratt, you had to respect her.

Greetings from the King and Queen

So within my first five minutes at Central I am being leaned on outside my classroom door by King Moller, while Queen Virginia III is circling me like a bird of prey. She's looking me up and down, from head to toe. As she circles me her confused expressions seem to ask, "What's wrong with this man, is he crazy? Is he sick? Does he know where he is? Did he just walk up on my floor twenty minutes late on the first day of school?" It was just the two of them, but I felt as though I was surrounded by hundreds! I tried again to hand them my get out of jail free card (the very real broken down car excuse), but it was looked upon like the rest of the money used in the monopoly game - "*counterfeit!*"

Now my thoughts became self-derogating. Why would I depend on a Vega to get me to my first day at Central!?! All the while Miss Pratt just kept staring, and Doc never stopped talking.

The royal visit seemed like it took about two hours in 100-degree heat, but in reality it was only about five minutes at room temperature. They disassembled me and then put me back together. As they walked away Miss Pratt, like the wife of Lot, as they exited Sodom and Gomorrah, turned and gave me one last glance. But instead of her turning into a pillar of salt, I did! Her expression seemed to say, "You better get a road map and find out where you are. This isn't high school, this is Central High School." I didn't know it at the time, but I found out later that there really was a difference.

Central High School, Doc Moller and Miss Pratt. I was about as prepared for that threesome as the Germans were at Normandy. With her expectations and Doc's demands, they asked me to do things I had never done. Since that was the case, I knew right away that to survive Central I had to find a way to become someone that I had never been.

A few months after my first day debacle, Miss Pratt had me in on another misdemeanor charge. Sensing that she had battered me consistently for quite a long trek, she called me to her office and said the oddest of things. She said, "Mr. Reed, I like you. I'll never show it and you'll never know it, but I just thought I'd tell you." Then she politely bowed her head and began writing. I sat there, stunned. Within a few seconds she jerked her head back up and in a sharp curt voice snapped, "Well go on, get out of here now!" She is the closest thing to royalty in a school that I ever met. Some people, with pride are All-American and that's great but Miss Virginia Lee Pratt with dignity, will forever be "ALL-OMAHA CENTRAL!" And that will suit her just fine... *I'll never forget her. What a lady!!!*

Those first day classes were accelerated. The class periods were more "get acquainted" time, then a quick bell would ring. It was sort of a walk-through, or as I related it to golf, a practice round. After Doc and Miss Pratt had given me my Scotland Yard welcome I just soaked in the atmosphere. Inside these walls it really did feel different, and the organized business of staff and students made me feel proud to be there. There was either a full faculty meeting or a math department meeting after school that day, I don't remember which. What I do remember is during the meeting I kept thinking the same thought - I had a mishap, got my butt chewed, and I'm still here. Wow, this must be home. That afternoon as I finished my first day, I realized that I had started my new life and in that short time I had learned my first and most important lesson - Omaha Central High School is like no other!

Chapter 8

STUDENTS UNDER THE BIG TOP

The blending and unique harmony of a diverse student body

OB

The distinguished Omaha Central A Cappella choir

Diversification

"They're all in their places with bright shining faces." That's the way we sang it in Monroe, Louisiana in 1954 on my first day of school in Miss Moses' 1st grade class at Carver Elementary. But now the seating arrangement had changed. My seat is facing the class and it is now my job to make all the faces shiny and bright. Though my first day at Central started a bit chaotic, once again the black and white film in my new life seemed to have changed to brilliant bright colors. I found myself holding to the notion that I remained in the magical Land of Oz. When all the teachers were in their places and all the students were in the building too, I saw the very best of what Central really was…"DIVERSIFIED". Right away its makeup seemed to be a tiny microcosm of that of the United States, particularly among the students. This became the part of Central that I would come to love the most.

At the advent of the 1980's Omaha Central sported a superb ethnic mixture. It was a diverse student body that seemed to reflect all that we were in the good old US of A. I was told that at one time back in the mid to late 60's, which was around the beginning of Doc's tenure as principal (1968) that the population of the student body was about one-half European, one-fourth Jewish, one-fourth African American with a sparse number of Latinos. The reality is that the United States is neither one-fourth African American nor Jewish, and the Latino population across the country was perhaps a little more than sparse at the time. Still, in my mind, this was a great mixture for a young person in Nebraska to be exposed to. At Central you were getting the full representation

All-State chorus 1981

OB

of ethnic, economic and societal groups interacting in real-time. This to me seemed to enhance the educational experience.

The blending of the cultures and classes of the students at Central was a great thing to see, particularly for someone who was only nine years removed from the *labeling of blood*. Things seemed so genuine and the everyday intermingling of the variety of lives, racially, socially and economically lent to ones thoughts that the world indeed had become a better place. Yes, Omaha Central seemed to offer up that glimpse of togetherness that I thought I'd never see in my lifetime. I was extremely proud to be in the midst of it all, as it seemed to be the norm in nearly every aspect of the school. Except there was one area that just didn't seem to be in step with the rest of the great visuals within the setting. It was the two cafeterias up on fourth floor that had me puzzled. All of the diverse interactions seemed to stop once students reached the fourth floor cafeterias. For whatever reason, the personable practice of eating lunch seemed to clearly create a racial divide among the student body and no one seemed to know why.

Voluntary Separation. The Dual Cafeterias of Omaha Central!

The dual cafeterias of Omaha Central was a staunch reminder to me that no matter where you go or what you do nothing will ever be 100 percent perfect. For as much as I loved the school, Omaha Central was no exception to this rule. While I found it fascinating, there was something within the walls that was all too much of a reminder of my days in northeast Louisiana. It was those dual cafeterias up on fourth floor. One was located on the **3side** while the other was adjacent on the **4side**. Upon first seeing them I thought, man the uniqueness of Central is on display again. However, the gathering from within confused me from the very beginning. The **3side** cafeteria always filled up with about 99 percent of the black students that ate lunch, while the **4side** filled up about the same with white students. It was not malicious, in fact it seemed innocent and harmless. From what I could see no one seemed bothered by it in the least bit, it was all routine business or as many students put it…"just the way things were". However, it bothered me a lot from day one. Again, I think it was due to all those bad experiences from my days in the old South, a situation I'd left nine years before and never wanted to see again.

Don't get me wrong, there was nothing preferential about it at all, the cafeterias served the same food for the same price and the rules and expectations were the exact same on either side. It was sort of a separate but equal scenario. This was okay for some, but within my past involvement inside the southern states that I once called home, separate but equal was never a healthy meal. Within such a scheme, inferiority and superiority complexes ran rampant and blocked out much of the promised outcome of fairness. It was this segregated picture of the 1950's South that I saw when I first looked upon the dual cafeterias at Omaha Central High. It was not a good portrait.

By this time I had fallen in love with Central, but having already seen this "separate but equal" business up close and personal I knew exactly what it led to. It starts with a separate few that eventually spreads to the many. It becomes more comfortable to separate in more and more areas, so more join in. Soon it becomes the norm for the upper classmen and the newer and less strong students are forced through optic perception to follow the crowd that looks most like them. The trendy choices to fit in are made visible by the strong, leaving little choice for the weak. They either go with what is perceived as their kind or fall prey the hellish throngs of peer alienation. Some may argue that there is nothing wrong with such, and maybe there wasn't. However, I saw Central as something different, something special. I felt that racial separation in any sense within its walls, in any setting, was beneath its standards. In fact, in this type setup, even if it only occurs during lunch, could lead eventually to an erosion of togetherness elsewhere, which could create a lack of cohesiveness school-wide. In that scenario some could begin to look upon the institution as biased, appearing to favor selective entities while seemingly being tolerant to some and totally intolerant to others. Whether it is happening or not, within this setting it could start a decay that could rot out a school's foundation from the root. To clarify; ***No school accepting such a social separation is able to deliver at maximum efficiency to the whole of its embodiment.*** (W.R.O.)

Omaha Central was better than that and I wasn't about to take the chance that it might become something less on the inside of two cafeterias then it truly was throughout. These dual-sided, neatly segregated cafeterias seemed to be a curious and out of place occurrence in a melting pot of people that seemed to otherwise work so great together in every other aspect. The students at Central were not separate that way in any other facet of their school life, so this particular circumstance was hard to understand. To me it seemed a kind of casualness went with it, as if some sort of built-in treaty had been adopted between black and white students. I asked around and no one had an answer. Many said they hadn't even noticed the separation. I talked to a few teachers, and many had hardly even seen the cafeterias and seemed a bit uncomfortable with my inquiry. None could explain the origin of the separation inside the dual cafeterias, while a good many had failed to recognize its very existence. Regardless, it seemed ridiculously out of place to me and quickly became one of the few things at Central that I came to disdain.

As luck would have it, in my third year I was appointed "The Monitoring Executive of Food Distribution and Consumption and The Chief Compliance and Enforcement Officer of The Northern Eatery" at Omaha Central High School. Or as Doc called it **"cafeteria duty on the north side!"** I loved the job. It was one of those *"I will work for food"* deals, as it came with a free daily meal. This was so ironic, I was now in charge of the only piece of daily routine that, to me did not live up to that *high standards of representation, befitting that of the expectation of Central High tradition.* I really could have left well enough alone and allowed the situation to continue. After all, no one else seemed bothered by it, not even in the least bit. But for me it was just too much of a reminder of the 1964 segregated Piccadilly Cafeteria back in Monroe, Louisiana. I felt compelled to at least make an effort to change the curious separation that was happening daily in each of the three lunch periods in the dual cafeterias of Omaha Central.

Once I put my mind to it and really got after it, things happened pretty simply and quite hastily. The process was a delicate one. You couldn't just tell students where to eat, even back in the grown up ruled 1980's. First, to make things work I found that I could only call upon that which I controlled, which wasn't very much at the time. However, there was one major group that I had total control over. So, I came up with a plan that would put them into play.

I ended up enlisting the popularity of the football team as the main catalyst for change and things happened immediately. In the almost "all white" north cafeteria, located on the **4side**, I proclaimed it mandatory that all football players eat on that side so that I could monitor what they ate. Of course they had little choice of meals in a school cafeteria, so they knew I wasn't monitoring their meals, but no one dared question my intentions. It helped a great deal that the man monitoring the other cafeteria, Mr. Stan Standifer, happened to be one of my assistant football coaches. I admit it was personal, I just couldn't stand even a hint of segregation within a place that I had come to love so dearly. I made it a matter of "football law", that all players needed to be monitored for diet during the entire year, even after the season. This meant they had to eat in the north cafeteria the entire school year. After the permanent migration of a team that was almost a perfect mix of 50% black and white players, along with their girlfriends and other groupies who followed them, segregation in the dual cafeterias soon became a thing of the past. A lot of the white kids that frequented the north cafeteria didn't like the jocks, so after the invasion, they migrated to the other side. A lot of the black kids from the west cafeteria didn't choose to follow the jocks as they migrated north. The result was the cafeterias taking on the look of the rest of the school - diverse and together. It left me bursting with pride.

One of my brightest moments at Central came when Mr. Richard Jones (Athletic Director) made a statement one day acknowledging my effort to change things. He looked me in the eye and then scanned the north side cafeteria, where he and I ate together nearly every day and said, "You know, this was a good thing you did in here." I came to love and respect Dick Jones and I miss the fact that he's not here to read this book. May God rest his soul! For the next eight years during lunch I was a prominent figure in the **4side** north cafeteria. For all those years the rules for football players and where they ate never changed. ***However, the dual cafeterias of Omaha Central most certainly did!***

Omaha Central
Aptitude and Attitude!

> "Each student must be pushed beyond their limits,
> challenged to do the right thing and NEVER lied to about their
> performance!"
> *- Dr. G.E. Moller in an interview at Panera Bread-*

O nce the case of the separate cafeterias was resolved, there was nothing at Central more obvious to me than the attitudes and interaction of the students and staff as they engaged upon their perspective duties. Everyone just seemed to blend within the setting. Of course, there were the usual clicks and picks that adorn every high school campus, but more than anything else the students and staff seemed to be together and respectful of one another. This was especially true with sports, which I have always seen as the great unifier. As stated before, the social attitudes of the student body at Central and the serious business nature of the staff was unlike any that I had ever encountered. This group, particularly the staff, seemed to be on another level as opposed to when I had seen them in other places.

I'd met some of the staff while they were teaching at other schools. When I met them back there they were sincere, serious and dedicated to the cause. However, here they were different. They seemed to walk and talk with a more sophisticated demeanor and carried a more professional attitude now that they were at Central. What a difference! It was true, once teachers dropped anchor at Central they became a little bit more high-stepping and sported a look of total confidence. Later, I found that it wasn't personal nor arrogance, it was more Barbara Streisand, "The Way We Were" from the top down.

In this place, attitude wise, you had to be all in to make it. There was no way you could survive Central while acting as if it was just another school. In this gathering of hearts and minds, teaching students while preparing them for college and other endeavors was big business, and everyone seemed to know that. Often times I would talk to students that had matriculated to higher places. They would tell me wide-eyed stories about how well equipped they were once they experienced the vast challenges that awaited them. They would tell of how prepared they were for the multitude of situations that confronted them, and how ready they were for the diverse cultures that seemed to be in every newfound setting. I always felt a pride in knowing that Omaha Central was not about just teaching and learning through books and classrooms. It offered a lifetime experience that seemed to fully encompass the educational experience it was sworn to uphold. Sure, there are all-girl's schools that are good, but our society is not all girls. There are all-boy's schools that are strong, but our society is not all boys. There are schools teaching 99% white students, and some that are teaching 99% minority students, but our society is not that way either. These can all be good schools, but none of them offered what Omaha Central did

> *The first duty of the school is to ensure that every student has access to a quality education.*
>
> *(W.R.O.)*

Giving a voice to the students. The diverse 1988-89 Student Council

in the way of real world and real life situations. As I spent more time at my new school, I found that this thinking wasn't narcissistic, it was all about attitude. A challenging academic curriculum, strong and energetic teachers, an eager-to-learn student body, business savvy administrators and quality extracurricular activities made Omaha Central High School everything an American high school should be.

As if things weren't already good enough, a few years after my arrival some-one noticed that it was time to move the buildings toward the new millenni-um. The serving of that notice ushered in a time of major renovations! The cranes, scaffolds and jackhammers moved in, but the teaching never stopped. Project after project, month after month, it went on and on, testing the pa-tience and resolve of every teacher, while challenging the attention span of every student. Teaching through noise, learning through chaos - it was a diffi-cult time for everyone. The staff and students were incredible throughout the entire reconstruction process and the results proved to be worth it.

Inside the dynamic Omaha Central courtyard

The west side was the first to go to the makeup room and the Central haters had to be eating their hearts out! A 1.6 million dollar Astroturf football practice facility was installed, including a synthetic polyurethane micro foam track. It was amazing and to add to the luxury, it was only about twenty steps from the west side lower entrance doors. At the time, it was one of the few such facilities in the midwest on a high school campus and for sure the only one in Nebraska. The next remodeling during the early 1980's was a modern-day upgrading of every single outer facing window in the building, offering a fantastic new look from the outside. The auditorium got new seats, while finishing touches were placed on a brand new gym. Even the inner floors and doors got in on the act, with facelifts that didn't disturb their nostalgic image. Then came the crown jewel of the renovation projects. The courtyard was sent into the age of contemporary styling and was fitted for a new glass hat, a spectacular sky roof that she wears proudly to this day. This touch made the Omaha Central courtyard far and away the most popular attraction on campus and the coolest commons area in the state. One that we were all very proud of.

Upon final evaluation, with all parts in place I made this final conclusion: For years Omaha Central has been recognized and renowned statewide for its diversity, academia and social aptitude. Athletically, it was revered for its basketball prowess and track dominance. In the midst of my evaluation I became acutely aware that I was standing between pillars of greatness and was poised to usher in a football program that would match the famed Eagle tradition…."Purple Rain" was in the forecast!

OB

These looks said it all as purple rain turned into "purple reign." Omaha Central 1984 State Football Champs.

61

The

2Two Side

"2Side Up, Dodge Street Down"
The 2Side was the second of the four-sided structures built.
Sitting atop a hill too steep, it caused Dodge Street to be
lowered. Completed in 1908, it faced Dodge Street.B

Central High To Central America

A transfer from Central begins a journey to tropical Belize

When Central High came into my life, I was overjoyed. When I left it, I was deeply saddened. But before long a new Central came into focus and it would offer sightings to some of the most beautiful places in the world. At Central High I navigated the streets and highways. In Central America I navigated the Caribbean Sea and found beauty beyond my dreams, with hardship living just around the corner.

My first stop was the island of St. Lucia where I made my home for several months at the scenic Windjammer Resort. My next stop was Barbados. Where on a week-long observation stay our hangout was the exclusive Sandy Lane. Sandy Lane a place so unique it sports a golf course that doesn't even have a club house. The residents just simply drive golf carts from their homes onto the course and play. The course was free but each lot cost about a million dollars.

These were two great places, but where I finally dropped anchor was a hidden little gem that wasn't an island at all. It was old British Honduras, a country that was now called Belize...

Chapter 1

THE JOY OF INTEGRITY, THE PLEASURE OF SUCCESS

Pleasure is temporary, while joy derives from God and is everlasting

Nicholas and Zachary

Two Fifth Graders

One night, while visiting friends, I sat down for dinner with two very talkative twin fifth graders. They were Nicholas and Zachary Keithley. The meal was great but at dessert they tried to force whipped cream on me, something I never eat. I don't think they'd ever met a person who didn't care for whipped cream so my "no thank you" spawned a very interesting debate. Somehow our conversation evolved and overflowed into a rather candid discussion about the difference between pleasure and joy. When asked about the comparison the twins went into a very serious and hesitant mode.

I could see that they were in deep thought, seeming to understand that besides me, mom, dad and two older brothers were also sitting at the table in anticipation of their response. Finally, Nicholas spoke up and in a very confident voice he said, "Pleasure is something that comes and lasts for just a little while, then it fades away, but joy is inside you, it comes from God, it's more real and it lasts forever." I was shocked at the statement and awed by the presentation. It was a deep, very sincere answer and later it sent me all the way back to my days at Omaha Central. I'd thought that being there was a pleasure but after I left, based on the young twins descriptions it must have been a joy, because it is still inside me. I still love the time, I still love the place and I still love the people. Like Nicholas said, it came from God, it's forever!

For Omaha Central football, as a staff we brought joy and it was a pleasure bringing it. That first year we lost three of the first four games but finished with three wins in the second half of the season. From there we never looked back. In just over a year after our arrival, the school whose football team hadn't experienced a winning season in nearly two decades was all of a sudden in the Class A (Nebraska big class) playoffs. The game went to a tie-breaker and we lost in overtime to Burke High. However, that night we won everywhere else and for the next 10 years, throughout the 80's we were the most talked about football team in the state. By the time we won the state title in 1984 we had become one of those well known high

> *What we do in life echoes in eternity.*
> *"Gladiator 2000"*

school football programs that everyone raved about. We were consistently producing some of the top players in the country and it only got better.

By 1990, more than 40 players from Omaha Central had been offered Division I scholarships and by then we'd had so many All-Metro and All-Staters that I lost count. By 1994, six Omaha Central I-backs had run the ball for the University of Nebraska covering twelve of the fifteen years that I or my assistant had lead the Central program. Also, during the 1980's, in five separate years the University of Iowa made an Omaha Central player one of their top recruiting priorities.

At Omaha Central the football program had changed for the better, but that wasn't all that changed for me. Through Doc's relentless push for perfection over the eleven years that I was there, I'd become a much better teacher also. Success was now expected at Central and every year it was realized in some way, shape or form. We became known as "the school with speed" and we showcased it every year, not only in football but also in both boys and girls track. Yes, things were great at Central High School throughout the 80's but as the 90's came lumbering in, I longed for something different; a new challenge, a new place, for what had become a new time.

After eleven of the best years of my life, in a place where I had been woven into its purple and white fabric, I was contemplating leaving. At the time I didn't know the joy, it was too deep to find, and like the kids said the pleasure only lasted for just a little while. I thought I needed a change. Four years later, Forrest Gump's mom said, "Stupid is as stupid does", and this was about as stupid as it gets. I had my reasons but it had nothing to do with anything negative. I felt that a good football program and a great tradition was now a finished product at Central.

That year, there was a quiet rumor murmuring throughout the system, that it was time to bring certain Omaha public schools to par level with Central. It all made sense to me and the rumors were strong enough that I believed them. I'd grown weary of the lofty football expectations at Omaha Central that came with the beginning of each year. I don't know why, I just had. Success comes and with it comes great pleasure and with that comes the question we all must answer; ***If the pleasure remains, does it remain a pleasure?*** Of course, two fifth graders have already answered that question, so there's no need to ponder.

It was indeed a privilege and a pleasure to teach and coach at Omaha Central High School for eleven glorious years. And yes, the joy of that time is still inside me and indeed will be there forever.

Integrity And Success

Omaha Central is a school whose very existence and reputation exudes great expectations for success. We only brought football to a level par with the schools already existent high level of expectation. While the football success was grand and we basked in its newfound status, Doc Moller never allowed me or anyone else to make it paramount. I was pushed by him at every turn to be better at being a teacher and a better man then I was at being a better coach. He challenged me relentlessly, especially in the classroom. I never felt as though I struggled as a teacher, but I struggled mightily to meet his standards and adhere to his demands.

At the time I didn't understand the push, but later, even as I prepared to leave Central, I realized what it was all about. I felt that for the most part I was pretty good in most facets of my life. However, Doc never accepted "pretty good." He didn't mind you being "pretty good", if that was all you could be. But if he saw a potential that you were not utilizing, he was on you like a twenty year old suit, "too tight." I understand easily today that I needed every push he was giving me, but at the time all I thought about was getting him off my back.

He always drove home the point that integrity made the man. I heard him when he said it, but it was only a courtesy listen. I think back in the day it was described as "in one ear and out the other". ***Webster defines integrity as: The quality of being honest and having strong moral principles.*** One never thinks about integrity or brag that they have it. It's just one of those things that everyone seems to assume they have. I thought I had it. Doc had presented it to me many times, never really mentioning the word, while offering up many complex examples. I didn't get the simplified version of the meaning until one day when I was asked to give a talk to the Omaha North High football team. There was a familiar man who spoke ahead of me that day and I listened to him intently. He was the former head football coach for the University of Nebraska, Dr. Tom Osborne. If you're wondering what he was doing there the answer is simple. Coach Osborne is one of those stubborn guys from the past that will go anywhere he feels he can help the future. I know, most probably think it to be futile and crazy but he just won't stop trying! Like I said, stubborn and that spells c-a-r-i-n-g.

That day in the room with the kids he brought up the word "integrity" and then simplified it to both them and me. He presented a rather detailed scenario involving one finding a lost wallet that contained $300 and the person's ID with no one around. He asked, what would you do? He then scanned the room and said very deliberately *"Integrity is determined by the things you do when no one is watching."* It's what Doc had been trying to teach me for all those years at Central. I finally got it. However, by then I had long since left Doc Moller, my greatest teacher and Omaha Central High, my eternal classroom.

The Odd Decisions Of The Program Builders

I can't explain it but some coaches just love to build programs and sometimes once they have they become stagnant within it. I think that I was of that sort. We're the group that when success begins to happen in expected repetition, we often lose the sweet smell of the aroma that comes with genuine appreciation. We begin to long for new challenges in new places. Places that seem to offer more freedom, and with our newfound reputations based on our latest successes, we can now garner more power.

During my tenure at Central the feeling of having become an established program with high expectations each year no longer excited me. For eleven years the pleasure had indeed remained, but did it remain a pleasure? I had begun to think not. During one of those last days of school I recall pausing to reflect on my life as a teacher and a coach within the four sides. I'd arrived at Omaha Central in the fall of 1979, a time when the football program was stuck in the mud, with no chance of getting out any time soon.

The players seemed to almost expect to lose and accepted it way too easily. Before my arrival, for almost twenty years each football season at Central had begun with low expectations and ended with a losing record. However, upon my arrival that would all change. With a great cast of assistants and a positive flow of hard-working players, Omaha Central became one of the most popular high school football programs in the midwest, consistently producing so many prime time runners that I aptly named it "I-Back High"!

The list was amazing and nearly made us famous. The blueprint was already there; Gale Sayers to Kansas, Phil Bates to Nebraska, and Danny Goodwin to Iowa State. All three of these great players had already been popular Central runners in the past. So, I started with their history, along with my knowledge of the great runners from my high school, Carroll High in Monroe, Louisiana, and built upon that. The running back position gained us instant fame and credibility, so we ran with it. However the overall program was about more than that. In the fall of 1979 we started something special and for eleven years I made sure it stayed that way. In 1990 my Offensive Coordinator, Joe Mc-Menamin followed me as head coach and he for sure got the memo and kept "it" going. And what is the "it"? ***Coaches make players, players make plays, plays make the game and we all become winners. (W.R.O.)*** We created a gem of a program with our focal point on players garnering scholarships. Our theory was that with that mindset, championships were sure to follow. That simple philosophy led us to create one of the most effective, player producing programs in the state's history. We were indeed "I-Back High". When I look back, even years later I am still overwhelmed at the consistent rate of high quality runners created by the program.

OMAHA CENTRAL HIGH SCHOOL

I-BACK "HIGH" HONOR ROLL

Year / Runner / College

1979, Gerald Paul, Nebraska Omaha
*1980, Terry Evans, Nebraska Omaha
1981, Pernell Gatson, University of Nebraska
1982, Nikki Paul, Info not available
1982, Byron Allen, Info not Available
*1983, Keith Jones, University of Nebraska
*1984, Bernard Jackson, Jr. College/Peru State
1984, Richard Bass, University of Iowa
*1985, Leodis Flowers, University of Nebraska
*1986, Leodis Flowers, University of Nebraska
1986, Curtis Cotton, University of Nebraska
1987, James Sims, University of Nebraska
*1987, Ronnie Barfield, UNLV
1988, Kelly Yancy, Oklahoma State
1988, Sherman Williams, Iowa State
*1989, Calvin Jones, University of Nebraska
1990, Bryant Gardner, Info not available

Year / Runner / College

1991, Jesse Value, Info not available
*1992, Damian Morrow, Wayne State
*1993, Damian Morrow, Wayne State
*1993, Ahman Green, University of Nebraska
*1994. Damian Morrow, Wayne State
*1994 Ahman Green, University of Nebraska
*1996, DeAntae Grixsby, University of Nebraska
*1997, DeAntae Grixsby, University of Nebraska
*1998, Ja'maine Billups, Iowa State
*1999, Ja'maine Billups, Iowa State
*1999, Lornell McPherson, University of Nebraska
*1999, Brandon Williams, University of Michigan
*2000, David Horne, University of Nebraska
*2001, David Horne, University of Nebraska
2002, Brandon Gunn, Iowa State
2003, Brandon Gunn, Iowa State
2004, Robert Wesley, Nebraska Omaha
*2005, Ronnell Grixby, University of Nebraska

Reference contributor: Stu Pospisil

* Denotes 1,000 yard rushing year

This charted reference of the runners is enough in itself to show how the relevance of Omaha Central football grew through the years. But they were just a sliver of the overall pattern of success that changed it all. Players like The Pauls', Gerald and Nikki, Nate Blanks, Sonny Jones, Tom Stawniak, Chris Sacco, Tony Avant, Doug Roper, Abe Hoskins, Sean Ridley, Eric Anderson, the Salerno's, Pat and Mike, the Smiths, Tim and Chip, Mancuso, Roper, Ball and who could ever forget Gerald Marfisi and the many others that were just as instrumental! In fact, the rapid rise of the program overall was due mostly in part to a beginning nucleus that included three very special players. When **Larry Station, Pernell Gatson and Dave VanMetre** showed up at Omaha Central in the fall of 1979 the football program would change abruptly.

After one year of their arrival as tenth graders, the school became something it had never been, a respected football program nationally. **Larry Station** to the University of Iowa. Larry was that defensive tough guy that every team needed. He became the mold that shaped every defensive player that followed. He has since been viewed as one of the greatest defensive players in Big Ten college football history and became a college football Hall of Famer. **Pernell Gatson** to the University of Nebraska. Pernell was our speed mold. He brought flair, with a flash and dash style that attracted more like him. He was a standout quarterback that was recruited across the country before choosing to play in the Big 8 Conference. **Dave VanMetre** to Cornell University. Dave was that glue that every good team has to have in order to be successful. He was a player that showed everyone how to make themselves special! He was loved by most and respected by all, a shining example of hard work, discipline and determination. He became an Ivy Leaguer and an NCAA Division I Academic All-American.

These three men flourished in life but not before becoming the catalyst that changed the football mindset at Omaha Central, a mindset that still exists today. I loved being their leader during such a successful and transformational time. It was a very special feeling, that brought with it new expectations and the attitude of winners, that kept on growing.

I could have stayed and followed the routine of satisfaction at Central forever but it was not to be. We had raised the bar so high that sometimes even we couldn't get over it. I took great pride in being a part of it all. However, the building of a program is what had excited me and I was less enthused about holding one together. So, like those heroes of the old cowboy movies after cleaning up the town, I thought it was time to ride off into the sunset.

I once heard this question asked of a man – "If you have it all here why would you want to leave?" The man answered, "*because having has not near the joy and excitement as wanting!*" I wanted to build something again, and with the public school's administration looking to bring other schools to the level of Central, I felt that this was the best time. My thought was that I'd rather be in a place working for success and relevance, as opposed to building on what was already considered one. I entertained the thought of, "you've done this once, then you can go to another place and do it again".

In December of 1989 I resigned as coach of the Omaha Central football team and put in for a transfer. A few weeks later I called a press conference and made it official. It would be a decision I would question for many years that followed. But regardless of the sentiment, by the end of January 1990 I officially got word that my transfer request had been granted. With the joy still in me I made preparations to leave the man and the school that had transformed my life. But before leaving I had one last job to complete. In the spring of 1990, as head coach of the girls track team, I would lead the Eagles to an unforeseen runaway Class A State Track and Field title. It was the happiest coaching accomplishment of my life and at the same time the saddest, because it was my last assigned duty as a Central High Eagle.

It was in the middle of the field at Burke High Stadium. Almost the exact same spot where I hoisted the first ever Omaha Public Schools state championship football trophy five years earlier. Jade Williams, Lisa Littlejohn, Yvonne Andrews and Angie Green had just won the All-Class gold medal in the 1600 meter relay and stood atop the podium in the middle of the Burke Stadium field. As is customary the cameraman moved in for the victory photo opt, when suddenly, the girls yelled for me to join them in the picture. I declined, but with them realizing the moment that I had not, they wouldn't take the picture without me. Their victory had marked the end of the 1990 Girls' Nebraska State Track Meet and also the end of my days at Central. I took a spot in front of the podium and they stood taller above. Then, the camera clicked and flashed brightly, but for me the day went dark. Because at that moment I knew as they did too, that my life at Omaha Central was over.

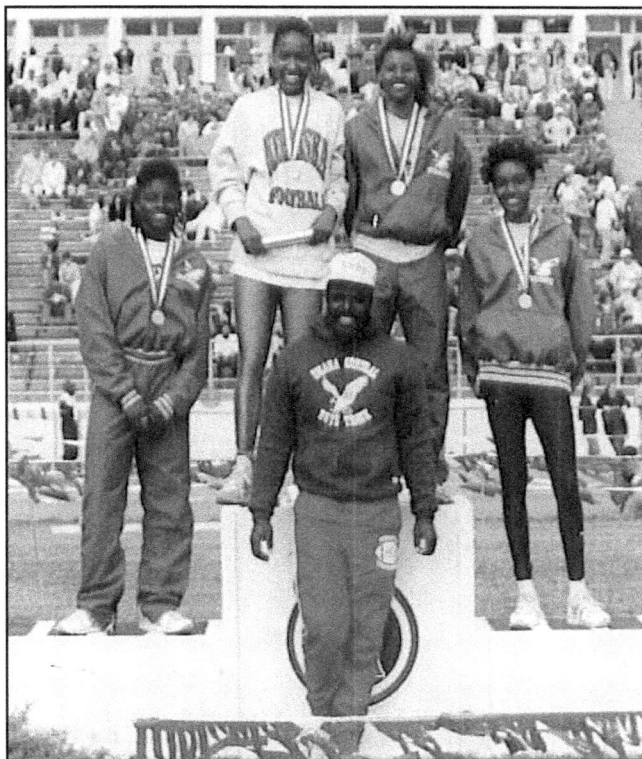

My last stand as an Eagle. In May of 1990 I was the girls head track coach of a team not picked to do much. However, the girls seemed to know that it was a special time and they indeed performed that way. We became one of the few schools that had ever swept all three of the Class A relays in the state track meet. Those feats helped pave the way to a run-away Omaha Central fifth straight state meet championship. It was my proudest and at the same time my saddest moments in coaching.

Chapter 2

SCOLDING WORDS OF WISDOM

A gift of knowledge from Dr. G.E. Moller

OB

Belief ???
Care, Give, Love,
Work, Respect, Discipline
Six words to belief, my greatest gifts from Doc

When I knew that it was time to leave Central I stood alone in room 320, looking down on Dodge Street. I was taking one last optical visit through downtown Omaha, from a third floor Omaha Central vantage point. I had come there with no thoughts of learning anything. Yet, during my stay I had gathered a wealth of knowledge, enough to propel me through three more life times. Most of it originated from my interactions with Doc Moller and though much of it wasn't pleasant, it resonated as some of the best lessons I ever received in life.

Doc helped me to cross that bridge called "Better" but before that he pushed me to start the journey. Every journey begins with the belief that one understands where he's headed and remembers from whence he came. I had not a clue when it came to the meaning and understanding of what I'd been taught and I don't think Doc knew either, what it was exactly that he'd been teaching. Before and since my time with him I've seen and met scores of school administrators. Still, Doc Moller ranks as the best I've ever seen. From the time I started school as a first grader, to the time I stopped teaching thirty-six years later, into this moment, no school administrator has ever impressed me more.

One of his greatest attributes was staring down anyone within his command, while giving them the cold hard reality of any situation. The things I learned from him came in broken parts that spread through eleven jagged years. They were strong lessons, dished out in fragmented pieces and were exactly what I needed. However, they came during times when I questioned their purpose and didn't see their worth. Because of that, it would take me several years to reap their value. When I finally did, I pieced together some of his strongest messages and like a beacon of hope, they guided me through my next life.

Once I realized Doc's motives, I understood his teachings. Later, I would structure his tight scrutiny and demands into an organized format. That format would become a formula of attributes and a system of values for all manner of teachings and business. It would become a conduit to those wanting to learn, eventually leading them to the single most important quality toward maximized knowledge. That quality is **belief**.

There were no other bosses at any other time in my life that placed such a high level of expectation on me. I didn't know how valuable it was at the time. However, the further life took me away from the school system, the better I understood the intent of his demands. I was grateful in the aftermath. Little did I know during my time at Central, that Doc Moller was challenging me daily with the foundation of a value system that would one day lead to **the root of acquiring knowledge.**

After our time at Central, I recall thanking Doc for his staunch lessons that pushed me beyond mediocrity. He took my compliment modestly in stride and said, "Didn't you sometimes want to just take a book and bash me over the head?" I said, "Of course not Doc, I just wanted to strangle you slowly!" When we parted that day, we both laughed all the way to our cars.

It was never a secret, Gaylord Moller was relentless in his push for quality and a stickler for planning and organization. Through the years he consistently challenged me to adopt certain values, then demanded that I live by them. Whenever it seemed I wasn't, he didn't remind me, he added more demands.

I really wanted to teach kids, but at the time I didn't see the necessity for his constant push. There were meetings after meetings, lessons after lessons and demand after demand. During this push, he laid out a series of values in the form of those demands. Values that I would later take advantage of, as the six steps used in the structuring and development of my golf school. In the operations of the school, I found that teaching was teaching and learning was learning, no matter the subject or situation.

It was amazing how everything so perfectly correlated. From the warnings, to the demands, to the close scrutiny and all the other disciplines, came a series of messages from Doc that would frame my third life. The messages usually began on his typewriter and ended on a note in my mailbox. He would summon me to his office and grill me on some lacking phase of my duties then send me on my way. On numerous occasions he would calmly but precisely attack me with an arsenal of perfected literary verbiage. It was a barrage of what I now know were words meant to motivate and guide me. These verbal attacks came hard and often and it seemed only perfection could get them stopped. Later, I recalled six specific words, from which I deduced a pattern. A pattern that helped to secure my approach to business and teaching. At the same time they would change my life for the better.

The first such word was **care**. For a good long spell it was all about caring, or in Doc's approach the lack thereof. "William, I just don't think you care." "William you have to care to be successful in teaching your students." Other times the word was **discipline**. "William, you do good things, but you lack discipline." For another period the call was for **love**. "You've got to love this job William, not just like it, you have to love it." I recall thinking to myself, "I can't love the job for hating you." I could hardly stand him during those years. These were the early years when I saw all of his scrutiny and demands as borderline harassment.

For a while, it was all about the word **work**. "Success as an educator only comes from hard work William." Still another time the word **give** kept popping up. "William you have to give your all. You have to give yourself to the cause." Give, give, give! Then there were those messages regarding **respect**, birthday cards, notes of wisdom, faculty meetings, speeches. For a time, it was all about garnering respect. These were six words of value that we all would do well to adhere to, especially if you ever desire to teach within any setting. I had such a desire and Doc's relentless push for excellence soon became my saving grace.

From the beginning I'd always been curious about teaching and learning. My first grade teacher, at Carver Elementary was Miss Moses. I hardly remembered a word she said that entire year. When I was promoted to the second grade, I found Mrs. Hill. She talked way too slowly and all I recalled from her class was my countdown to 3:00 p.m. When each day I heard the two most anticipated words of my young life... "class dismissed."

But that following year, third grade came with a change of schools but more importantly, a change of perspective in my teacher. Those first two years I was frightened of what I didn't know but Miss Jenkins made me fearless by teaching it to me. She impressed me right away by not having smart seat sections, average sections and slow sections within her classroom. It was amazing how I blossomed in her class that school year. It was 1956, the time I've always recognized as my first year of school. It seemed in those first two years I was "**at**" the school. But when I found Miss Jenkins at Lincoln Elementary, for the first time I was actually "**in**" school! More importantly, I was learning like never before.

For a long period of time I pondered in thought. What did Miss Jenkins do that was so different from the two teachers that preceded her? That question haunted me for years and finally one day, I got it; *"I believed in everything she said and trusted in everything she asked me to do. I took in her teachings with a kind of certainty that left no doubt that I was acquiring real knowledge. What it said to me years later was that once I believed in the teacher, I became better at learning."* (W.R.O.) This meant to me that belief, in my simplistic world of education, was the root to acquiring progressive knowledge to one's fullest potential. Meaning that once a student believes in the teacher they will bring attention, focus, and respect to consistent learning. So, *when you find ways to get students to believe in what you're teaching, they will become better students of learning and you will become more effective in teaching.* (W.R.O.)

For an expanded amount of time I've held to the theory that belief is the destination to effective learning. But until I met Doctor Moller I never knew the road to getting there. I realized I had found that road one day in 1996, while driving along I-80 East, headed toward Des Moines, Iowa. I was en-route to Richfield High School in Minneapolis, Minnesota. I'd been invited to address the student body and faculty during a student and teacher in-service day at the school. My subject that day was *The Root to Acquiring Knowledge* and as I motored along the highway I was contemplating my speech.

I had set my mind to my presentation, *The Root to Acquiring Knowledge*, which I surmised was ***belief.*** That's when it hit me! All those demands that Doc Moller had consistently pushed on me came rushing to the forefront. I asked myself, could his demands have been the values that lead to the root of learning?

At that moment just off the interstate in Des Moines I spotted an empty parking lot. To my surprise it was the Adventureland Amusement Park. I pulled off the interstate near the park's hotel and began writing. Once finished, I had taken six of the most popular demands from Doc Moller's thrashings and collectively tried them on for size as the values that led to ***belief.*** They were a perfect fit! With that, my speech for Richfield High was in place, along with the connective values that were the catalyst to the installation of ***belief.*** I went back to those six most frequent demands during our Central days; <u>**care**</u>, <u>**discipline**</u>, <u>**love**</u>, <u>**work**</u>, <u>**respect**</u> and <u>**give**</u>.

I thought of them in a particular order and then arranged them as such. I felt the first order of business was to ***care,*** so I made it first. I saw giving as a by-product of caring, so I listed ***give*** second. Next, I felt the combination of caring and giving created love, so I made ***love*** third. My thought was that once these three attributes were in place, they had to be followed by ***work***. I then said to myself that if one could follow through with these four values then they would be respected. So, ***respect*** became number five on the list. And then there was six. I remembered Doc's staunchest demand, ***discipline***, discipline, discipline and with that the list was complete. These six values would become my greatest gifts from Doc. Though their presentation was often time met with cloaked contempt back in the 1980's, they eventually became the life lessons of my future. So, for the people who decide to teach, which is all of us at some time or another, here were Doc's demands of me that together is the formula to inducing belief.

*In order to teach and better insure learning; number one you must <u>**care**</u>, not just for some things but for all things and everybody. Number two, you must be willing to <u>**give**</u> unilaterally. When you care and you give it teaches you to <u>**love**</u>, and* *love, which ignites the greatest energy known to mankind adds the passion that is needed for success. When you care and you give and it has taught you to love, then you must understand* __*work*__*. Knowing that you must work in order to achieve those results you crave. When you care and you give and it has taught you to love, and you understand work, people will* __*respect*__ *you. And respect my friends is what all living beings seek. When you care and you give and it has taught you to love and you understand work and indeed you are now respected, you can then demand* __*discipline*__*. Discipline, that subtle order of getting things done. Discipline, that rare ability to resist all manner of temptations. So, when you* **care** *and you* **give** *and it has taught you to* **love** *and you understand* **work**, *indeed you are* **respected** *and have demanded* **discipline**, *then people will believe in you. That* **belief** *will open up avenues for those you teach that will lead them to a healthy, productive and enthusiastic path of learning.*

In an interview I had with Doc Moller, he said, "The most important quality a teacher can possess is energy." He went on to say, "Some teachers are not good enough to keep around, but not bad enough to send away." ***What I put forward here, is that if any one of the above attributes are missing then you become a presenter not a teacher, and within that vain description, you will never rise to the level that is your highest potential.*** *(W.R.O.)*

I had gone to Central with football dominating my thoughts, but Doc Moller placed life and the classroom above everything else. After I'd left Central his barrage of demands and push for perfection had made me more passionate about teaching and a better person in life. When I think about those ageless demands I feel a longing for time spent and a vague curiosity of time missed. I feel like the kid that moved away from his family before he was ready for the world. That family was headed by Doc Moller and despite my premature departure, he has always left me with the feeling that I am still a part of it. This was nothing he did in kind for me, it's simply the kind of person he is.

The forest... the Omaha Central family.

What I've always respected most about Doc Moller, is that he has never been one to take the measure of a broken twig and make it the legacy of the entire tree. Broken twigs fall and are swept away with the wind, while the tree remains in all its glory, still standing, always growing; fading in the fall but returning each spring to be more vibrant and more productive than ever before." (W.R.O.)

Chapter 3

A CENTRAL HIGH GOOD-BYE

Few saw the surprise ending, none saw the new beginning

Leaving Family

I had coached and taught young men and women at Omaha Central High School for eleven years and in that time I thought it was all about me making them. However, once I was gone I realized it was actually more them making me. I found that my success wasn't in coaching or teaching this class, these teams or that person. It was more about the entire scope of the Omaha Central mystique. I found success, not only in football but with the constant demand for excellence from Doc Moller, I had also become a better teacher and a more efficient person. Back in my time, Central was not a place for lone wolves. Once there, you were a part of a whole, which was a family within four sides of tradition.

They say you can never be homeless until you lose your family, and I concur. I didn't realize it at the time but the embodiment of Omaha Central had come to be family to me. After my departure I found that *"**Sometimes you can look at ten thousand acres of trees and not understand that together they combine to make the forest in which you thrive."** (W.R.O.)* At Central we weren't just a collection of trees, we were collectively a forest. ***That's how it was for us, steady growth, consistent production and perpetual, positive change. Like the trees, every year we'd shed a little of who we were, while gradually growing into who we would finally become. (W.R.O.)***

I'd made the choice to leave Central but I had been anxiously nervous since. When it was finally time to go I wasn't ready, everything just seemed bad. In fact, the only good thing that ever happened after I decided to leave was ironically, Doc Moller asking me to stay. After my departure there was an emptiness that I had not expected. It was that lost feeling of having left a family.

During those last days at Central I was sick to my stomach. I remember being afraid for the state track meet to end, knowing the finality it would bring to my life within the four sides. But the meet did end and with it, so too did my time at Central. On the Monday after the state meet Doc called me to his office one last time. There he tried to save me with a final sincere request. "You don't have to leave, you know", he said with that signature, puzzling half-smile. However, when he offered up that olive branch, it was more a grand gesture of letting me know that there were no hard feelings and he was still there if I needed him. He knew even if I wanted to I couldn't accept it. By then I had committed to the transfer, and there was no turning back.

In his office that day I couldn't help but think about that first time I was there. Eleven years before, I'd come with fists clinched tight, ready for battle. I recalled him standing up and my surprise at his slight stature. That final day the stature was still slight, but now the aura it projected was that of a giant. There we were, meeting once again in a setting I'd become so familiar with. Now, as I listened to his words they seemed to come from a sincere place and a loving spirit. No matter what he said that day, all I heard was, "I care". When I stood to leave his office my hands were shaking and my heart was breaking and I knew I was leaving a great place and an even greater man.

When I stepped outside his office I was overwhelmed with emotion. I felt his sincerity and more than ever I understood what he was truly about. Doc Moller **cared** for the teachers, **gave** to the students, **loved** the school and **worked** to meet his own standards of protocol. He is indeed **respected** and through it all he demanded **discipline.** From it all **belief** did derive and at least for one proud soul that belief would maximize his learning. That was how we said goodbye. Now came the time to leave him and the four sides, along with the rest of the Central High family. It was one of the hardest days of my life.

In the end, I did not ride off into the sunset as I had envisioned. Instead I wandered into a rare obscure darkness of faded glory and forgotten memories. A Central High good-bye was meant to change and rejuvenate me. Instead it crumbled me into a thousand pieces that would take a new lifetime to put back together.

The Move To South High

When I moved to South High School in the fall of 1990, nothing felt right. It wasn't the school. It was that joy thing that the twins spoke of, Central High was still inside me. That brief semester that I was assigned to South would not extend my career. Instead it would mark the finish of my days as a teacher and coach for the Omaha Public Schools. What would follow was perhaps the most tumultuous period of my existence, a period that would force an ending that spawned an awakening after my dying. This all led to a rebirth of my soul and eventually the creation of a better man.

There's a legal gag in the details of that controversy. The circumstances are sealed and I'm sworn never to discuss those scrambled times. One of the good things that came within this period was the fact that it offered a full view and a clear definition of life. It is fair to concede that everything I was, am and ever will be I owe to the Public School System of Omaha Nebraska. For it was the cause that brought me here and for that I am eternally grateful.

I started at Omaha Tech, came from Benson and jumped to South High. In between it all, I think that God sent me to Omaha Central and never intended that I teach or coach anywhere else. It seems all the years before Central were just a passage to getting me there, and anything after that was not for me to consider. As a coach, I tried to throw myself onto Benson and I was rejected; when I asked for Omaha Tech I was refused; Finally I forced a move to South High; where in 1990 the ship called "My Life" sank in murky waters at ***The Burt/Cuming Divide;*** latitude 41° 16' 2.88" N, longitude 95° 57' 37.45" W. ***(The TAC Building)***. There it would remain submerged for the next three years.

Chapter 4

LIFE TURNS TO A LITTLE WHITE BALL

How golf became the skill, business and enjoyment of my new world

Golf: The New Beginning

The pleasure of working in the Omaha Public Schools was gone. But the joy of school, students and teaching, well as the twins said - it's inside you, it comes from God and it lasts forever. Soon, another school would be created, new students would appear and the teachings, though a different subject, would still be the same. The new subject was golf, it was always there but was lost deep inside me and it would take an eight year old to finally dig it out.

All through my childhood I was fascinated by the game of golf. So much so that against all odds, as a thirteen year old kid, I designed and constructed my very own miniature golf course. It was a course that weaved through the south side of the housing project where I lived. I was a happy kid that absolutely loved golf, but for a long period of time I had to keep it a secret. For me like every other kid in the area, sports were <u>The Usual Suspects</u>; football, baseball, basketball and track. Golf was the worst. In fact, inside my neighborhood back in the 1950's golf was taboo and anyone caught trying it was usually downgraded to subhuman.

It sounds a little cruel but later in life I would find out that there was a method to the madness. It seemed golf was one of those elite things that in the Jim Crow South were not too accessible for blacks. So, parents just subtly steered you away from it. The message from them was, "we don't push kids toward things that are impossible to have". Sadly, golf was one of those things. Despite the negative connotation in 1961 I secured a set of clubs in a very curious and bizarre way. No, they weren't stolen. They were thrown away by an angry golfer at Bayou Desiard Country Club. Little did I know that single event would lift me out of a death spiral three decades later.

Golf: A New Life That Reunited Me with Dr. G.E. Moller

Sometimes life is like being in quicksand. You're alive but you can feel yourself slowly sinking. (WRO) It was the way I felt the first three years away from Central. Then came golf and it wasn't long before I began creating a new circle of life. When the circle was complete, to my joy and amazement I would eventually be reunited with the man that commanded the four sides for twenty-seven years. In 1993 I had been out of teaching for almost three years. I was floundering about in life, driving down many avenues but not knowing which way to turn. I remembered that old adage that if you could find something to do that you truly loved, then you'd never work another day of your life. One day, after a bizarre encounter with an eight year old, I stopped and formulated in my mind all the things I loved outside of family and relatives. I considered hard working and enthusiastic kids, teaching, coaching and yes golf. If I could put those things together, then according to the adage, I indeed would never have to work again. Later, I would find those four special things that I loved so dearly could only be bundled in but one place - "school"!

In the fall of 1992 I created the parameters that outlined the creation of a unique golf school. In that instance I had put myself in the position to capture all the things that I truly loved. The school was up and running by the summer of 1993 with 400 kids eager to learn. That was how it blew up. However, how it was ignited had a lot to do with that bizarre question I mentioned that rolled off the tongue of an eight year old.

The Sixth Fairway and A Question from an 8 Year Old

For a good long time my faith had been fading and then luckily I found a cause inside the world of golf. Once I grabbed hold of the potential, I ran with it. But how it came about began with the deepest, most captivating question that I had ever been asked. To add even more drama and intrigue it came from an eight year old. It was a question that pierced my soul and eventually snapped me out of a downward spiral, rekindling my spirit.

Two years after my departure from Central a young man and an eight year old boy walked across the 6th fairway at Fontenelle Park Golf Course. It was kind of odd but not unusual, people often cut off the seven extra blocks it took to go around the golf course, to get to Fontenelle Boulevard. By walking across the middle of the number three, four and six fairways at the golf course you could save a lot of time, but it was dangerous. I'd heard that years before as four or five teens walked slowly across the three fairways, some irritated golfers felt justified to hit balls at them. Their aggressive exhibition was followed by several gun shots back at them. Though no one was hit, I heard the run back to the club house darn near killed all four of them. Later, it would take multiple police units to retrieve their clubs.

With the knowledge of that past history in mind, as this couple crossed I waited patiently. Curiously, the man stopped mid-fairway and the child began walking toward me. The lad seemed unsure of his mission as he approached me and was working to gather himself upon arrival. Once he composed himself, as much as an eight year old could, he proceeded with the question his companion had undoubtedly told him to ask me. Now, close enough for me to touch him, in a much more mature voice then I expected, he said, "Excuse me mister but didn't you used to be Coach Reed from Central?" The question staggered me, I had to think about it for a moment, and feeling a little awed and confused by it, I answered in a panic, "Yes." Then I thought, did that mean yes I was or yes I am?

The whole episode had discombobulated me. This was the 6th fairway at Fontenelle Golf Course, a short par 5, about 520 yards and seldom a problem for me. As the little kid walked away I tried to refocus on the task at hand. After one of my patented drives down an un-irrigated fairway, I found myself only about 165 yards out from the target. If I could hit the narrow green with an eight iron, I would be assured a birdie or perhaps maybe even the big bird. But on this day that wouldn't happen. I kept thinking about that kid and his powerful, but puzzling question. "Didn't you used to be Coach Reed?"

With that thought still lingering I smacked my 8 iron against the Titleist DT ball. It was a line drive that careened off a water hydrant and landed in the middle of an untrimmed pine tree. After my drop, I skulled the ball across the green, then duffed it to the edge, where I promptly three putted for a snowman (that's an 8 in golf). Every golfer knows that one of the saddest things imaginable is building snowmen on the golf course in mid- July, as the heat index threatens the century mark. After the sixth hole disaster, with head bowed and shoulders slumped, I took that long triple bogey walk to the 7th tee. During that walk I began to question my life, and at the same time doubt its worth. I couldn't help but wonder, if I was no longer Coach Reed, who or what was I then? As I readied myself to play the 7th hole, I eyed the par 3 green and composed myself. I knew this shot better than I knew my way home. It was a 167 yard piece of cake that I ate for dessert every time I played the course. However, on this day my shot was still climbing to its apex as it reached the green, and it sailed into the back bushes, never to be seen by me again.

In golf you are allotted five minutes of search time before the ball is officially declared MIA. As I trampled and searched the hillside behind the green, I found myself knee high in weeds at the corner of Fontenelle Boulevard and Pratt Street. Frustrated and exhausted, I gave up the search. The Titleist golf ball was officially MIA and I realized so was I.

It was early evening and the traffic was speeding by like Nascar. Suddenly a blue car passed and the passenger yelled out "you suck!" Dazed and confused I thought, dang, how did he know? Without finishing the hole, I began walking toward the number eight tee box, which takes you back uphill toward Fontenelle Boulevard. I could see that eight year old and his elder off in the distance. As I watched them fade out of sight I barely caught a glimpse of a passenger in the car going right past me. He yelled out, "Hey, Coach Reed, what's upppp…..???"

There it was, three major encounters in three golf holes. The day had turned from playing golf to real life and with two holes to play I had officially lost interest in the game. "Did I use to be Coach Reed, did I truly suck at life and really what was up?" It was the late summer of 1992, I had been away from Central for less than two years and already I was nobody. Have you ever been lost and didn't even know it? Like just walking or driving and all of a sudden, out of nowhere you run into a dead end and think, oh my God, I'm lost! That's what this was like. I was lost in life and didn't even know it.

I'd never had a drink in my life, but that night I staggered off the golf course like the town drunk, still dazed by the question. When I finally arrived home I saw a commercial on TV that featured several young children and unbelievably, they all looked like that eight year old from the sixth fairway. Although none of them actually were, their faces seemed to ask his question, "didn't you used to be Coach Reed"? Indeed I felt lost and now I knew it. There I was in the middle of my life moving without purpose, unenthused about living, yet not ready for the alternative. Still, like every human being I was dying, one day at a time.

> *Satisfaction is; getting what you want then appreciating what you have.* (W.R.O.)

Since leaving the public schools I was yet to find my way. I was lost in life with no idea of which direction to go. I'd forgotten that I was lost and now an eight year old had reminded me of it. That night after my three close encounters of the third kind at the golf course, I sat down at the kitchen table and began writing. When my wife awoke for work at 6 a.m. the next morning she was surprised to find me still writing. Throughout the night I had written the inner workings of a golf school for kids. It was the pages of something I'd been thinking about for a long time and just hadn't been motivated enough to do it. Now the whole program was right there on the kitchen table. I saw strong possibilities for a new beginning that had all started with a weird question, "didn't you used to be Coach Reed". ***And it came from an eight year old.***

The Reedway Golf School

When Doc Moller first visited the site that had become my golf school, I hadn't seen him in nearly ten years. He had that patented puzzled look on his face and like old times it was followed by a barrage of heat seeking questions. His puzzlement was expressed in a confused statement, then came the rapid order of questions. "I didn't know you could do this! Where did you learn this stuff? Who taught you all this? Where did it come from? You, a golf instructor, how?" These were all great questions and I think this book is a great forum to answer them in. From my entry into the world of golf, to the school I created, from the places it took me, to the people I met... golf literally saved my life.

One of Doc's biggest questions when he first visited my golf school was "How did a golf school and William Reed ever become a merger?" The answers come easy now. I had teaching skills, a caring for kids, a God given ability to coach and an eight year old that had stirred my being. In one night's sitting I wrote the internal workings of a unique golf school for kids. That was how it all got started, "on paper"! But as everyone knows life doesn't happen on paper. *Instead I see life as a collection of events and a series of deeds, with the by-products being, blood, sweat and lots of tears! (W.R.O.)*

In my journey to become once again relevant, there came an awakening seven years before the new millennium. It signaled that it was time to move to a new life. That life was clearly golf. By autumn of 1992 I was poised to start my very own golf school. I got the blessing of the local and National PGA (Professional Golf Association) and great advice from the USGA (United States Golf Association). The support came easy once I got the backing of Mr. Bob Popp, who was the recently retired director of golf at the famed Omaha Country Club in Omaha, Nebraska. He was also the 1982 National PGA Professional of the Year. Mr. Popp helped me tremendously in garnering respect. When the inner workings of the school were complete I offered a great appreciation to those who had helped and felt an abundant sense of accomplishment.

I had gotten every wish that I ever could have hoped for in the golf school's development. And "just like that" I was in a new world, starting a new life. I was thoroughly satisfied when the creation of the school was complete. Now, it was time to find a home and quality instructors. In the spring of 1993 an inviting

Opening day, 1st period Reedway Golf school 1993. Session #1of 5 at the Practice Tee.

old spot next to the Benson Golf Course, (the former site of the old Skyview Drive-In) was converted into a golf driving range, called The Practice Tee. This had always been a dream setting in my mind for such a project. Now, two smart and energetic young men, still in their twenties and owners of a very profitable lawn service had taken the leap of faith to do just that. They were Jeff and Tim Banghart, young men with great business IQ's, enough money to venture and both loved golf immensely. I, with my new idea, approached them on making my golf school a part of their new range. They accepted and it was a perfect fit. Thus was born the Consistency Golf Academy, to later become Reedway Golf Inc. More than 400 kids showed up that first summer in four different two week sessions and we serviced over 4,000 students over the next eight years, including a lively group from my hometown of Monroe, Louisiana. Things were wonderful during those days and I was reborn in the process.

Dena, and Naomi Rennard

A year or so into the program a little eight year old girl tugged at the back of my shirt. When I finally felt her presence I turned and looked down. There stood the cutest little kid you could imagine. Holding her little mini golf club she looked up at me and said, "Excuse me sir, but are you Coach Reed?" Immediately my mind flipped back to that eight year old from the sixth fairway two years before. I took a long pause and then a deep breath and with a sigh of relief I said "Yes, yes I am!" In a perky voice she said "I'm Dena Rennard and I want to learn how to golf!" Her older sister, Naomi was right by her side.

The two of them would become two surprise packages that I would open up in amazement every time they came to the golf school. They were two of the best human beings one could ask for in any school setting. At the time their father, Doctor Stephen Rennard was a Professor of Internal Medicine in the pulmonary and critical care section of the department of internal medicine at the University of Nebraska Medical Center in Omaha, Nebraska. He had sat and watched me teach for weeks and finally one day approached me and said, "I have never seen anyone teach anything with the professionalism, knowledge and enthusiasm as you do with golf." Immediately my mind went back to Central and Doc Moller who always demanded those three things of me and everyone at Central. To say the least I was overly flattered by Doctor Rennard's compliments. A few weeks later he would enroll his daughters, Naomi and Dena in my school and they would remain for the next six years. These two super, special kids were part of what I had always imagined for the school and no one since or before could say "Coach Reed" with more pride and respect then they. To top things off, as if written in some made for TV movie they both enrolled and graduated with honors from, you guessed it, Omaha Central High.

While the student list that first year was amazing, the employee roster was even better. I landed two of the best golfers in the state to sign on to work each session; Melissa Johnson, one of the top female golfers in Nebraska (University of Missouri golf team) and Troy Martin, the number one golfer at Kansas Wesleyan University. They were a dream come true, more than I could have ever hoped for. These were two bright and attractive students that any golf course or school would have been blessed to have. The list of instructors also included Todd Hotchkiss a certified basic golf instructor and Miguel Thompson a UNO graduate and quality golfer from Augusta, Georgia.

Reedway Golf School daily session 3. Youth girls

Both brought great instructions to the table. Tony Tubrick (now owner of Classic Golf Omaha) was an equipment specialist and Randy Jensen was an informal historian, offering golf stories to the kids that were sure to amaze. Class A golf professional Charlie Mahon joined in the fun and later one of Omaha's best golfers of the 1970's, Steve Sargent did the same. With all the pieces now in place all we needed was a format and a set of operational guidelines. For that I created the <u>Youth Golf Program Guide</u>. This was followed up by the series, <u>The ABC's of Golf</u>; seven books written by me on teaching kids the game of golf, including a 100 page <u>ABC's of Golf Training Manual</u> to complement the books.

The golf school days included four class periods per day, with five instructors each handling four kids per class. That totaled about 80 students per day in four-2 week sessions. We taught over an eight week period that began the second Monday in June. The summer workload included three weeks in June, four in July and one in August.

This truly was a creation from pure scratch and I loved every minute of it. One morning I awakened to the fact that we had taught over 400 kids that first summer both in camp and individually. It was an amazing feeling, I was back in the teaching and coaching business and boy did it feel good. A new life in golf had begun and I couldn't have dreamed where it would eventually take me.

After the second year of the school I had a grand banquet for the kids, with Coach Tom Osborne of Nebraska coming in as guest speaker to support me in my new endeavor. It was a smashing success! The banquet room was full, but more importantly the kids loved it. Young Jayden Lombardi and his sister Tessa were a big part of those first camps. Tragically, Jayden just 16, was killed before the start of the second session. So, I dedicated the banquet to him and enlisted the United States Marine Corps to help in the dedication to his family. His father, Kim followed the dedication with a crusade of his own, targeting teenage drinking. His campaign continues to this day. That night was like the rebirthing of me. I had used all those tough lessons presented to me by Doc Moller. They had worked and I felt a pride like I never had before.

Coach Reed and competitive golf team members

When the last person left the banquet room that night I was there all alone and I would take my first deep breath since leaving Central in 1990. It was within those moments that I knew golf had become my life. I was a different person, a brand new man. For the last time I saw that eight year old kid, standing in the sixth fairway at Fontenelle Golf Course. I could no longer see his face but I still saw those curious brown eyes, searching my soul, asking that biting question; "Excuse me mister but didn't you used to be Coach Reed from Central". I could only imagine, if he had asked me after my golf school opened, my answer to him would have been a resounding "YES... I STILL AM!"

How A Magazine Expanded My World Of Golf

Indeed golf had become my new light to the world. From playing, to teaching, to creating projects, golf was my life throughout the nineties and into the new millennium and I might say that life was pretty good.

The golf school was averaging about 350 kids per summer and I was now using two locations; one was located in far Southwest Omaha, at a place called the Four Tees and the other still at the original site near Benson (The Practice Tee). I had also started an indoor school at Classic Golf that attracted kids throughout the winter and I was teaching about a hundred women (the moms) in the fall. The routine was perfect, I had settled fully into my new life and thought it couldn't have been better.

The golf school was still flourishing and I was using up time by the barrel, teaching and coaching seven days a week, when a new project was thrown into the mix in 1997. That new project put my life on full overload. Out of time and out of mind, I was forced to drop the fall school for moms and abandon my indoor winter program for kids, in 1998.

With the success of the school and my newfound reputation for teaching golf, I had begun to engage new people and with them came new opportunities. One of the more dramatic of those opportunities began when Paul Bryant introduced me to Steadman Graham. Yes, *that* Steadman Graham. After being introduced, I ended up giving him a series of golf lessons followed by joining him for a couple of rounds of golf. That all led to me being invited to his annual golf tournament in Chicago, "Athletes Against Drugs".

The night before the tournament I met Gayle King (yes, *that* Gayle King) on a boat ride that originated at Chicago's Navy Pier. She spoke of Oprah Winfrey's desire to get involved with a magazine for and about women. I'd already thought of possibly doing something like a magazine for women anyway. So, I perked up when Gayle said Oprah would be entertaining ideas in that direction. Based on the more than 100 women I'd recently had as students, I felt I had a natural group that would serve as the perfect reference bank.

After gathering all the details from Ms. King, the next day I met Tina Mickelson (sister of Phil) during the tournament. It was being held at the famed Cantigny Golf Course in Wheaton, Illinois. Tina and I played together and before the end of the round we agreed to create the magazine together. The magazine would feature women who play golf and those things that most interested them in life. Tina would eventually bow out and I was left alone to complete it. I wrote most of the articles, designed it, directed the photography and searched out every single advertiser. I called it The Lady Golfer magazine. Once finished I self published it and had 15,000 copies printed. The magazine was published in June 1998. It would take me nine months to complete it but I can say without doubt that it was worth it.

In 1999 The Lady Golfer magazine put my new life into hyper drive. It put me in front of people I never imagined meeting, took me to places I never imagined going and had me doing things I never imagined doing!

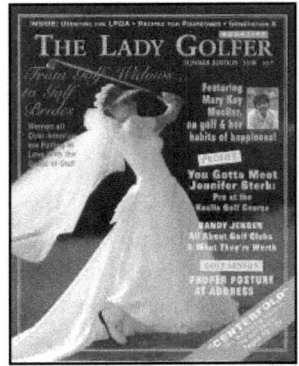

While the magazine did not fit into the plans of Oprah and Gayle King, it did allow me the opportunity to meet some amazing people. People like: Mary Lou Walker, owner of Garbo's, a popular hair salon in Omaha, Nebraska. She is the toughest "sweet woman" I ever met and one of the great entrepreneurs in Omaha. Bob Broderick, a former Kiewit executive and high ranking Level 3 investor. Bob Broderick and his wife Margaret still rank as two of the nicest people I've ever sat down with. Yves Menard, Sue Marchese, Mary Kay Mueller and many more. All great people that I would not have possibly met if not for The Lady Golfer magazine.

After putting me in front of people locally, the magazine would then carry me back down to my home town area in Northeast Louisiana, where I met Roy Bechtol, designer of the famed Barton Creek Resort in Austin Texas. Roy is one of the world's great golf course architects and land planners. From there it took me to a meeting with Tom Kite, the 1992 winner of the U.S. Open Golf Championship. Then it sent me down the Caribbean, to places like Belize in Central America and the islands of St. Lucia and Barbados.

Yes, from Oprah Winfrey's beau, to Phil Mickelson's sis, to one of the top golf architects in the world. The Lady Golfer magazine changed my life again and opened doors to me meeting some of the most fascinating people I could ever have imagined. These were significant times and many life changing relationships were born from them. However , I thought none were bigger for business than my meeting Greg Siaperas. Greg was the owner of a company called Golf LLC of Omaha, Nebraska. The company owned several golf courses in the Omaha metropolitan area including Skyline Woods, Lakeview, Fox Run and a little project still in the planning stages in Ashland, Nebraska called Iron Horse. He had some great ideas for the magazine and expressed interest in owning a part of it.

Later, Greg and I would form a partnership that consisted of a contractual deal bringing me on board as a member of the Golf LLC team in exchange for him getting percentage rights to <u>The Lady Golfer</u> magazine. My job within the company was to evaluate the services and status of existing properties owned by the company and find or create new ones where possible. When this all hit it was the summer of 1999 and while it was all happening I was still going full bore with the golf school.

By the end of the summer of 2000 my life had become jam packed and sadly I had to say goodbye to the school and the kids that had given me new life. My toughest task to closing the school was saying goodbye to those two little girls who six years before had tugged at my shirt. Now, leaving them was tugging at my heart. They were teenagers by then, but six years later Naomi and Dena Rennard were still in my school.

Leaving the school was tough, but the arrangement with Golf LLC was a great deal for that particular time in my life. I was made an instant member of the Skyline Woods Country Club, rubbing elbows with some pretty nice people there. I had free access to all the other properties and was treated like royalty. At Golf LLC, I was hearing about the planning of the housing expansion project at Skyline Woods and details of the new Iron Horse development in Ashland. A few months into my time with the company, I was told by an old friend in Louisiana of a golf/lake project being proposed near our hometown of Monroe. The project was being set up just outside the town of Delhi, in a place called Poverty Point, just thirty miles from where I grew up. It included a lake to be surrounded by housing, with the nucleus being a golf course. This kind of project was right in line with what Golf LLC was looking for and what I was charged to do.

> *If you dream a dream of creation and find that you can do it alone, then your dream is too small. (W.R.O.)*

Immediately I left to explore the possibility of our company to go to

Louisiana to create the dynamic project. Also bidding for the project was a company out of Austin, Texas called Planned Environments which was the affiliated owners of Bechtol Russell Golf, headed by Roy Bechtol and Randy Russell. Roy as mentioned previously is the original land planner for the world-renowned resort project Barton Creek. As he and I jockeyed for the Poverty Point project we became instant friends with a mutual respect for one another. He wanted the project but didn't want to see me a loser. I wanted the project and didn't want to see him not get it. In the end we compromised and concluded that he and his company would do the land planning while Golf LLC would handle all the construction.

I rushed back to Omaha with the good news. However, it was not so good sounding to Mr. Siaperas. Greg said he had an agreement with Gene Bates, a high profile golf course architect, land planner and his partner, Fred Couples, a world renowned professional golfer. He explained that Mr. Bates was already active with Golf LLC in redesigning Skyline Woods Country Club and the development of the Iron Horse project in Ashland, Nebraska. He went on to say that any golf course project that involved Golf LLC must have Mr. Bates and his team as the primary architects and designers. I explained that we couldn't get any portion of the project without compromise and that it was imperative that we share with the Planned Environments group. Having none of it, Mr. Siaperas made the comment that it seemed with my insistence to bring Mr. Bechtol into the mix that perhaps I needed my own company. His tone was not conducive to that of a partner and with that, we parted ways.

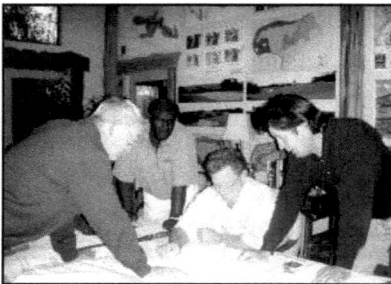

Going through the particulars of Marquis' Bay of St. Lucia - Randy Russell, Coach Reed, Tom Kite and Roy Bechtol

When I called to tell Roy what had happened, to my surprise he echoed Mr. Siaperas' comment and said "Okay then let's form that company, you and I together." All of a sudden I found myself in the land planning and golf course development business. My job still was to find projects and bring all parties to the table, the land owners, purchasers, funding sources and community. I felt it was a new brand of work for me, but in retrospect I'd been doing it all my life. I loved it and found some great projects in the interim. Roy and his Planned Environment's team did acquire and complete the Poverty Point Project and I did some minor, behind the scenes consulting with the project manager. The Poverty Point creation still flourishes today. It included housing, a five mile lake and a golf course, called Black Bear. All designed and created by Roy Bechtol, my new best friend.

Soon after Poverty Point, I made a play for our first big project. It was a 19 million dollar beauty in St. Lucia, of the Caribbean Islands. We went all out to get it, even bringing in touring pro Tom Kite as adviser and consultant. In a group session with Morgan Stanley in New York City during the early fall of 2000, we were chosen for the project over Bob Petralia and his group. It was like a coup; we went in, offered a better project, in a faster time, for less money and had a power point presentation to back it all up. As a finale, we rolled out a six foot by four foot conceptual master plan depicting housing and a golf course resort in living color. The Petralia group had come with three yellow sheets of paper that they slowly put away as we made our presentation. With Roy Bechtol carrying the ball that day, they never had a chance.

Roy and I got the call as we took in a meal at the famed New York Plaza Hotel. Oh, happy day, the project was ours! After winning the Caribbean project Roy and I had lots of fun and consummated a special bond during that time. On the way back to our hotel we just needed to celebrate. So, as we passed an apartment for sale in the Trump Tower, just for fun, we walked inside as potential buyers. Roy who really looked the part of a Texas oil tycoon, posed as one and then introduced me as Sheik Reed.

I could hardly hold in the laughter as the guy opened the doors to a place that looked like something out of a fantasy dreamland book - the price? 2.3 million for 2,300 square feet. We laughed, scurried from his lair and in the name of schoolhouse rock, we described it with adjectives!!! We left New York City in a hail of glory and within a few short months we dropped anchor in the Caribbean Sea, just off the shores of the island of St. Lucia.

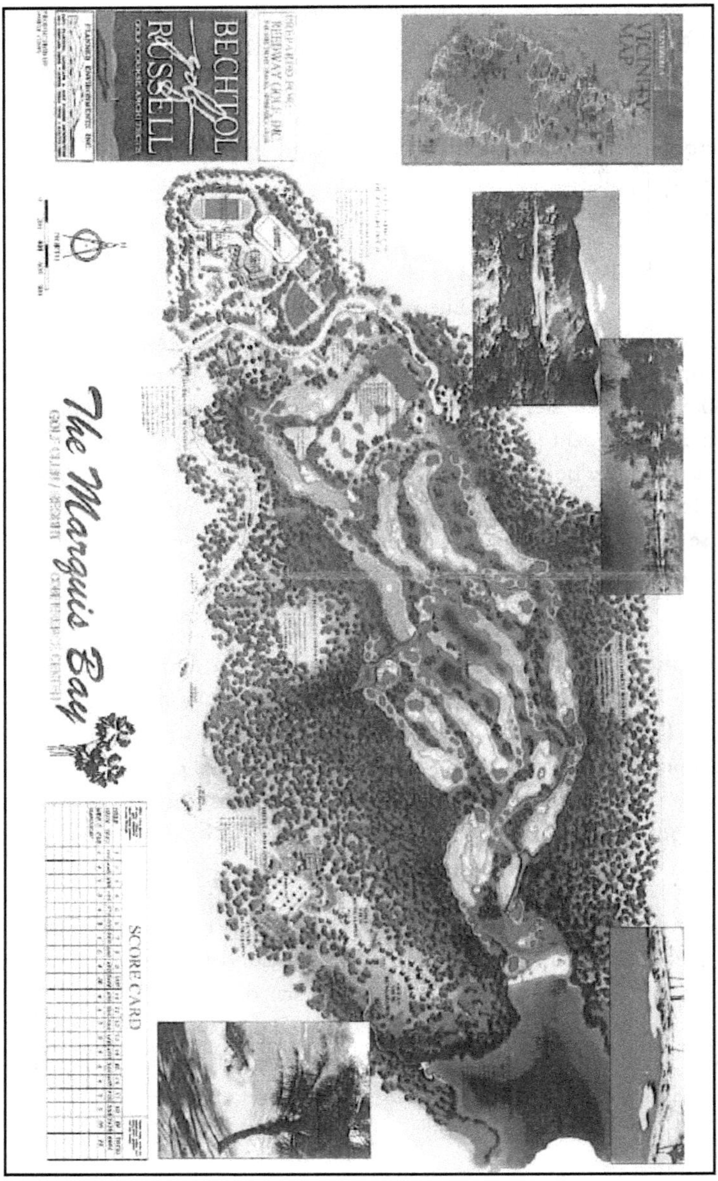
BECHTOL
RUSSELL
VICINITY MAP
The Marquis Bay
SCORECARD

It was early 2001. To us we had pulled off the deal of the century and we named our project "Marguis' Bay." With plush greenery, waterfalls and an ocean side view, it was a magnificent piece of land. During our stay there we bedded down at the famed Windjammer Resort and also spent time at a secluded paradise called Jalousie. It was the time of my life, working, planning in St. Lucia and negotiating the investment deal with the Morgan Stanley financial representative, who was there from New York.

We were all set and scheduled to close the deal in New York City on Monday, September 17, 2001 in tower number two of the World Trade Center building on the 43rd floor. However, on Tuesday, September 11th both towers had gone down, and unfortunately our beautiful Marquis' Bay project went down with them; as did all 25 floors occupied by Morgan Stanley on that terrible day. Yes, Morgan Stanley lost much in the catastrophe and within their misfortune we had lost our financial partners.

When the bellowing soot and smoke of the twin buildings came tearing down the streets of New York City the buildings had fallen into rubble and the dream that was our beautiful Marquis' Bay project, was buried beneath it. It would never surface again.

Chapter 5

FINDING BELIZE
When we lost the island of St. Lucia, we found the country of Belize.

The ancient and historic Maya Mountains in Southern Belize

The World Trade Center Goes Down - Belize Comes Up

The fall of the Marquis' Bay project left Roy and I scrambling to find another project. That project emerged rather quickly, when I met a former American Air Force major named Byron Thurston. Major Thurston lived in and was a citizen of Belize, Central America (formerly British Honduras). I met him through an acquaintance out of California, a panel home distributor named Mary Flowers. She set me up with Major Thurston by phone and the next thing I knew, I was landing in Belize City, right behind Hurricane Iris! I arrived in Belize during the second week of October, 2001. Iris had beat up the south region, down in the Toledo and Stann Creek districts, but the Belize City area was almost unscathed. I hit the ground running and jumped right into the project talks with Major Thurston. The first lesson from Mr. Thurston was that non-military folk were not allowed to refer to him by his military rank. We were only allowed to call him Byron. He had a ranch that was primed for a golf course project similar to the one we had plans for in St. Lucia. However, it took me just twenty-four hours to figure out that he was not a man I could deal with, even if I wanted to. He seemed to scold his wife, Armeade, with every word, even when he was being nice he showed little respect for her. He talked to me as if I was an errand boy and hardly allowed me to get a word in edgewise. He boasted of his power in the states as well as in Belize. Referring to himself as the right arm of the Prime Minister. My breaking point came when he stopped the meeting with the six of us involved, put in a World War II video and demanded we watch.

After that second morning at his ranch I'd had it. I left the place seething in anger. When I finally reached the main highway I was picked up by a very talkative jitney driver. After the story of my adventures with Byron Thurston, he said the man I needed to see about projects in Belize was Wilfred Elrington, Attorney at Law. While meeting with Mr. Elrington, he told me I needed to sit down with Arnaldo "Popi" Pena, a major landowner in the country. Upon meeting Popi, he told me that we needed to meet the prime minister, Said (Sa-eed) Musa. After meeting Prime Minister Musa, he thought that I

> *Often times we end up where we weren't planning to be.*
>
> *(W.R.O.)*

should meet his Deputy P. M. and after that, Popi introduced me to everyone. "And just like that," I was no longer at Belize, I was in Belize. Rapidly, I came to be known by all simply as "The Corch," not Coach, but "Corch", and I loved the place. I loved all the beauty and potential that came with being there.

Golf... Belize's Missing Link
"Present Day"

Two years has passed since my arriving here in Belize, it is 2003 and when I talk to people back in the states who haven't seen me for a while they are dumbfounded and confused when I say that I am living in Belize, Central America. I'm seeking land projects here and even though it seems to rain everyday from May until September, it's still a paradise waiting! Upon arriving here it hasn't taken long for me to realize that this small country has big possibilities. Known for its spectacular scuba diving, Belize, Central America is home to the second largest barrier reef in the world. The country can take you from one of the most exotic resort settings in the world, Ambergris Caye, to the ancient jungles and Mayan temples of centuries past. The clear blue water, coral reefs and an abundance of thousands of sea creatures, small and large, has made it one of the most popular and fastest growing vacation destinations of today.

Personally, I thought the place had everything, but to my surprise there was a missing link. Surprisingly, this grand vacation dreamscape does not have in its landscape one golf course, not one!! That's not a big deal for some but was a shocker to Roy and I... really? The entire country of Belize doesn't have one golf course on the mainland? Nor does it have one on its most popular island province, San Pedro, which houses Ambergris Caye, 40 miles out in the ocean? Recently, I've come to know that perhaps the country could claim one golf course within its boundaries. It sits on the isolated private island known as Caye Caulker. However the place is so exclusive that it's hardly meant for ordinary mankind. In fact the only way to access it is by helicopter, uninvited boats are not allowed to approach.

I mentioned weather earlier because even the rain is spectacular in Belize. The towering thunderheads that begin each May are like a daily show and are always followed by a warming breeze and then bright warm sunshine. During my two years here, the temperature has only twice been above 85 degrees and never below 65. From the Maya Mountains in the south, to the free zone up north in Corozal, out west to the capitol, Belmopan and back east to home in Belize City, I've been all over Belize these past two years, seeing land, meeting people and intermingling with the politicians on a daily basis. When I first told Tim Cook (one of my favorite, former players, class of '83) what I was doing, he called it spreading the Central legacy from C to shining C (Central High to Central America). It's amazing the places life can take you, I have quickly immersed myself inside the culture, life and times of the old British Honduras **"Who would have thought it??"**

Chapter 6

AT HOME IN BELIZE

Beautiful time, beautiful place, beautiful people

Popi's unfinished night club and restaurant in the sea.
The Bellevue Hotel is in the background with my living quarters just to the right

Life in Belize

With my wife recently deceased in the spring of 2000, I have little reason to rush back to the states. So, I have plunged myself headlong into creating a resort project here in Belize and for these past two years it has been like home to me. I live east of downtown in Belize City, in a boarding house adjacent to the Bellevue Hotel. A walk out my front gate across a two-lane street and I am in the Caribbean Sea. We lost everything in St. Lucia when the Trade Centers went down, but then Belize came up and life has begun all over again. It's where I am today during these first days of November, three years into the new millennium.

Life here in Belize is far from routine, however I try not to ever get too far away from the regular citizenry. Belize City is an urban throw back city during the day, but a somewhat dangerous place to be at night. There is no middle class here and that shows up vividly. Jobs are scarce, salaries are sad, making the economy a tunnel without a light at its end. In fact when vacationers are walking around with two or three hundred dollars in their pockets, they have in their possession about a month's salary for the average worker. It's a known fact here that inside the wrong place at the wrong time, some have been known to try to take away that salary in whatever way they can.

A quick economical scan will show an average paying job here will constitute ten hour work days at about $1.50 an hour US. Take that modest salary and the fact that gasoline in 2003, is more than $6.00 a gallon. Telephone costs in Belize are more than just a chat. Local calls must be prepaid at 35¢ per minute, with out-of-the-country long distance requiring prepayment also. Phone minutes must be purchased like groceries. I usually buy the 20-minute long distance packages for $100.00 US. Yes, that's an unbelievable $5.00 per minute. Unlike the USA, seeing people with phones attached to their ears at 35¢ local and $5.00 a minute long distance is a rare sighting in these parts!

In fact, shopping is crazy all around with no sense of consistency anywhere. You can find a beer for as low as 50 cents but a cake may cost you $60.00. I saw a turkey for 50 bucks and they don't even have a Thanksgiving here!

Needless to say with the gas situation, there are a lot of walkers and bicycle riders. The automobile population is strange here also, as most of them are white and in this year (2003), the latest model and style in the country is the 1993 Toyota Camry. Most of the cars that come into Belize were sold in the U.S. ten years ago.

> Home... that place
> you hold the key to,
> while it holds the key to you
> (W.R.O.)

Don't get me wrong, I'm not complaining, despite all the differences my life is good here. When I wake up each morning my first stop is always breakfast at the Bellevue Hotel. Popi is always there by the time I arrive. Afterwards, there's usually an agenda of business for him and I, that could take us anywhere in the country, on any given day. Our Wednesdays however, are pretty consistent as that is the day the cabinet meets in the capitol city of Belmopan, an event Popi often attends.

Other than Wednesdays, just about every other day Popi takes me to a new land region that he either owns, controls or has connections to in some way or another. He has an island about forty minutes out in the ocean from Belize City called Calabash Caye; there's land in the southern region that he owns near the Maya Mountains, and dense land he has in the rain forest a few miles south of Belize City. There are thousands of acres of prime farmland that he controls up north near Corozal and thousands more in other places that we have visited these last two years.

A few days ago we spent the entire afternoon surveying and exploring a piece of land that he owns adjacent to the airport. This, along with his 800 acre island, seem to be the hot items of the month. Yes, Popi keeps me hopping here in Belize. With him every day is a new adventure. Though most of my time is spent with Popi, on some occasions I get to spend time with my other good friend Wilfred Elrington, mostly on the weekends. I thought I'd seen all of Belize, hanging with Popi, but Wilfred showed me an entirely different side. He contends to this day that we are forever brothers, after we both survived when the boat we were in sank off the coast of a small remote cove down near the Sittee River in southern Belize.

That sinking was the prelude to him taking me down to a place called Placencia, a piece of land in the southeast corner of the country that is absolutely breathtaking. Having been in a boat that sank that morning and then viewing the splendor of Placencia that evening, I felt as though I had seen heaven and hell, all in the same day. On another occasion he took me on about a hour and twenty minute boat ride that took us within a stone's throw of Mexico. The place that day was Belize's crown jewel of the Caribbean, Ambergris Caye.

As I see it, Belize, Central America is two countries in one. First of all, life on San Pedro, where the popular Ambergris Caye resides is a paradise for thousands of tourist each year and is amazingly beautiful. Places like Placencia and the Maya Mountains are a tourist dream, and the Great Barrier Reef is a scuba divers' oasis! However Ambergris Caye is 40 miles out away from the mainland, Placencia is but a sliver barely attached to the southeast corner, the barrier reef is about 6 miles offshore and most of the other hidden attractions are far, far reaching.

This brings us to the real aspects of the country, not where people visit but where people live - Belize City, Belmopan, Corozal and Dangriga - all places on the mainland and all places in need of help. Those places comprise the Belize I know and where I reside, while trying to make a difference in this country of scattered beauty and grand opportunities.

As stated, the mainland cities make up the real Belize and they resemble more 1964 downtown inner city USA then paradise. Back during my days in Louisiana, I lived the 1964 inner city story, so in a way here in Belize, I have access to the results. This sort of makes me someone to be listened to in the country and many do. My connections here are strong. Arnaldo Pena'(Popi) is the most influential landowner in the country and my best friend. Wilfred Elrington is not only a close friend and confidant but also my lawyer and soon to be the country's Minister of Foreign Affairs. The three of us came together on the tail of Hurricane Iris in October 2001 and we are collectively working to create a special project down in the southern region of Belize, extending from the Northern Lagoon all the way down to Gales Point.

Chapter 7

LEAVING BELIZE
A scurry back to the states

Popi's undeveloped island, Calabash Caye. 800 acres

112

The Call
"Present Day"

It's Tuesday in Belize, November 4, 2003. I am awakened by telephone in my room at the historic Bellevue Hotel in Belize City. It's the hotel owner, Popi Pena'. We are scheduled to take our long awaited trip down to Southern Belize today to view two properties. Popi wakes me shouting the words "Johnny Cakes, Johnny Cakes", a Belizean breakfast that everyone knows I can't resist. Ribbon cane syrup made right in the city from home grown sugar cane, along with an awesome marriage of waffles and pancakes to form the Johnny Cake. Miss Janey, the restaurant cook, always saves a good helping of the Johnny Cakes along with eggs, sausage and bacon just for me. The ladies in the kitchen appreciate the fact that I absolutely love their cooking.

When Popi announces "Johnny Cakes" I admit it has ignited my energy and ended my slumber. We have a full day ahead of us today, an adventure that will take us down into the southernmost region of Belize. The trip is an overdue inspection of two pieces of land called Plenty and Uncle Sam, located in the Maya Mountains. Popi is a late night-crawler and he kept me up into the wee hours last evening. However, despite that habit he is always an early riser. The excursion this morning is a trip down the Caribbean to the Sittee River. We both know that an early departure is necessary, if we are to beat nightfall coming back. I'm showered, dressed and walking into the restaurant just as breakfast is being served. I feel super! Good people, great food, superb weather and the Caribbean Sea only ten steps from the front door.

After the hearty breakfast, it's about 8:30 a.m. We're now ready for our expedition and my cell phone is ringing. It's a call from the states. The caller on the other end is telling me of an extremely important day that will happen tomorrow in Omaha, Nebraska, next door to the old Cedar Hills Golf Course where I used to play on occasion. She is explaining that my old principal, Dr. Moller will be there. Immediately I know I have to be there too. I haven't seen Doc in quite a while but now my mind is quickly filling up with the memories of our past times together. Without him fully knowing it, he had come to mean so much to my past, present, and future life. I've finished the call and I'm sure Popi can see that my mind is no longer focused on the trip to the Maya Mountains this morning. Instead I just told him that I need to get to the airport immediately. This beautiful morning of sweet serenity has all of a sudden turned into a three-alarm fire emergency. I am scrambling to my bungalow and Popi just sent a helper to get the car as he is unloading my gear from the boat. All plans have changed, I have to get home, and I have to get there in a hurry!

> No matter how fantastic life may be, sooner or later we all have to leave it.
>
> (W.R.O.)

Change of Plans, Homeward Bound

A few minutes ago, all I could think about was the trip to the Maya Mountains. Now my thoughts are consumed with wanting to get back home to see my friend and life teacher, Dr. Moller. Belize is a very different place socially, as they are not so apt to pry into one's life happenings. So, the cooking ladies quickly join in with me and my scurried desperation to leave without asking a word. They even offered up a sort of snack bag to take with me. Popi just had the car brought around, now instead of walking out to his boat we are packing up his SUV.

Ordinarily trying to get out of Belize on this late notice could be problematic, but with a pocket full of standby tickets and the most influential land broker in the country breaking down interference, I know I have a chance. I'm grabbing a few things and stuffing them into my bags. We're headed to the airport, its 9:00 a.m. There's a flight scheduled out at ten - what luck! This flight is nearly always full but on this day it's very sparse and better than that, it's also running late. After making a few last minute calls to Omaha I've checked one bag, presented my ticket and now I am official. I'm able to board with little delay and within 15 minutes I find myself high in the sky leaving Belize. Amazingly I am homeward bound.

Day Dreaming...
The Plane Ride Home

I have a full row of seats to myself as we reach 30,000 feet. As I relax on this smooth floating plane, last night's late hours, along with the soothing satisfaction of the Johnny cakes begin to take their toll. I now feel the sleep mode that I left back at the Bellevue Hotel creeping back in. I really need a nap, but I can't sleep for thinking about my whirlwind life and how it has brought me to this moment. As the plane begins to level off, it is eerily quiet inside and as I look down on the clouds my mind is floating within them as they carry me to a serene place of deep, deep thought.

The thoughts are of old Braniff Airlines and the 707 plane that first took me from Louisiana to Denver and finally to Nebraska. I'm also thinking of my wife, children, football and Central High School. But mostly I'm thinking of the things that are bringing me back to Nebraska at such a torrid speed, Doc Moller and the days when he brought his grandsons to my golf school. I was flattered when he gave me the opportunity to teach them the game of golf and I'm thankful for those days when he tried desperately to teach me the game of life. I am chuckling inside now, at how he had even allowed me to teach him a little of the game and actually paid me for it! Can you believe it? After our long past relationship and lopsided confrontational meetings relative to teaching, Doc Moller had paid to be a student in my class. This was Haley's comet, an event that might come around once in a life time, "Only in America".

My chuckles now turn into full laughter, but the laughter soon shifts into tears. I find myself strained in this multitude of jumbled emotions. I am very tired but still can't sleep. Why is there such laughter and why is that laughter followed by so many tears? To answer these questions my mind has begun to retrace their origins and reflect on the last twenty-four years of my life. A time when I was bombarded with a barrage of screaming notes that demanded I become better than I had ever been. I came to dread those notes, while at times despising the messenger, only to find out later that they were a concerted push to excellence by a caring man of principles.

Now half asleep and half awake on this Boeing 727 I'm thinking about flying, trying to memorize the flight attendant's script. No matter the attention to the now, my mind just carved out a route of its own and is drifting back to a time lost to new horizons. However, never forgotten are the timeless memories from so many years before; Memories from the day that I met Doc Moller in 1979 to my eerie decision to leave Central High School in 1990. The year's numbers mean little, just a start and a finish. However, that space between the years represents everything in an 11 year lifetime of hopes, dreams, successes and failures. Wow, it seems like 100 years ago but I remember it like it all happened yesterday.

Before 1922 the Register (school newspaper) staff was also in charge of producing the Omaha High School yearbook called, The Register Annual. However, in 1922 for the first time the yearbook sported its own staff and promptly changed the name. This new name became The OBook, with the O representing the word Omaha in Omaha High. Eighty plus years later it is still one of the most organized and uniquely informative high school yearbooks anywhere. I know, because my life at Central span through eleven years of these great publications.

From the fall of 1979 through the spring of 1990 the essence of my life was within the OBook pages. No, there's not an article about me in every book and my picture doesn't appear within it any more than any other faculty member. But as written previously, Central became my family and during that stretch each of the books speaks to the family members of each of those years. I lived in these pages along with thousands of students and scores of teachers, administrators and other skilled workers. To this day my eleven years inside the prestigious pages of the corresponding eleven OBooks still ranks as the most memorable span of my sixty-five years on this earth. When I think about it, most of the things that happened there can be summed up in a stack of little notes that Doc Moller sent me and the cries of my wife that finally reached me.

(The next section speaks to "family first" and ask that you listen to your principal and hear your spouse. Lessons I finally did learn.)

OB

My 11 years of yearbooks from 1979-80 through 1989-90.

The 3Three Side

"Tennis anyone?"

The 3Side was the third side to be completed in the four-sided Omaha Central High School structure. At one time it sported multiple tennis courts as its yard. Facing 22nd Street, it was completed around 1910.

Hail To The Mollergram

Things I learned from a Lady and
Doctor G.E. Moller

In the beginning months of the new millennium, I sat with my wife and four children in a room where the silence was only disturbed by the pinging of the respirator. They were the last minutes of my wife's life. My children, having for years watched death being played out over and over again in the movies or on TV thought they knew what was coming. They thought maybe they were prepared, but in the end none of us were. This segment is about an avalanche of strong messages from Doc that eventually made me better and it is dedicated to my wife for helping me to see the need.

Throughout my years at Central I was sent a series of boldly scripted communications that kept me walking on eggshells every single day. I absolutely hated them and for awhile wasn't too far away from feeling the same way about the distributor. I once described him as Napoleon Bonaparte with a typewriter! The only difference being, instead of an army, he had a faculty and nearly two thousand souls to protect. If I just once could have caught him wrongly admonishing me I would have nailed him to the wall. But I never did, not once. Later, I would come to know why. All the time I thought he was doing things to me with those bold, irritating, in-your-face notes. I understood later that he was actually doing things for me. This segment is about those notes and how they pushed me down so that one day I might eventually get up!

*From the plane through the scattered clouds I can see nothing except the
ocean blue below. I think we started out over the Caribbean Sea and are
now over the Gulf of Mexico. We're making good time. I'm thinking about
personal things; children, coaching, wife and Omaha Central in the 80's.
There I learned so much from Doc, but it didn't register for years. I heard
so many cries from my wife that went unheeded. These were personal lessons that I missed in those years, but are the guiding lights to my life today.
Those exasperated looks from my wife said everything. However, it was
those biting little notes of discipline from Doc that "WERE" everything!
I wanted to strangle him at times but he would have still been right, so I
just let it go. I guess, as I think about it, in the end he taught me what true
discipline is all about and so did she!*

When the job at Omaha Central became a reality for me, I was determined
to make it a success and I was willing to devote hours and hours on seeing it
through. Immediately, I wanted to change the climate of football and how it
was looked upon at the school. I didn't like it but the stale atmosphere was
certainly understandable, since there had not been the fragrance of a winning
football season in more than eighteen years. It was clear that the expected outcome relative to football for most students and faculty had become a foregone
conclusion. Fortunately, I was already familiar with the drill and knew that
in order to access change I had to enlist constant focus and consistent effort,
along with lots and lots of hands on time.

Any successful person of substance can tell you that when one moves toward changing a negative result that has become an accepted norm, there's
always particular sacrifices. This means that some areas of importance would

definitely end up being neglected. For me those areas of neglect just happened to be the two that mattered most and both should have superseded all others. They were family at home and teaching at school. Unfortunately in my zeal for success on the gridiron I was not giving nearly enough attention to those two areas that I loved so dearly. As a result of this miscarriage of judgment I was consistently reminded and prodded at every turn, by a wife who dared and a principal that cared!

The Reed Family 1985: standing- Aarian, Marcie, Dar; sitting- William, Kalisha, Linda

OB

Inside his office, Doc's greatest tool was his typewriter

Chapter 1

PERSONAL LESSONS LEARNED THE HARD WAY

Tough lessons from a man, apologies to a lady

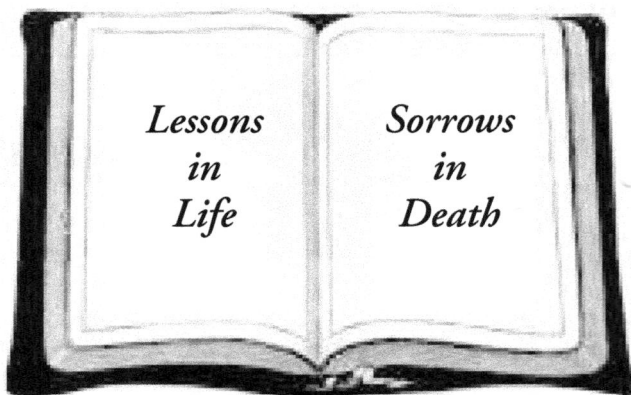

Lessons in Life   *Sorrows in Death*

The Good, The Bad And The Brave
Self Derogated...Unregulated

Nothing is more humbling than learning life lessons twenty years late. All you can think about is how long you've been wrong and how many suffered because of it, including yourself. I am proud to say that I learned so many valuable life lessons from Doc Moller and a lady. That lady just happened to be my wife. They were good lessons and very important lessons. It's just that it took me so long to understand their true meaning. To Doc I say thanks, to my wife I say I'm sorry.

The year is 1979 the class is 1980, and I would spend the rest of the decade and one year not only married to my wife but also married to Omaha Central High School. One might also say that I was married to many other things during that transitional period of my life and what a topsy turvy time it was. I was teaching five classes a day with four extra duty periods, while coaching football and track. I was a scratch golfer, swimming pool manager and played about a hundred softball games a year. We had a beautiful house in an upscale suburban neighborhood, three beautiful children and one on the way. Most men who were crowding their forties back then were walking for exercise, but me, I was still running the 40 yard dash in 4.6 seconds! It was pretty obvious that in sports and in life I was moving way too fast.

> We don't always get to do what we want, yet we are responsible for who we are.
> **unknown**

My plate was full and then some, and in my world of ignorance I thought life was good. It intensified in 1984 when Central had become the only Omaha public high school to ever win a Nebraska statewide football championship. Also, by then I had coached four high school All-American candidates. I was still a scratch golfer and was still playing about a hundred softball games every spring and summer. What more could one want? It was seemingly the American dream for me. But for my wife Linda, well that was another story.

I was home about one fifth of the time and felt tied to all the so-called important and unimportant clutter in my 1980's life. That life was my children, football, math classes, golf, wife, softball and track, possibly in that order. She hated the situation and I've come to know why. All those things that I thought made me something special, she came to despise. She detested me as a football coach, hated golf, didn't care anything about softball and began to care even less about our marriage. It was clear, we were walking in opposite directions, and I for sure, was headed the wrong way down a one way street.

I wish I could go back and grab that 30 year old maniac (me) and shake some sense into him. I wish he could sit down for a minute or two and talk to this William Reed. My, my, how much would he learn? First off, he'd learn what I first learned from Doctor Moller, without him knowing that he was even teaching it at the time. It was taught silently through his actions and interactions with his wife Betty and left me with the bold impression that; *"life begins with priorities and is defined by choices. Priorities must always be with family and all choices must begin with them in mind. No matter how big you get you must never outgrow your family, particularly the spouse that watched you scratch and squirm your way to so-called respectability."* (W.R.O.)

I think that when you have learned something wise from a humbling circumstance, as I did, it gives you the ability to act and help others. When you have the ability to act, it now becomes your responsibility to carry out such acts. So, for that reason I am sharing that somber time in my life, those first years at Central. It is with hope that perhaps one might learn to walk life forward from one who walked life backwards for far too long. The message is that; *"you can't do everything you want. At some point you have to sacrifice and do those things that you need to do in lieu of the wants."* (W.R.O.) Had my life been a movie back then, it would have been titled, <u>The Good The Bad and The Brave.</u> I often played the part of the good, sometimes the brave, but never once cast myself as the bad. It was an exciting motion picture but was labeled fiction. In the reality of my life Doc was the **good**, while I was too often the **bad,** and my wife remains eternally and forever the **brave**.

Linda: The Home Of The Brave, Courage on Immanuel 6

This segment of the book will end with a thank you to Doc Moller but will begin with a tribute to my wife, who was the victim of my success. I am often tormented by the thought that I could have done better and the reminder that I should have. It's a proven fact that life can at times get away from you and mine was a smorgasbord of false delights. The truth is that the lives of football coaches can be a nightmare to many of those who love them the most, and mine was no exception. After a time in that turbulent life I found myself in one of the saddest and scariest places in all of Omaha, Nebraska. It was the sixth floor at Immanuel Hospital. A place featuring dedicated professional healthcare workers, loving and caring families, and patients that were on the edge of hospice. I lived there for a week, hardly leaving the floor, never once leaving the building, while my wife lay terminally stricken with breast cancer. I recalled once having a compass in my life, but it was either damaged or just plain malfunctioned sometime around 1978. I thought with all my glorious talents that I should have the right to move at will, my will, in any direction I chose, with no restitutions. I was wrong and I'm still haunted by that sometimes renegade period of my life. My wife suffered through my transgressions and later she proved to be ten times the person I ever was or ever could be. In 1997 she was diagnosed with breast cancer, and in the year 2000 on her way to her 50th birthday, she succumbed to that dreaded disease.

In those last years we were just as close as we had been in high school and she showed me what real courage truly was. Without bickering or crying, without anger or hatred, she left me and this world, with dignity and pride. But before she did, she told me a story of goodness and greatness, not of her but of me and the one thing she thought I always managed to keep primary. She said that my greatest strength was my love for our children and that made her comfortable, despite my shortcomings and her unfortunate plight. My wife was a great and courageous person, and you and I can only pray to be as noble as she in our journey down the silent halls of death.

Her brother, Tom Harvey, the former longtime Associate Superintendent for the Omaha Public Schools, had been the bridge that brought us to Omaha, some 30 years before. Later he and I would both sit helplessly in that room on the sixth floor at Immanuel Hospital as the respirator was being shut down. I had asked Linda once if she was dying. She, being a registered hospice nurse herself, offered these profound words. With fortitude and conviction, she said, **"Everyone is dying William, it's just that we all have different dates."** And everyone knows how right she was. A few months after that, she passed away and her words have never left me. "We're all dying!" That dark description of life and where it's headed is just one of the many things that helped me to tell this intertwined story of Doc and me. All those things that she screamed for me to be, Doc Moller was at the same time trying to make me. Most of us can live tough, talk tough or act tough. But only the truly valiant can die tough. As a sports enthusiast I've had the privilege of watching many athletic events. They are all preceded by the national anthem, which always end in the same four words. "Home of the Brave." Do you ever wonder who lives there? I think thousands of great people do, including one named Linda Faye Reed. May God always bless her and all the mothers of our children.

Doc Notes

As it was at home, my life was a scattered mess in those early years at Central. Though Doc Moller always seemed to be very entrenched and devoted in one's duty, honor and family, he never really nagged at the staff about their personal lives, unless it leaked over into school business or performance. If things weren't right and he felt it, he had this way of asking you a question that actually made a statement. So, when you answered it, whether silently or aloud you would immediately realize that he had not asked a question but rather presented a challenging statement about the problem at hand.

I was the recipient of many such cloaked questions, which in reality were cutting statements. They were delivered most of the time within the context of one of those carefully transcribed, soul-searching notes he would send. One of which I received sometime toward the end of my time at Central. However, I didn't decipher it until years later while I was sitting in that lonely hospital room at Immanuel Hospital. The note spoke of winding roads and unending temptations. It spoke of loyalty, respect, wasteful hypocrisy and the handling of forbidden fruit.

It asked a few questions that made loud statements that were meant to direct, excel and nurture ones being. It included, among other things, the words "honor your wife." Few really pay attention to such things these days. But in March of 2000 I sat sobbing in a lonely private waiting room, cowering underneath a bed on that dreaded sixth floor at Immanuel Hospital. The empty and helpless feelings as my wife lay dying became an open passageway to my brain that finally let in some sense. Her silent warnings, along with Doc Moller's lead by example messages about life and wife, now made explicit sense.

In the weeks that followed I wept over those unheeded warnings from my wife and scoured my mind trying to remember more of Doc's sincere life messages, dating back two decades. I had reconnected with him a year earlier (1999). Even before then I had already used some of his school administration teachings within the concepts and creation of my golf school. They however, were mostly business booster messages and indeed did help. But while the memory of those messages served me well, what I sought afterwards were those transcribed notes of discipline that challenged my being and strengthened my resolve. These were those same tough notes that in the past I had so dreaded. Now, I saw his disciplines for what they truly were; ***forced enhancements which eventually fueled the source that led to my second term of life.***

Chapter 2

UNDERSTANDING THE MESSAGES

How simple notes of discipline became
legendary messages of triumph

> 2/18/85
>
> William, William, William
>
> Please meet in my office at
> 3:05 p.m. today.
>
> Doc

Exploring Doc's Disciplinary Notes

Iproclaim that Dr. G.E. Moller as a principal was one of the great disciplinary note writers of all time. I absolutely hated when he'd dropped those atomic scripts with drone-like precision on unsuspecting victims. Remember the feeling you get when you meet a patrol car while doing 75 in a 55 mph zone? It's that immediate look in the mirror and that sinking feeling when the lights begin to flash behind you as he swerves around to chase. That was the exact feeling I got when Doc walked passed me and observed something wrong. He'd maybe smile, talk to me for a bit, while never mentioning the shortcoming. However, I knew that I was wrong and I knew that he knew it also! Yet, he says nothing. So, just as with the patrolman I'm holding to the hope that perhaps it's just a warning. But on most occasions the patrolman writes you up and unfortunately so did Doc Moller. Usually before the end of the same day there it is, the note waiting in your mailbox describing in detail your misguided lapse in judgment. Mine always began with my first name being written three times; William, William, William. This became the universal code in my life that would forever signal, that something within my judgment had gone terribly wrong at Central.

It was a couple of years before I found out that those little notes on colored paper had a name. By then they were coming in bunches and about drove me crazy! To the staff, outside of Doc's presence, the notes were known affectionately and sometimes scornfully as "Mollergrams". I received several such notes from Doc as those first years passed by but had no knowledge that a connotative name had been attached to them. Until one day, I opened my mailbox and found it filled with all manner of mail. As I removed the contents a blue piece of paper floated to the floor without

> *Understanding is the first step to knowledge.*
> *(W.R.O.)*

me seeing it. As a courtesy it was picked up by a fellow teacher, Cheryl Brown. With a startled look as she picked it up she said, "This is a Mollergram!" Then she handed it to me as if it was radioactive. Then with a sad face and a shake of the head she said, "Good luck man" and her facial presentation sadly whispered "its been nice knowing you – bye!!!"

I'd been getting the notes for over two years but had never once heard about this Mollergram moniker, so I inquired about it. What I found was that everyone seemed to already know what I did not. Apparently Doc didn't appreciate the characterization so it was more of an in-house teacher thing than a universal brand. But despite the cloaked intention Mollergrams were definitely a part of Omaha Central lore. In fact when I asked my friend Stan Standifer, in the P.E. department about it he perked up immediately and replied, "Man I've been getting showered with "Grams" since the day I got here." "What, I thought, he's familiar enough with the term to use the short form?" Wow, I don't know who in the world ever thought of the name, but whoever it was should receive a Pulitzer. The name is genius because that is exactly what they were. As soon as I heard it I quickly thought about all those notes I'd been receiving. After a brief scanning of my brain there was no doubt, they were definitely Mollergrams!

I could explain the interaction of Doc and I in an assorted variety of ways. However, I think the best way to describe what he did to me, for me, and about me is through the eyes of these screaming notes that first haunted me, and are now a daily blessing. These menacing notes that I resented, disdained and professed at times to be torture. These jackals posing as words and naturalized as Mollergrams, have turned out to be the most important lessons of my life.

It took me two years to know they existed, eleven years to get away from them and the rest of my life to decipher their meaning. Through it all I became better while using them as positive tools to help me along. These were Doc's little bombs and now they've become my big explosions. I thought them devilish at times, but now I shout with joy, "God bless the Mollergram".

Defining The Mollergram

When a superior relative to your employment decides to make written evaluation of your performance or the lack thereof it is usually silently evaluated by the employee victim and screened for its scorn. We check it for unwarranted cruelty, non factual content, unnecessary premise and an over reactive display of power and authority. There was no exception to this rule when it came to Doc, myself and this so call Mollergram business. I took it as something he enjoyed, abused and took pride in messing in one's daily life. However, I felt awful when I found how far that was from the truth. I disdained these Mollergrams with a passion but never tried to define or understand them. After years of receiving them and many more years of search and recovery, one day I asked myself, "what exactly is a Mollergram, what was its purpose and what does it accomplish in the end?" Somewhere in the mist of that question the answer came gushing out in a simplistic manner.

A Mollergram is a note deriving from the desk of Dr. G.E. Moller. Though mostly typed it could be handwritten, outlining minor or critical defaults involving your performance as it relates to a particular negligence revolving around Central High School. It was an internal doctrine that was based on communicable consistency and equal treatment. It offered and promoted awareness, protection, rehabilitation, accountability and was a perfect agent in record keeping. It was Doc Moller adding his own brand to a civilized chore that predated mankind. A chore that is the order in life known as "discipline".

It seems the plane has leveled off and things are very smooth now. The beverage cart is making its way toward me but I'm still thinking about Doc and his practice of sending those piercing notes. Notes that nearly always found me in some disciplinary context. Now, my mind is creeping back to my childhood thinking about how his notes and their name related to another time in my life. A time when another type "gram" hit me with even more intensity.

From Life Changing Mailgrams To Life Building Mollergrams

At the advent of my teenage years, during the summer before I headed to 9th grade I was caught up in a semi-gang situation that resonated from a Monroe, Louisiana housing project called The Foster Homes. I think the place was so named for the Fosters, one of Monroe's most prominent black families. However, having to say I lived in The Foster Homes, always evoked the first thoughts of orphan. But you learned to live with it and you got use to explaining it. During the days of our little gang thuggery we ran rampant and justified it with grandeur of our TV hero, Robin Hood. We gave much of our bounty to people in need. So in essence we assumed we were robbing from the rich to give to the poor, just like Robin. Of course this is not a very popular stance in today's society and soon we would learn that it wasn't so hot during that time either.

When J.B. a 6th grader in 1962, was caught at school wearing a $200 Rolex watch that slouched on his slender arm, he was immediately escorted to the principal's office at Lincoln Elementary School, and thus the party began. That day they put him in a private room and the only reason he ever stopped talking was that they ran out of reel to reel tape! That next morning the police sent out more than 25 mailgrams by courier that read: *"Your minor son has been cited with a juvenile summons and must be brought to the juvenile detention office within 24 hours of the issuance of this summons or a warrant will be posted for his arrest."* This was high drama and it would be the first time that I would worry about receiving a mailgram in my mailbox for doing something wrong.

It was a hot June afternoon and that mailgram courier just kept on coming, making deliveries all across the neighborhood. There were rows and rows of buildings facing each other with four units attached to each one. You could see the courier as he parked and walked between them. He would get out of the car with papers in hand, walk between the buildings in search of a particular door and then he'd stop and place the summons in the mailbox. You could hear the shouts and screams, as all hell broke loose upon every delivery. I sat petrified that afternoon, worried sick that sooner or later one of those deliveries would find our mailbox.

My mom just knew I wasn't involved so she spoke to the horror of it all in the sense of, "how could they?" However, I knew better, so I would ease to the window to watch the courier's every move. I was dripping sweat upon every delivery and my heart was pumping five times its normal rate. Lee Daniel, Freddy, William H, Richard Lee, Wilbert, John Pomphrey and others had already received one. The mailgrams started about 2 p.m. that day and at 5 o'clock they were still coming! My friend Ervin Turner and I still talk about those hours to this day. It was three hours of pure agony and several months of worry to follow. Even the innocent were sweating in fear, watching the mailboxes. Everyone was scared, waiting for that life-altering mailgram that would send you places you didn't want to go. Places that were sure to change your destiny in life forever.

For Ervin and I the mailgrams never came and even now neither of us can understand why. But as we sat inside the Tri-District Boys Club, that he created several years later, we could look out the north window and see the housing project where we grew up. Now 36 years old with birthdates only two months apart we went back to the day of those awful mailgrams 22 years before. Those kids, our friends, that were picked up received 1-2 years in reform school. John Pomphrey who was the only "so called" adult in the group at 17, was tried as such and sentenced to five years in Angola Prison. During those days many times a death sentence to a young teenager.

As Ervin and I sat there reflecting on that hideous day, I had one year earlier coached the first Omaha public school to a Nebraska State Football Championship. While Ervin had just won his second term as Ouachita Parish Commissioner (police jury as named in Louisiana), we took a count by naming all of the young kids we ran around with before that mailgram summer. The number came to 32 and then we counted again. Of that 32, nineteen were dead by the age of 30. Most were violent deaths, some were lost in Vietnam and almost all of them were the kids that received those mailgrams that day.

With that awful story in mind I was later confronted with that same kind of anxious fear as I would walk to my Central High School mailbox some mornings. The mailgrams of my life in 1962 had now become Mollergrams of the 1980's and their daily impact was just as nauseating. I'd often find myself hoping against hope, holding to the possibility that maybe the delivery would pass me by. Back in Monroe that day, I was polarized by the thought of receiving that mailgram. Now as an adult, I was sometimes experiencing those same anxieties. Of course it wasn't life or death and certainly nineteen lives wouldn't end before their time, but ask any teacher at Central and they will tell you, that no one, and I mean no one, wanted to receive that "gram" from Doc that said: "Please meet in my office at 3:05 p.m. today!"

At the onset of my years at Omaha Central, I was hit with so many Mollergrams that I was totally convinced that Doc Moller was out to get me. However, years later it became apparent that each note he sent me told a story and asked that I be a better and more efficient person. There came a time when I asked myself the question, "what was he really up to?" What I learned later in life was that I was being taught some of the most valuable lessons that a teacher or a coach could ever receive, "**non-acceptance of mediocrity.**" Today that push propels me to strive to be better than I ever knew I could. In fact, whenever business or personal things bring me into contact with other individuals, I always ask myself the question, "Could this person work for Dr. G.E. Moller?" The answer is usually "no". Either way, once I ask the question and process the answer, I am better able to evaluate the person and navigate the situation. I don't know if a mailgram from the courier that day would have changed my life back in 1962. But years later I know for sure that a series of Mollergrams most certainly did!

Receiving Mollergrams

For a long period of time I surmised that if I was receiving this many notes weekly surely Doc didn't have time to write any others. I began to explore a bit further and found that I was not some lone isolated victim. There is no one at Central that escaped it. Doc would send a Mollergram to the Pope if he came to work at Central and didn't fulfill his duty. My thought was always that the World Herald newspaper of Omaha has an entire network in place to acquire data and then release it in the form of printed words. Where was Doc Moller getting the time to investigate, produce and distribute this odd intelligence piece known as a Mollergram? I even talked to a female teacher that expanded on things. She told of another such communication from Doc that had been aptly named the "Mellogram" which is a note of praise or congratulations written on the same type note pad. I think the notes were color coded based on Mello or Moller but I can't speak to that. Someone once said that certain bright colors were Mellograms, while other less brilliant colors were used only for Mollergrams. Again, that I can't verify, however I can verify that mine came in a variety of colors called "abundance." I was being bombarded with so many that I couldn't take time to decipher colors, I could only deal with content.

Those notes were Doc Moller in all his psychological savvy. Of all the notes he ever sent me, of all the times he ever addressed me, to this day he has never referred to me as Coach Reed. It was always William and sometimes Mr. Reed. Why? Back in the 1980's I never thought about or understood what he was doing until later. I think it had to do with him driving home the point that William was the person, Mr. Reed was the teacher and Coach Reed was the coach. Since he never addressed me in a coaching setting he never had grounds to call me coach. So, his subtle way of prioritizing the order of my dutiful life as it related to Central High School was person, teacher, and then coach. This was not surprising to me at all, as his covert messages were always clear, simple and effective. I have to say that Doc Moller was often amazing in his wit and masterful in his approach via the Mollergram.

Typically, here's how he charted and expedited communications to me. When a note began with the heading Mr. Reed, it usually meant something nice or official, a Mellogram, if there was such a thing. If it began with William, it mostly called for something general or routine. Then there was the big one, the three *Williams deal*. Which meant I was in deep. "William, William, William." When I saw the triplets I didn't have to read further, I just headed to his office at 3:05, took my regular chair and it was officially the hot seat from there! He later told me that the three Williams were his way of saying that he was exasperated with me. Whenever I was called to his office I could always feel the magnitude of the problem by the reactions of the secretaries. As I headed back to Doc's office I had to pass them first. There were usually three or four at their respective desks, Wanda, Martha, Ginny, Opal, Mrs. Rosenthal, all nice ladies. If I was in for a Mellogram they were usually bright eyed, with smiles and hi's or hello's all about them as I passed. However, if it was a "Mollergram" they seemed to know it and as I proceeded pass them one by one they lowered their heads as if I was walking to my doom. I couldn't blame them because in retrospect, many times I actually was.

Around the year 1984, I recall Doc sending me a Mollergram requesting my presence. The school had begun to be overrun with college football coaches with recruitment in mind. These guys were popping up everywhere, hanging around the building like vampires, just hoping for a bite. At times they would show up unannounced, loiter outside my class until the bell rang and sometimes even interrupt class. It was a cluttered jungle, a virtual circus and I knew it didn't sit well with Doc. Their rambling football recruitment visits seemed to display some form of disorganization, something that was almost unholy in Doc's world. I knew it was coming and finally there it was, on white paper though. Ah, a Mellogram. The message: "Mr. Reed, please meet in my office 3:05 today."

The way the note read I knew it was not a big deal, I felt safe. The meeting ended up being a strict set of new rules for all visiting college coaches, I could live with that. They were to check into the office before going to any other part of the building and if I was not free, or an assistant coach was not available to accommodate them, they were put in a temporary holding room in the main office until such time that one of us became available.

That same week, Johnny Majors of Tennessee sent a coach to visit. Cletus Fischer of Nebraska was already there, as were five or six other coaches waiting in the "holding tank", including a Penn State assistant and Terry Donahue, head coach of UCLA. Cletus and the coach from Tennessee spotted one of my football players in the hall, circumvented the rule and had that player direct them straight to me in a third floor math class. I had cafeteria duty coming up so I sent Cletus there and I was working on getting the Tennessee coach back downstairs. In the process the bell rang and now two or three other coaches are waiting to get directions to where they might go after spending a couple of hours in the holding tank.

I am not nearly prepared for this type of traffic. By the time I offered instructions to the last coach it was about five minutes past the time I should have been in the cafeteria on duty. Then, as if summoned by some unearthly force, Doc walks by. He glanced, didn't stop, didn't even hesitate. I moved toward the stairwell and spotted a coach down the hall speaking to one of the players. That was off limits for that time of year, so I walked down to break up that violation and again, Doc walks by. I'm now about 10 minutes late for my duty in the cafeteria and there's four coaches waiting and again that unearthly force summons once more and Doc walks by a third time without a word. At this point there's no doubt in my mind that this is big, big trouble!

Now comes those three hours of sweat and anxiety that I had back in Louisiana as a kid. Is the Mollergram in my mailbox? Will Doc understand the circumstances and let it go? Will he follow through as he always seemed to? It looked bad but there's a possibility that I might be able to get by with this one. It was a troublesome period and I didn't want to deal with a visit to his office, having just left there with a warning three days before. I'm hoping for that break I got back in Louisiana, when the courier kept coming back to the Monroe projects but never left a mailgram in my mailbox. I had that same scary, sick feeling.

Can it be that I might make it by this time too? Taking my time, that afternoon I walked to the office after school that day with a sick anticipation while cautiously wondering, is there a Mollergram in my mailbox? When I finally reached the mailbox area, I slowly and meticulously slid the box open and there it was. After some twenty years my luck with mailboxes had run out. A full-throttled gram written on faded purple paper, beginning with the greeting, "William, William, William."

The next day as the summons stipulated I surrendered in the main office and right on queue the secretaries lowered their heads as I passed each one. This officially made it Dooms Day! The lecture and pounding I received that day had to do with duty, punctuality, planning and priorities. I was reminded of the necessity for having a cafeteria monitor and the perils that might have happened due to tardiness. It didn't matter that I had three strong intelligent aides on duty, it was all about the supervisor. I was reminded that day of the consequences for putting college coaches ahead of students that I was assigned to monitor. I was told how careful planning might well have prevented the entire incident. Those were the charges and I was guilty before the last sentence was read.

The punishment was another intense revising of the rules. Now, coaches that came to visit were not allowed to see me during school hours, period! If a coach came from Miami and arrived at Central at 8 a.m. he'd have to wait until school dismissed to see me. Of course this wasn't said in the meeting, it was sent via a "Mollergram" post haste. It was very sad one day to see Nebraska

Coach Tom Osborne pacing the floor in what resembled a holding cell inside the main office. But those were the new rules and I didn't dare try to bail him out, for fear of violating my Mollergram probation.

Things are getting a little bumpy aboard the plane as we seem to be descending in altitude. I think I'd better buckle up. Sitting here locked down on this plane reminds me of that seat I always took in Doc's office. It was seldom pleasant there and most of the time I was not even aware of the offense.

OB

139

Chapter 3

THE MOLLERGRAM REBELLION
The Battle of 1983

A Coaching Debut Interrupted

I can make light of the so-called Mollergrams today but back in that beginning year of 1979 and those that followed they were no laughing matter. During that time I was consistently trying to make sense of what was happening. I had never been prodded like that. The meetings came fast and furious for me and they were always preceded by that mild descriptive summons note "The Mollergram." I was hit with five my very first week at Central, including an unforgettable one for punctuality. I recall daily check in time as 7:25 a.m. The Mollergram that afternoon indicated that I clocked in at 7:26 a.m. This after waiting my turn behind five other teachers. I was upset over what I deemed as pettiness, but it mattered not. Those five were followed up with yet another gram, this one indicating that I had received five for the week... really? Perhaps I had broken some sort of record I presumed.

A week later it was football game day and I was oblivious to everything else around me. You might say that I was in my own little world. To me this was a historic day and I wanted to live every minute of it five times over. As I checked my mailbox that Friday I admit I was thinking more about my first football game as a high school head coach than I was my five math classes. I was nervous in anticipation of the night to come and there it was again, "damn it," another Mollergram, and on "my special day"!

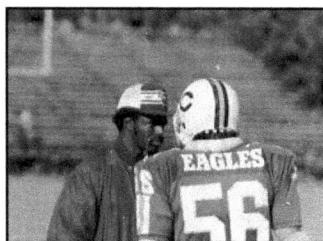

OB

Coach Reed offers defensive instructions to Dave VanMetre

This one was to make sure that I was aware that he knew where my mind most likely was that day. "What?" This was baffling. His note made it clear that if such was the case I might not last too long at Central High. To me, this was borderline harassment. I was outraged and outdone! Was it possible that the man could read minds too? Though seething with scorn, I took the invasion of my mind like a man and moved forward. After all he was right, and although I wanted to strangle him, he would have still been right, so I just let it go.

The Mollergram Revolution

One week after my debut as the head football coach at Omaha Central I am hit with yet another gram and then another. This avalanche of Mollergrams persisted throughout the year and when he sent me his longest, most biting one to date, I said enough! This was more than just a Mollergram. It was a full throttled, two page bomb he dropped on me this time for some miniscule mishap. A bomb that I characterized as petty at best and ridiculous in scope. This to me meant war! It was time to rebel this trash, time to make a stand! I remember my head being hot that day. Steam came from it, as the water boiled in my brain. Fire blew from my mouth, while sweat poured like a faucet. I was hot! All I could think about that day was how to retaliate. There is no way that I will just sit this one out. The Mollergram revolution was officially here, it was war and Doc Moller was going down once and for all!

I figured the best way to go was to bomb his bomb with one of my own. So, I decided to flip the script and give him a dose of his own medicine. I figured if I sent him an anti-Mollergram it would catch him off guard. I mean a piece of literary writing that will top any gram he had ever sent. I decided to attack this menace pen to pen, paper to paper, man to man! My note will be bigger, better, more intense, and totally rebellious in every sense of the word. It would be the Revolutionary War, the Civil War and World War II all rolled up in one. No way will I let this go this time, no way!

> No matter the foe, there comes a time in life when you have to stand and fight.
> (W.R.O.)

When I arrived home that evening I went straight to the basement and ordered no disturbance. In my rage I grabbed a pen and paper and with no typing skills I hand wrote my attack. It was an eight page assault written on long legal size paper. It was a three hour chore that finished in a rebuttal that retaliated with all the firepower I had. It made his type written two page "mega gram" look pale in comparison.

The next morning, I stood stern near the faculty mailboxes and gave my rebuttal one last look. Yes, in all its glory this was my declaration of independence. After the re-read of my strong retaliation the football side of me took over, and I "spiked it" into his mailbox! I didn't know if he would read it or not, but boy did it feel good to slam it down in his mailbox. Bang, take that! Then I aggressively slammed it shut. I strutted around all that morning with the <u>Dirty Harry</u> look and my <u>Terminator</u> walk. Head high, hands clinched, daring anyone to get in my way.

All that morning I felt strong, as though I had slammed that mailbox and reclaimed my manhood. I figured he'd be about a week just trying to absorb the shock of it all and by then I'd be ready with phase two. I just knew I had caught him off guard. I envisioned having him in a boxing ring against the ropes pounding away, looking for the knockout! I thought, "bammm, that'll shut him up for awhile." That noon hour I strutted down to the main office area just hoping to run into him. I wanted to give him my poison stare. I didn't see him so just for the heck of it I checked my mailbox, knowing it would be empty. But no, it wasn't. Strangely and surprisingly my rebuttal letter was already back in my mailbox.

At first I thought he was afraid to read it and just returned it in fear, but when I opened it right away I was confused. It looked like a bird with red paint on its feet had walked all over it. I thought to myself, what is this? Then it hit me, "No way!" It was my letter and it had been checked and scored with red marks. I was aghast at what I saw. My great letter of combat, my declaration of war dissected like a science-lab frog and was now being used as a weapon against me. It had been graded like a test and then noted with an indication that I'd made 55 grammatical errors within the scope of its content. Did I mention Dr. Moller was an English major?

This was craaazy!!! I was flustered and losing ground by the second but didn't want to sound the retreat. I thought what the hell do I do now? Before I could gather myself he delivered his knock-out blow. Attached was a Mini-Mollergram that read; ***"Such grammatical presentation is not consistent with the high standards of expectations befitting that of an Omaha***

Central teacher. " "Say what?" I was dumbfounded to say the least. The battle had reached a new crescendo, I'd been wounded and metaphorically speaking, I was bleeding profusely. Not knowing what I might be hit with next, I had no choice, it was time to sound the retreat. I immediately hid the letter in panic, looking nervously all about me, hoping no one else peeked over my shoulder and saw all those disparaging red marks. I felt like a ten year old school kid that had just failed his 5th grade language test. I read through my would be rebellious masterpiece one last time. I noted the red markings, took it down to the coaches' restroom, burned it, then flushed it immediately.

That was it, my rebellious rant and twenty-four hour revolution went up in smoke and down a toilet in the downstairs locker room of the new gym. It was over and as of that day neither of us has ever spoken of it again. I mean really, how does one respond to someone who just found 55 grammatical errors and misspellings within the context of an eight page letter? Answer: You don't. You lick your wounds and learn not to constantly write capital N's and misplaced commas within the body of a sentence, an old habit of mine when I wrote in anger. With that the white flag went up. The Mollergram Revolution was over. Though it wasn't a contested battle, whatever it was he had won. I wanted to strangle him, but if I had the outcome would have still been the same. So I just let it go. About two weeks later, after things had settled, I was once again at my mailbox and wouldn't you know it... yep, "ANOTHER MOLLERGRAM."

After the smoke had cleared and the dust had settled, years passed and so many of the hard knock lessons from Doc began to take hold. I often pondered the things that happened in my actions and interactions with him throughout those great and sometimes turbulent years within the four sides. I can feel the things I learned back then, still hear his lessons in sounds and I can see the templates of the Mollergrams that left an indelible impression within my being. To be clear these lessons were not guided teachings directed only at me, but more a philosophy that played out in his life as an administrator every day.

I can't say that he knowingly and specifically meant to impact my life in the way he did. If that were so then some might assume he should take responsibility for my shortcomings as well and that would be cruelly unfair. I only know of things that were done by him and how I was affected by them. These were positive things, good things and solid tools for life. Whether it was done purposefully, accidently or unknowingly, what I know is that I learned much from him and continue to, even as all these years continue to pass.

As the plane rumbles through turbulence I'm reminded that I am still airborne. I am thinking about some of Doc's needlepoint Mollergrams and my overdue interpretations of their meaning. What was it that prompted their delivery and what did I learn from their content? One by one I can think of several. One by one I can recall their delivery and every story behind each one of them.

Chapter 4

LIFE, FAMILY, JOB
No need for books!
Everything I ever needed to know
I found in a Mollergram

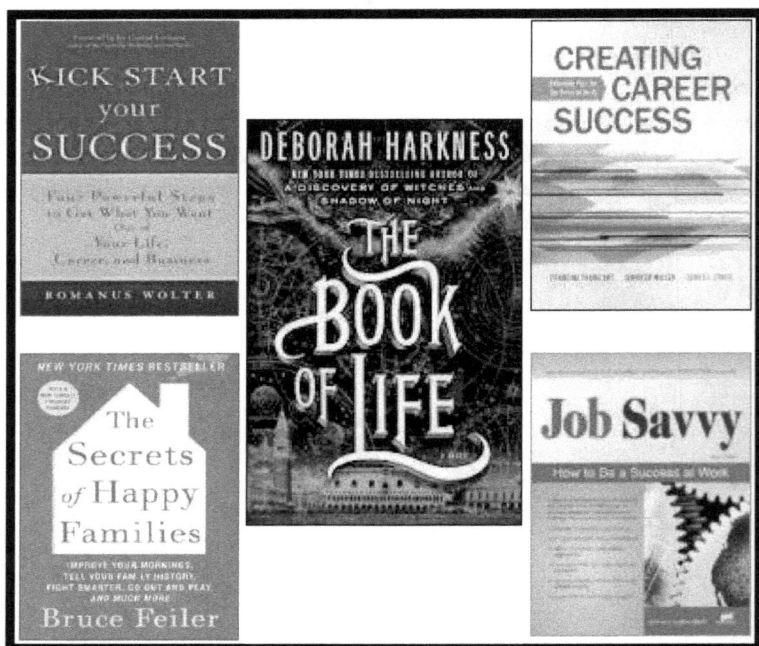

Mollergrams: Serious Messages, Serious Business

So many times Doc sent his messages to me and so often they went unheeded. They just kept on coming but were not really getting through. I've playfully and in some cases scornfully referenced the mocked notation "Mollergram". However, in the process I don't want to diminish the seriousness that came with the presentation of those communications. They all came during some very serious and challenging times for both Doc and me.

The reason I can make light of the word Mollergram from lost times yesterday is because I believe and understand the true meaning and intent of their purpose today. Some of that representation came within a complex package that took me years to decipher. However, once I did I began to use them as life tools and today my life is better for it. What follows is my interpretation of a few of them along with stories that will expand on their usage. They will all be concluded

> *The content within the message far outweighs its source.*
>
> *(W.R.O.)*

with a **"direct message"** of what I learned from the situation overall. Each of the **"message notations"** are my original and personal interpretations presented with the thought that someone might learn today through my oversights of yesterday and thus may find a clearer path to the goals they seek. If that number is one person, then this book would not have been written in vain.

Eight Great Mollergrams And The Messages They Sent

<u>Mollergram 1</u>

It is fair for your leader to demand your very best effort and that effort must end in a positive result.

During my first five years at Central I was pushed and tugged at like a rag doll by Doc Moller. I tried to enlist all manner of reasons for his behavior toward me. My thoughts were - he didn't like coaches, could be prejudiced, narcissistic, mean and unsympathetic! You name it, I thought it. Yet, I never considered any reasons for mine toward him. In truth, all that ever happened was his demanding my best effort. Not some of the time, but all of the time.

We were in charge of advancing the lives of the future and when placed in that situation everyone must give their very best effort and there must be someone in place to make sure that they do so. The principal that is **not** willing to step into the face of the strongest personalities under his command is doing a disservice to the students and faculty he is sworn to guide. Doc didn't allow my efforts to be just effort, he required my best at every turn and it had to show results. Looking back on it today, he defied being the type of principal that sought to make friends with everyone involved. He attacked shortcomings and scolded lack of effort with a vengeance, no matter the person or circumstance.

The message was this: *"The primary function of a principal is to ensure that the function of the teacher is primary". (W.R.O.)*

Mollergram 2

Beware of the leader who too often accepts mediocrity.

My first years at Central were pure adjustments. I had taught school in other places and really hadn't worried so much about the level at which I operated. I had a pretty significant work load and if things got too hard or just plain too much, I'd explain to the principal or assistant principal and everyone would understand. But within the four sides of Central High School in front of Dr. G.E. Moller mediocrity was unacceptable, no matter the reason. I often wondered did this man know that I have five classes, cafeteria duty, hall duty and courtyard duty during school and a big football coaching job after? Does he know that I have a wife and four kids at home? Does he know I'm trying to bring the Central High football program back from the dead? Doc never gave in to that kind of silent whining. He expected me to not just do, but to excel in every endeavor and I rebelled at every turn. However, he never allowed me to get away with insinuating that because of effort toward one duty, the others were excused during that period. As years moved, so too did my understanding. I finally came to the conclusion that this man would not be satisfied until I showed superior performance in all areas of school and life. I now know that those high expectations he handed out in the name of excelling were all about him first caring, and then preparing one for the next level, whenever it might come. Today I cherish his non-acceptance of things that were not done correctly. After all, what is an administrator really saying to you when you are allowed to perform at a subpar level and never held accountable for such?

I recall in football having horrible luck in 1983 with star running back Keith "End Zone" Jones in the backfield. It was a tough year losing three games by a total of six points and barely missing the playoffs. Doc called me in along with Athletic Director Dick Jones. I thought to myself, this could only be routine because it concerned football and Doc could care less about how I performed in football. Well, I was wrong again. He emphasized teaching those five math classes and manning my duty assignments at maximum efficiency at all times, which was normal for him. However, what wasn't normal was him showing equal concern for expectations in football. I was shocked, I didn't even think the man knew what a touchdown was, or for that matter that he cared. Now, to my surprise here he was sounding like a color commentator for CBS sports. He had knowledge of everything that had happened during the season and was commenting in depth about pure football stuff. I was in shocked! When he commented that people close to the program had bigger expectations than the results of what were happening, I was caught totally off-guard. He went on to say that people close to the school expected a lot more from my coming.

I asked, "Are you saying what I think you're saying"? Even with three losses that year, I thought any negative comments about the season were completely out of line. Four seasons at a school that hadn't had a winning football season for 18 years, and in my second year falling one game short of making the state semi-finals, losing to Burke in overtime! The following year making the play-offs again after being rated statewide number one for the first time in school history. I thought we were due a parade but apparently the Central estate needed more. I left that meeting with a new knowledge. Doc Moller has high expectations for football also. I will admit that my focus on winning football games changed after that meeting. I was mildly insulted by it at first, but I must say everything that had to do with coaching was a little more intense going forward. The very next year, 1984, we became the first Omaha public high school to win a statewide championship in football. When I reflect, I think of the curious smile that Doc gave me the day after we won the State Championship game. "Good job William", he said with an oh-by-the-way tone. From that time on there was never another word uttered about expected success for the rest of my time at Central. I got a nice Mellogram from him that day and then quietly headed to my second period class. That year told me a lot about Doc and even more about me. For him, I now understood that mediocrity was not acceptable under any circumstances. For me, I found that I could indeed meet his expectations within the scope of each of the circumstances that concerned us.

The message was this: *"When we get these jobs of magnitude we must understand that there is always perceived notions of high expectations. In the interim we should not get angry at the guy that reminds us of that, we should only respect his concern and refocus to the task at hand." (W.R.O.)*

Mollergram 3

There is no favoritism within the boundaries of expectations in lieu of a job well done.

When Gaylord E. Moller gave you a task the expectation level was always very high. You were expected to perform without deprivation or mental reservations. You must get the job done or feel the wrath, and don't expect him to offer up any high fives for doing what you were assigned to do. The fact that you'll never hear about what you did is silent acknowledgement that praises a job well done. This manner of governing didn't just apply to some; it applied to all souls on board. Doc never played favorites! I think for him that was like some form of blasphemy. As the years passed I found that anyone could be sitting in that seat in his office at 3:05, with door closed!

One day I saw Vicki Anderson storm out of Doc's office, seething with hostility. From that moment I knew that no one was exempt from the disciplinary enforcement of one G.E. Moller. My thought that day was that if you were willing to push those buttons, then nothing could escape scrutiny within his command. Miss Anderson was Central High hierarchy, very nice and extremely respectful. She was truly one of the "good guys" within the walls. In fact, she was selected as the National Representative for teachers statewide during that time. That meant she represented all teachers at all schools across the state, but inside and out she was first and foremost all Central. She wasn't quite the queen but she was definitely in the queen's court. She had that way about her that always seemed to suggest that she was a little more Central than most. She just always seemed to be in the know all the time about everything school. I just couldn't see Doc having to ruffle her feathers. However, it reinforced what I think were Doc's three greatest attributes as a principal: disciplined leadership, open fairness and total consistency.

> *The acquisition of knowledge should last a lifetime.*
> *(W.R.O.)*

Paul Pennington was an ambitious teacher on the rise and eventually ended up as Central's athletic director in later years. I thought him to be sort of untouchable in his role as a Central High nobleman. I recall vividly a year when Paul was caught in one of those infamous Mollergram showers. It was never pretty when Doc was on your trail shipping out daily Mollergrams and was even worse for those who weren't used to it! For about a month stretch Doc was relentless in his pursuit of Paul. I never quite knew what had happened during that period but every time I saw Paul he was nervously looking over his shoulder and constantly worried. He was a little jumpy, sometimes sweating, shirt-tail hanging out, eyes dancing. I knew the symptoms, it was a Doc Moller barrage that I was all too familiar with. **"Mollergrams! No known antidote."** The fact that Paul (a made man at Central in gangster Lore) was now the hunted really surprised me. I felt really bad for him. However, I must admit that I was a little happy too. I think everyone is happy when the state trooper that turns on his lights behind you ends up passing by in pursuit of another vehicle.

Doc lived and breathed righteousness, with no favorites and absolutely no favors. *Playing favorites, on the job or in life is a sure fire sign of weakness and it distorts one's ability to lead.* Doc Moller would never paint himself into such a corner.

The message was this: *A great leader never skews the lines and must be practical and fair in their dealings. These consistent actions evoke the broad range of respect that one must command in order to lead others." (W.R.O.)*

Mollergram 4

The order of life that is discipline begins with consistent punctuality.

I don't want to say it but I have to; Doc Moller taught me the true meaning of punctuality. Okay there, it's out! I was one of those guys that figured if I showed up five minutes early on Monday then I had the right to be five minutes late on Tuesday. That theory was like having someone throw you an anvil while you were treading water... if you grab hold, you're probably going to drown!

In the space he guarded, Doc Moller offered little room for tardiness. The mere thought of it seemed to discombobulate him. In a word he once told me that it was just plain irritating. Then he explained that it scrambles the mindset of those who are expecting you at a particular time. He called it annoying, upsetting and just plain unprofessional! He took it as something so simple to do that if you didn't, it was either on purpose or because you just didn't care. Doc treated being late like you were stealing his lunch money! He saw it as being more like showing up to work with wrinkled clothes, uncombed hair and your shirt tail hanging out. To him being late was just plain tacky!

When he had finally exhausted the Mollergram deliveries to me on this particular subject (punctuality) he called me in on it. Two minutes here, five minutes there, one minute passed, he was just annoyed with it all. When all the while I was thinking, those numbers seems close enough for me. With that thought process it wasn't long before I was back in his office; 3:05, closed door, same seat. He stunned me immediately by telling me that I had too much clutter in my life. "You're late mostly because you're trying to do too many things at the same time," he said, "You have got to prioritize the things you do or the tardiness will persist and this will be taken to the next level!" I was thinking, would that be Mars or Jupiter? Really! Give me a break! Quickly though, I saw that it was not the time for smart-alecky comments. Doc was thoroughly angry while I just couldn't get myself worked up to defend a one minute tardy. It was pointless to me.

I argued my point but he refused to let me win the tardiness debate. I even came up with this beauty: sure, other teachers are here on time but how many stay three to four hours after school every day, like I do? The look he gave to that was one of utter disgust. It seemed to leave him speechless for a few seconds. However, this rare mute moment didn't stop another Mollergram from penetrating my mailbox. The punctuality battle lasted a little while but I knew all along that it was never a defensible position. In the end I took his advice and tried some corrective measures. The results turned out to be another healthy learning experience and since then I have played it to my advantage at every turn.

The message was this: *"Accountability and dependability are by-products of punctuality. Nothing can be worked and done before it is first started... and the best way to start is on time. (W.R.O.)*

Mollergram 5

Punctuality is graded by the second not by the minute.

Regarding punctuality: In the 8 o'clock start time there's no difference between 8:01 and 8:15, in both cases you are late. Doc blindsided me with this hard lesson early in my tenure at Central. Check in time was 7:25 a.m. and I was written up for 7:26. This was too picky as far as I was concerned and I was irritated to say the least. A "William, William, William Mollergram for one minute? Give me a break! A 3:05 closed door meeting for 60 seconds, really? REALLY??? This was nuts! I walked into Doc's office that day and gave him my, "are you serious" look, followed by a gyration of disgust and an arrogant baritone voice of defiance. He just sat there, quietly and patiently, allowing me to vent and get it all out and boy did I let him have it! I gave it to him loud and tough and since he offered no defense, I got after him even stronger and louder. "One minute!" I said, "are you kidding me"? What manner of harassment is this"? I went on and on until I finally ran out of combative phrases. I stopped and rested my case, then gave him my patented scowl face, piercing his eyes with my penetrating stare. This was my three dimensional mean look, usually reserved for when someone was talking on the green as I three putted from five feet! Finally, I mimicked the Exorcist and mumbled in a hideous monotone, growling and snarling between the muffled words. Sitting there that afternoon, I was sure I hated this man. I finished my audible sounds and snobbishly rested my case. I then crossed my legs, reared back in my chair then folded my arms in total disgust. He took in my stare for about ten more silent seconds, then calmly moved forward in his seat, leaned over his desk toward me and in a mild, deliberate fashion he spoke in a calm but stern voice. He said, "I want you to go back through this morning, from the time you awoke, until the time you got here and think about all the places you could have saved ONE MINUTE! Find one, just one, and we wouldn't be having this conversation!" He looked me straight in the eye and paused for my reply... I never said a word, while all the time thinking of about 15 places I could have saved that minute! I had never played chess before but I clearly knew it was checkmate! He had me. My three dimensional scowl was replaced by a cotton cloth towel, that I promptly tossed into the ring. After my delayed pause and my new subdued look he squinted his eyes, then gave a nasty sneer and said in a loud voice, rather rudely as he slapped his hand to his desk, "INEXCUS-ABLE"! he yelled. Still, I never said a word and I thought, yep, he's right. I wanted to strangle him but he would have still been right, so I just let it go.

The message was this: *"You make time for those things that are important, in doing so punctuality becomes a non issue." (W.R.O.)*

Mollergram 6

Within the scope of your job assigned duties trump all others.

This Mollergram showed up in the wake of the Division I college football uprising at Central High. I had cafeteria duty and a study hall. But by now I was established enough at Central to assign helpers. In both cases I used the time for what I thought was the more important duty of talking to coaches about getting Central football players into college scholarships. I really thought that those days of the *holding tank* had gone after we won the state championship in 1984-85. However, after delivery of the Mollergram, I found myself in Doc's office, yet again. 3:05, closed door, same seat. I remember Doc acting like a court room prosecutor that day, badgering me on what I considered a trumped up, lapse in duty charge! I tried to tell him that what I was doing at the time of that alleged duty lapse was extremely important, but he'd quickly go into trial mode, interrupting me by saying, "Just answer the question!" "Were you or were you not, outside the cafeteria during your assigned duty"? I responded, "yes, but I was talking to..." "Just answer the questions" he stated over and over again. I was never able to defend the position, so I had to take the plea. I left his office frustrated but with a clear understanding, that in a subordinate situation assigned duties trumps all!

The message was this: *"When you are assigned a duty by a superior, you are not left with the choice of prioritizing it within the bounds of its importance to you". (W.R.O.)*

Mollergram 7

Criticism is personal but must not be taken as such.

The one thing about Doc Moller that always stood out was his unyielding and relentless manner of criticizing. He was fearless in his attacks, if you deserved it you got it. Later I would learn that his criticism was always directed toward critical duty lapses and teaching gaffes. These attacks mostly centered on decision making. Doc always thought it imperative that teachers make the correct critical choices. Mistakes in judgment, missing assigned duties, making a bad presentation, showing up late, were all things he would make you look small on. He'd give you a chance to defend yourself with explanation of why such a gaffe had occurred but as you were speaking he made this really curious frowning face, as if totally amazed by your weak defense.

Doc looked toward the decisions made by teachers as critical to the survival of the school's reputation. Too many bad decisions by teachers could turn a good name into a bad one in no time. Maintaining Central's great respect level and its prominent reputation was always his highest priority. There was no way he would ever allow it to be said that Central took a step back under his watch. Any fault or misdeed threatening such was something he'd attack with extreme malice. Usually a strong face to face meeting followed up by an explicit Mollergram.

The message was this: *"A credible person (Doc Moller) making criticisms, were no more than critical reactions to critical people, after they've made critical mistakes in critical situations. It had to be done." (W.R.O.)*

Mollergram 8

Henceforth all outgoing communications will be regulated.

Communications formulated in the name of the school and sent to entities outside the school, regardless of content, is a direct reflection on the school. With that statement in mind all material leaving the school in the name of the school must always be sent with positive content of the utmost quality and accuracy. In other words, one teacher can send out one bad communication and it could affect the daily workings of the entire school. When I arrived for my second year at Central I never really thought too much about what I wrote or how I wrote it. After all, I was a Math teacher and a football coach. I figured if I was making a sensible point with no usage of profanity it was a decent presentation. This subscription was okay when I worked with principals at other schools, but with Doc Moller at Central, no way!

I was feeling pretty good after I finished my 1981 Omaha Central preseason football letter to parents and fans. This was my 3rd annual Central High football state of the union presentation to all concerned. Once it was all written, typed and packaged I saw it as a sparkling piece of literary perfection! I felt pretty proud of the wording and once ready for shipping I took it in to the main office for envelope and stamping. At some point my package was sent to Doc's office or as I sarcastically referred to it back then, "The Central Customs Agency." There the package was review scrutinized then promptly rejected. Sentence structuring, a few loose punctuations, a couple of improper uses of the words there, their and they're. It was "the usual suspects," I was charged with simple battery, accused of assaulting members of the Grammar family. A family Doc protected like his own! I was formerly charged and a stop was immediately put on the package.

The Mollergram I received that day was direct and to the point. New rule: All written and printed material sent out of the building relative to anything concerning Central High School must first be sent to the main office for review and clearance. In other words "customs inspection!" And the Customs Inspector General was who? Of course that sly, sadistic, English major principal himself, Dr. G.E. Moller! Again, I wanted to strangle him but like before he would still be right, so I just let it go!

Once the inspections began, getting outgoing letters passed his scrutiny was like trying to pass the bar examination with The FBI acting as monitor. Many times he would measure it and score it 2 or 3 different times before he would release it for mailing. Each time returning it to me, asking for modifications after adding his own. And how did I take to it all? It was a bit humbling, somewhat degrading and I thought a little overdone. To be honest, I detested it!!! I can still hear him saying; "you can't write things like you talk". This was something he constantly reminded me of, yet I hardly knew what it meant. There was rejection, after rejection, after rejection. It was utter frustration and at times I felt the entire process was unnecessary, demeaning, and a complete overreach of authority.

When I think about it, in those days I saw things pretty dramatically and was misinterpreting messages all along the way. Doc's rejections weren't personal and in the end they were more for me, than against me. Today I'm proud of all those rejected mailings. When my written communications were scrutinized, my skills improved, and not only did the school benefit, so too did I. In the end I understood that his scrutiny was making my presentation to parents better, thereby making my message clearer while enhancing my skills in the process. My writings were always great and the ability was always there. I just had to realize the importance of application and proofing.

What did his rejections do for me? Later I wrote seven books on teaching kids the game of golf, along with a 100 page instruction guide. I created, wrote and published a ladies golf magazine, The Lady Golfer. I've written over 3,000 golf quotes, a complete 150 page project guide and reference book on the country of Belize and many other printed works, most of them edited by me with Doc's scrutiny in mind. Oh yes and I'm writing this book and enjoying the ability to do so in a proper and articulate fashion. Doc once commented that I had excellent writing skills and great substance, but I should be a bit more careful grammatically. I don't know, but that might have been a compliment! What I do know is that this was one of those situations when he dared me to do better and challenged me to change ragged habits. What he consistently said all along was: "You have talents in many areas, refine them and you will be better off for it".

I am proud to say that before I left Central I actually won my right to send letters out without his approval. Some may view that as miniscule but for me it was monumental. No fanfare came with it, one day in passing I heard from one of the secretaries that he had stopped requiring my mailings to be sent to his office. By that time I'd long since gotten where I didn't take it personally anymore. Still, that release to freedom told me a lot about his motives and I accepted it as a sense of accomplishment. It was one of those hard lesson learned that keeps on giving. I was forced to do better and now the results felt super!

I was beginning to feel like Dr. Moller was at all times trying to help me succeed at what was to come. I now took on a different view of his motives and actions and felt a sense of reason. Could it be that Dr. Moller, my superior, my principal and sometimes preconceived nemesis was now and always was my most important friend?

The message was this: *One should place serious importance on presentation that represent themselves and their affiliations, especially when that presentation is written. (W.R.O.)*

These were just a few of the stories behind the man and the life messages I learned from him... via "The Mollergram"

GREAT NOTES FOR TEACHERS
They Came From a Mollergram

It would take me six books to write about all the Mollergrams that I either know of or received. It would take even longer to tell the stories behind them, their meanings and contributions to my life. Since I can't cover them all, here are a chosen few of the more important separate "messages" (without stories) that I received via the Mollergram. It is important to point out that these are all notes I received from Doc, mostly in a disciplinary context. I've cleaned them up a bit to protect the innocent. Primarily, these were presented over the years as either strong advice or stern reprimands as it related to the following of rules or some other mishandling of duty on my part. In other words at some point I had to be written up for most of these things or warned for not following through in a way conducive to the deed at hand. Later, following through with any one of them made me a better, more efficient person. Not just for teaching but for all walks of life. I submit to anyone who subscribes to being better at who you are and what you're doing, that you may be well served to take heed.

Note: the following is literary substance presented by Doc Moller at some point during my tenure at Omaha Central High School. These are not direct quotations from Doc. Rather, they are my own interpretations of how I perceived the meanings of a particular note (Mollergram) that I received personally from him.

(W.R.O.) - *William Reed Original*

- *Greeting students outside your door as they enter class creates a healthy start to the day. (W.R.O.)*

- *A teacher involved in extracurricular activities is working overtime for the cause. (W.R.O.)*

- *The art of written planning keeps you in control as you head in the right direction. It also serves as an insurance policy for those you teach. (W.R.O.)*

- *No matter how big your heart is, as a teacher you can't save everyone from personal disasters. Attempting such weakens your foundation. (W.R.O.)*

- *Unsociable teachers are deficient by nature. (W.R.O.)*

- *High school coaches must not be allowed to grow bigger than the classes he or she teaches. (W.R.O.)*

- *The game is not as important as your second period class. (W.R.O.)*

- *A school cannot run on 100% energy, you must give more. (W.R.O.)*

- *Leave no questions of the space that divide teachers and students. Your job depends on it. (W.R.O.)*

- *The security of the school and the protection of the students are every teacher's number one duty. (W.R.O.)*

Over the years through this maze of Mollergrams I came to this final conclusion!

The educators of the world can only lay out in open presentation the educational and situational values that may aid in one's life further down the road to success. (W.R.O.)

Such was my pathway to the knowledge that coagulated from the leadership of one Dr. G.E. Moller. While it took awhile for the transfusion to take, when it finally did I found myself armed with a sack of seeds that might be cultivated into a budding success. By the time my tenure at Central was over, everything I ever needed to know about life, family and job I had learned from the messages in a Mollergram. And what I learned more than anything was **"appreciation."** That appreciation is for the man who sent them.

Once again my thoughts are broken inside the coach section of the plane. This time I hear a question from the flight attendant. "Yes, I'll take a Sprite. Thank you." Man, that strong fizz offered in this can of Sprite reminds me of the time I drank one during halftime of 1984 Nebraska State Football semi-final game in Fremont, Nebraska. As the musical group, The Dells once sang, "Oh what a night".

Chapter 5

A MOLLERGRAM
PUT TO GOOD
USE

How Doc's lessons in punctuality
led to the tardiness that took us to the state
football finals

Omaha World-Herald

Tuesday, November 6, 1984   21

All-Omaha Final
Records Fall in Eagle Win

By Stu Pospisil

Fremont, Neb. — Omaha Central unleashed a record-setting performance Monday night to blow past Fremont 42-20 and into the Class A football championship game.

The Eagles, who will play Omaha Burke in the title game Saturday night, set Class A playoff records with 367 yards rushing and 553 total yards in rolling to their 10th win of the season.

Bernard Jackson also joined in the record-breaking as he rushed 17 times for 210 yards. The performance bettered the Class A individual rushing total of 192 yards set in 1981 by Burke's Victor Breakfield.

Setting The Stage

I'm still chuckling about those Mollergrams but I'm thinking seriously about their importance and how so many times I put them to use. Like the night we played Fremont in the Class A Football semi-finals in 1984. Man, now that was a night to remember. A reverse Mollergram slam! The punctuality lessons of the early to mid-eighties became one of Docs most persistent teachings and they eventually got through to me. Being on time became an organizational tool that I even used in football, except the one special night when I wanted to be late. It was the "Big Tardy Game" of 1984, Omaha Central vs. Fremont High.

I never felt completely organized in football practice until Doc drilled punctuality into my brain. Now I was using it to my advantage. I never imagined how much smoother and more precise practice was when you say you will start at a certain time and it happened that way. But even better, you say you will end at a certain time and that happens also. I started practicing that philosophy during the 1984 season, and it just so happened we won the state championship that very same year. The players seemed to be sharper, better attentive and a lot more disciplined when time schedules were met. They seemed to show more intensity and often operated at a much higher energy level. This was all good and it worked, but the most gratifying of my punctuality lessons from Doc was the night that I used it in reverse.

It was the 1984 Nebraska Class A state football playoff semi-finals in Fremont, Nebraska. On this night, for the players this game was as big as it gets. Fremont was loaded with the most lethal passing tandems in Nebraska state history, Gerry Gdowski and Chip Bahe. These were two stud athletes that could do everything in every sport. They were the enemy but man were they fun to watch! Both would later start multiple years in division one college football for the University of Nebraska Cornhuskers. Notwithstanding Central wasn't exactly the sisters of the poor. We had a total of

> Sometimes it's better to be late than harassed on arrival.
> (W.R.O.)

eleven Division 1 players on the team that year, including six that were offered scholarships to Nebraska also. They included; Sean Ridley, Richard Bass, Bernard Jackson, Art Thirus, Shawn Starks and Tony Avant. Leodis Flowers, a sophomore, Eric Anderson, a hard hitting Junior, Bruce Cullum and Michael Page along with two others were also Division 1 scholarship players. So, we weren't so bad either. There was some bad blood in the air that night and I had heard that the whole town of Fremont had shut down in anticipation of the 7:30 start. I'd been told that they had all sorts of things waiting to heckle and annoy us with upon our arrival. I'd sent a scout over at 6 p.m. to assess the atmosphere. He reported that the stands were already filled. "We want Central, we want Central", was the cry. "beat'em Tigers, beat'em." I could hear all sorts of crazy chants over the walkie-talkie and they were the exact things that I didn't want the players to see or hear that night before the game.

An Irregular Routine

It was customary for a team to arrive for a game being played at 7:30 p.m. around 5:45 p.m. You go in finish dressing and come out for initial warm-ups, beginning around 6:15 with kickers and punters. At 6:30 the whole team comes out stretch, warm up, get ready. At 7:00 everyone's busy, you run a few offensive plays and the defense goes through certain sets - base, nickel, dime, 4-3, 54, and so on. The game clock begins at 30 minutes and then counts down to kick off. By that time the crowd would be in a frenzy hooting and hollering at the opposition.

But on this night all that would be different. I would use what Doc had described as irritating and confusing. Something that frustrated him to no end... tardiness!! I mean just downright being late. While all the town of Fremont waited to boo, yell and heckle, I had sent only a team manager to the game armed with a walkie talkie. The team instead was taken to an empty back parking lot. The place was lit pretty well. I had the buses, in a dual configuration for lower light and we did our pregame warm-ups about a mile from the stadium. We punted, kicked, ran plays, caught passes and prepared right there in the parking lot. Everyone in the stadium, our fans included, were feeling just as Doc said people felt when people they expect at a certain time were running late. They were all losing their minds with confusion and anxiety.

It was 6:30, no Central, 6:45, no Central, 7:00, no Central. Now the officials are worried. 7:15 p.m. still no Central. Dick Jones, Athletic Director and even the cheerleaders began to worry. And the people from Fremont, who had been so roused? Well, they were now feeling the effects of the BIG TARDY. Instead of the attention to the game at hand their attitudes had now changed and they began to anticipate a forfeit on the horizon. The stadium was eerily silent and as the clock ticked down the Fremont team and fans were thinking that the game was not going to happen. Then the chant started, "forfeit, forfeit, forfeit." By 7:15 we had loaded the buses and were getting our "*mean*" on as the buses proceeded with caution. My manager, with the walkie talkie at the stadium, was having the time of his life. He was doing a play-by-play of the coaches, players and fan reactions. He was really into it, interjecting his own countdown of the clock. It's 7:24 and we are unofficially about one and one half hours late. The Fremont team had stopped warming up, their coaches baffled, and the fans absolutely reek with confusion. Everything that Doc had told me about being late was playing out. It irritates people, confuses them and is just oh, so annoying.

The Eagles Have Landed

The time is 7:27 and the Eagle has landed. The team is at the stadium. We are perched directly behind the Central fan's bleachers. Ready to take the field, as the clock is counting down; 2:28, 2:27, 2:26. The officials are waiting in the middle of the field with Fremont's royalty captains, Gdowski and Bahe, The irony is that Gdowski's Dad is head coach and Bahe's Dad is athletic director. They are out in the middle of the field, either ready for the coin toss or ready for the refs to hoist the ball and award Fremont the victory. At 2 minutes to kickoff I sent my three captains into the stadium and out to the field. They came walking out of the darkness, into the stadium like three gunfighters from an old western movies. The Central fans, worried that they had made the trip for nothing, spotted the trio and erupted in a thunderous roar. A roar of spirit, pride, and yes relief too. Oh, I'm telling you they were beside themselves. I could see the Fremont stands. Their fans were still locked in confusion, thinking, "Can they do this? Are they just going to play with three people, what's going on here?" Fremont wins the coin toss and our captains trio retreat back into the darkness. Now with just 30 seconds left on the clock, the purple and white of Omaha Central, complimented by contrasting grey pants with eagle wings on both hips, came prancing into the stadium arm and arm, locked together like the 300 Spartans. They were stepping in double time chanting the Spartan chant, all the while a boom box is blasting Prince's hit song "Let's Go Crazy". And that's exactly what we did! They unlocked arms and just scattered, like a swarm of killer bees. The kickoff team goes straight to the field, the rest of the team break to the sideline... 15, 14, 13, 12, 11, 10, 9 now the ball is ready for play and boom goes the kick. The BIG TARDY GAME was underway.

We were so hyped until the very thing we had practiced all week to stop happened on the first few plays of the game. Gdowski to Bahe "Touchdown!" We countered with a tenth grade half-back pass. Leodis Flowers to all-state wide receiver Tony Avant... 72 yards. Touchdown! We traded touchdowns again and that was it! Bernard Jackson, Richard Bass and Leodis Flowers followed Paul Flaxbeard, Art Thirus, Mark Buckner, Jim Lee, David Day, Shawn Starks and the rest of the "O line" on a mission of destruction. It was a relentless ground assault that crushed all in its wake. It seemed as if Fremont was still wondering if we were going to show up. By the time they realized we were there we were already gone.

We were tardy that night and Doctor Moller was so right, Fremont never recovered from the emotional stress of someone being late. It was supposed to be a toss-up game but instead Omaha Central won 42-20, with a Class A state record nearly 600 yards of total offense, including 367 rushing! Had we wanted to, we could've put up 800 that night. By the end of the game it was like Little Bill beating up on English Bob in Clint Eastwood's, "Unforgiven". **Fremont never had a chance.**

In the mist of it all I learned that anxiety, confusion and frustration usually accompany most tardy situations. Today punctuality is an extremely serious part of my everyday life. Whenever I'm going to be late my focus always goes immediately to those expecting me. I worry about their feelings and take measured actions to avoid confusion and frustration on their part. But more importantly, these days I simply make every effort not to be late in the first place.

Four years after the big tardy game Fremont head coach, Gerry Gdowski Sr. and I coached the Shrine Bowl in 1988 as opposing head coaches. We enjoyed each other so much and had the best of times. I recently saw him again at a golf tournament. We hugged, laughed and talked about times past. Including those two dynamic kids of his, Gerry Jr. and track star Linda and my four time state track championship daughter, Marcie. That day football never came up, but I'm sure that neither of us will ever forget, the night the Central High Eagles showed up late in Fremont, Nebraska! Like I said " Oh What A Night."

Still though Gerry got the last blows in, when he coached the North Shrine Bowl team to victory over my South team. Also, incredibly he raised five children and all were Valedictorians of their high school class. I never understood it??? All that brilliance, coming from a father that can't spell Jerry and left the "a" out of Gdowski. It seemed that on the night of my deep exploration into the world of tardiness we both won something that was more than a game, it was called friendship.

I can feel the plane lowering in altitude. We must be getting close to Houston. My mind is still locked in on the Mollergrams. All those lessons learned from those important miniature cuts of paper. Their worth to me today can't be measured. It's amazing how much I use them now. Often times I'll think of one of the notes and its lesson will resonate in my brain. Then it will emboss itself inside my being, waiting for its chance to either be used in enhancing my life or aid in me helping someone else's. Most of the time it was hard to accept them but today I embrace them at every turn. Doc Moller, through his Mollergrams, reminded me continuously of the importance of being all you can be, all the time on time. It was not so good to get them in the disco 80's, but today it's so gratifying to have them, here in the new millennium. Though the goal was always to get the Mollergrams stopped, it was kind of sad when they finally did. I can remember that last one that I received from him. So many years have passed since then but the memory marked not only my last Mollergram message from Doc but also my last days as an Omaha Central Eagle.

PATRONS ARE REQUESTED TO FAVOR THE COMPANY BY CRITICISM AND SUGGESTION CONCERNING ITS SERVICE

WESTERN UNION

CLASS OF SERVICE	SIGNS
This is a full-rate Telegram or Cablegram unless its deferred character is indicated by a suitable sign above or preceding the address.	DL = Day Letter NM = Night Message NL = Night Letter LCO = Deferred Cable NLT = Cable Night Letter WLT = Week-End Letter

NEWCOMB CARLTON, PRESIDENT   J. C. WILLEVER, FIRST VICE-PRESIDENT

The filing time as shown in the date line on full-rate telegrams and day letters, and the time of receipt at destination as shown on all messages, is STANDARD TIME.

Received at

"Mollergram"
William, William, William
Please meet me in my office at 3:05 p.m.

When demanding notes of discipline are sent to us in an effort to identify and point out flaws, they usually derive from a hand that thinks we matter. *(W.R.O.)*

Chapter 6

MY LAST MOLLERGRAM

Doc's obsession: The process connecting parents and teachers

May, 1990

William,William,William,
One phone call?
Doc ☹

Parent Phone Calls

In my last faculty meeting at Central Doc once again interjected a plea that had become a staple in the staff meetings at the end of each semester. Once again with deep passion, he aggressively pushed his agenda detailing the importance of "parent phone calls." Doc believed vehemently that the positive connection from teacher to parent was just seven numbers away. This single belief perhaps defined him more-so than anything. When he committed to an idea that he believed in, he rode it ceaselessly, no matter where it took him. It was within this belief that he felt that if every teacher made just one positive phone call per week to an unsuspecting parent, it would eventually touch a majority of the households that make up the Central family.

> *The saddest part of any great thing is its ending.*
> *(W.R.O.)*

Doc felt strongly that a healthy communication between teacher and parent was a positive formula toward bridging the gap between teacher and student. At times he seemed almost obsessed with the notion and preached it like a sermon! To me however, that notion seemed more like going to trial than to church. In the world of Omaha Central, the court of parent phone calls was reconvened at the end of each semester and I dreaded every single trial! Doc really couldn't force teachers to make the calls, so it was more of a strong request than a superior demand. However, deep down inside as a faculty member you knew he expected you to do it! He would go so far as to read aloud in faculty meetings, the names of each and every faculty member along with the number of parent phone calls they had made for that semester.

I can recall sitting there in the group that consisted of mostly low rated phone callers. All of us just cringing at the importance that Doc put on that singular aspect of our expected duties, while we had usually neglected it. John Keenan –39, Dan Daly –41, Virginia Lee Pratt –52, Carolyn Orr –20, Jo Dusatko –25, John Waterman –35, Vicki Wiles –27. Bayer, Martin, Stommes, McMeen, Lincoln, Roeder, all names in double figures. Stan Standifer –3, Joe McMenamin –7, William Reed –1. I was abysmal at this phone call business and Doc made sure I knew it. A Mollergram landed in my mailbox after every one of those faculty meeting trials. Today I freely confess that they were totally justified and my effort in the program was pathetic.

I had about fifteen calls one semester, but they were all to the parents of Marcie Reed, my daughter. Usually to check on dinner or to see if my wife would be picking her up from school that day. I told Mr. Jones of my little devilish plan to turn the calls in as sort of mocking the process. He said, "Try it at your own risk, parent phone calls is not a subject to play with when it comes to Doc Moller." I quickly aborted the idea.

For eleven years Doc preached the phone sermon at the end of every semester. My high score was maybe three. This phone business wasn't just a happening it was a full blown process. First of all, to become qualified for recognition it didn't just require making the phone calls, the procedure also required a registration form with each transaction. You had to make the call, fill out the slip, drop it in his mailbox for credit at semester's end. I loathed the process and detested the role call at the end of every semester. Poor Stan and I would slowly lower our heads as Doc began that dooms day role call that singled us out like vagabonds each semester. I remember the tension in my body when he reached the P's - Plata, Pennington, Perina, Pritchard, Pruss. Now here it comes, Mr. Reed one phone call. I suffered through that roll call twenty-two times and was always in the bottom one percent. I'd leave those meetings feeling as though I was wearing the scarlet letter, only it was purple. Don't get me wrong, I talked to dozens of parents at length all the time. So it wasn't so much the calling and talking, I think it was more the organized process requiring documentation and reporting.

I played stubborn for a long time but eventually I had to face it, this was a great policy that made perfect sense. Good enough sense that a principal should not have to push and tug to get one involved. I pretended not to see the worth as the years went by and basically chose not to participate. At times I felt it disproportionately easier for some teachers based on the academic level of the students they taught. This gave me an excuse to not do it and really that's all it was, an excuse.

I received a certain Mollergram after every semester's sermon on parent phone calls, so it was only fitting that it would be my "last". The gram would begin, William, William, William, One phone call? ☹ My last week at Central was no different. True to Doc's nature and character, even when he knew that I wouldn't be returning to Central, it was still there - three Williams in my mailbox along with a notation of one phone call, accompanied by one sad face. This would be Doc's last Mollergram to me. I know now that even in the end he was still trying to make me better, this time through accountability!

What I learned from my last Mollergram was this*: "A positive phone call to an unsuspecting parent goes a long ways towards bridging the gap between home and school." (W.R.O.)*

Subscribing to Doc's Phone System

As fate would have it, after leaving Central, three years later I opened my own school. A private golf school that serviced more than 400 students that very first summer. I had seven loyal instructors on staff throughout the sessions. However, none quite understood one of my staunchest requirements which involved all four sessions. At the end of each session all instructors, including me, was required to designate a student for parent phone call some time after the last session. They were to offer praise or concern and a quality report of how well the parent's child was progressing.

Along with that, they were required to make a note of the parent they called and drop it in Coach Reed's parent phone call box the following day. I know, it was hypocrisy to the max! I'm almost ashamed to say how powerful an impact that little gesture made in creating an outstanding image for my new school. Every time a parent came up to me to say, "Coach, you and your team are so professional and I can't say how much it means to me when you stop your busy days to call parents like me about our child's progress. Your school is a class act." I would always look around very nervously when a parent praised me in public for having such a policy. Worried that Doc might pop out at any moment and say, "William, William, William couldn't you have made just one phone call per week? Just one, that's all you needed to do." These days I must confess, Doc's obsession is a great tool when it comes to education and a grand policy for all manner of life.

OB

It would be years later, but I eventually found out that his smile was genuine.

My golf school flourished for seven years and I never had less than 300 students in any of those seven. During those years the policy of one phone call per day, per instructor, never left the teaching manual. I can't remember my first Mollergram from Doc, but I certainly remember the last. I kept it with me for a long time. But like all things of the past you have to eventually let go. Though the paper is gone the message remain and I still embrace Doc's phone policy in all walks of life. I will never forget my time within the four sides and I will never forget those gut wrenching days, when Doctor G.E. Moller took the time to send me a Mollergram!

The plane took a sudden dip and shook me awake. The captain just calmly spoke of the approach to George Bush Intercontinental Airport in Houston, Texas. He gave a weather report and asked the flight attendants to strap on their seatbelts. A short time later we're back on American soil. The late departure from Belize and the crowd at customs almost caused me to miss my connection to Omaha. But I just made it. The small plane landed in Omaha less than two hours after takeoff. My plane trip is over "I'm home."

With Omaha Central hiding in the background and the Woodmen Tower dominating the skyline this was our neighborhood in the 1980's... downtown Omaha, Nebraska.

The

4Four Side

Actors, Athletes and Actresses

In 1930, the side entrance to the 4Side offered access to a new gymnasium and auditorium. The two stylish facilities weren't just on the 4Side, they were the 4Side.

The Principal, The Letter & The Coach

Respecting the principal, praising the grandpa and honoring the man with a letter from the heart

The first time that I saw Doc after our days at Central, he was in the mode of grandpa. It was a role I'd never seen him play. His co-star was his grandson, a bright, young energetic twelve year old named Ben Hofmeister. They had come to my school for golf lessons. Ben and I hit it off right away and the seven lesson session was very positive. I can say without reservation that the reunion with Doc was great! However, the bringing of his grandson for me to teach was even greater. It kindled my spirits and uplifted my soul. We laughed and joked about old times at Central. Him even ragging me about having the audacity to actually be on time for the first lesson with Ben. He even signed up for a lesson of his own, allowing me to rag him on his inability to accept positive criticism.

It was a great time that summer of '99, but four years later sadness would rule. I'd come to understand just how good of a principal he was and how much he had pushed to make me good also. I now knew that there was caring involved in all he had done. So today, I still respect him as the principal, praise him as the grandfather and will forever honor him as a man. I'm sure for him that acknowledgement would be enough in expressing my admiration, but I took it one further. I sat down on a sad and gloomy day and wrote him a letter from the heart, putting it in writing and making it all official.

Chapter 1

DEFINING DR. G.E. MOLLER

The man who was always busy…just doing his job

OB

178

The Principal

After all is said and done, for the rest of my life, Doctor Moller will always first and foremost be seen as my principal. From the western Nebraska towns of Alliance, Valentine and Gering, to his bold decision to come east to Omaha; his is a time of leadership that took him from the Emperors chair in the Roman coliseum to the arena floor, face to face with the gladiators! It was indeed at times a fight for survival. From the rural towns of similar type people in western Nebraska, he was catapulted into the school house storms of urban Omaha's blackboard jungles. It was 1963 when he started, a time when Omaha Central High and many schools around the country like it, was on the edge of revolutionary change. In that year the country was flourishing, while at the same time for some decomposing. During that time, the country was actually living and dying, all at the same time. He began his career at Central as assistant principal, within a three month countdown to the worst tragedy in the history of the United States, the assassination of John F. Kennedy. Five years later he became principal in the grips of 1968, one of the most tragic years ever recorded.

Gaylord Moller saw three decades of young lives coming together in ways few thought was ever possible and he worked to shape those lives and prepare them for the mystery future that awaited. In the panhandle towns of western Nebraska, one can remain hidden from many of the world's affairs. However, in the mainstream of the downtown urban asphalt jungle of 1963 Omaha, Nebraska, hiding only left you in plain sight. As an educator he brought with him to that jungle a rule and always stuck to it. He let it be known that amidst the chaos of the urban sanctuary that he was chosen to command, you could always find him poised and focused, on "simply doing his job."

The things that brought he and I together were dramatic, funny, confrontational and in the end, tragic. He would spend nearly three decades as Central's leader and leave a legacy that few could imagine while so many would benefit. His resume' reads as follows; ***He was the longest tenured principal at Nebraska's strongest tenured high school through the toughest tenured years. Enough said!***

I sat down with him one calm morning and somehow got him to talk about his life as a son, a father, a husband and yes, as the Principal! This is the beginning of that interview.

Panera Bread... The Interview

It was an autumn Thursday morning, one that resided within the month of witches and goblins. It was a day that I was poised to sit down with Dr. G.E Moller for a rare interview. That day I met with him perched in the back of a place called Panera Bread, in the midst of the rattles of pots and pans and the smell of freshly baked bagels. He had chosen this place and it seemed appropriate enough for where he might spend a morning having breakfast. When he walked inside I could tell that his stride on the ballroom floor of life had gone from the Quick Step to the Viennese Waltz. He just kind of shuffled in. Yet, as I watched him enter that morning, even in a shuffle at eighty plus years of age he still possessed that rare aura of control.

I just watched him for a few minutes. He had arrived fifteen minutes early and relying on past history he didn't even consider that I might already be there. So, when I walked up from the back of the venue to greet him you could immediately tell that he was curiously surprised that I was already there. I set the meeting for 9:30 a.m. Knowing him and that obsessive time fetish of his, I knew he would get there exactly 15 minutes before, so I came at 9:00. On cue, upon seeing me his first words were, "What are you doing here so early? You're not supposed to beat me here." I said, "It's not the old product anymore Doc, this is the new and improved William Reed brand." And with that the loud laughter from two old mates was resurrected.

Now, all things seemed normal and I could feel the unmistakable genuineness of this man of my past. I first had to have him understand that though he had chosen the venue, it was I who had called the meeting, so it was I who should have been in control. However, true to years past, he would have none of it. He quickly jumped into the breakfast line and immediately pulled his wallet. I said "No, this is on me", but he reacted just as he did when I gave him his first golf lesson in 1999. Back then, whenever he did something wrong he would attempt to let me know what had happened before I could comment on what was really wrong. Now, he was taking over my breakfast invitation in the same manner. He made an order then quickly said to the cashier, "get him what he wants also." I immediately put my money away, ordered a muffin, grabbed an orange juice and gave him his space. I thought to myself, that after all these years he was still the principal, always in charge, still placing things in his own order, while allowing the pace to move only at his speed. I said to myself, at least now I was certain that this was not an imposter, it was the principal, Doc Moller still taking the lead.

The Setup

When we sat down for the interview he was apprehensive upon seeing my assistant (Marlon Wright) with the video camera and tape recorder in front of him, so immediately he began interviewing me. "What is this about?" he asked, "What is all this stuff you have in front of me and what are you going to do with this material when we're done?" I knew if I told him that I was writing a book that included him, he would probably want to read it, evaluate it, check for punctuation, grade it and then make a decision as to whether it was worthy of release. No way could I tell him I was writing a book to honor his deeds and describe his legacy from my perspective. He would have bugged me to death had he known that, so instead, I quickly made up a story of the interview being part of an assignment for a class I was taking. Now his barrage of questions intensified and took on a new direction. "What school? What kind of class? Where, when, how?" I had to quickly get him out of the question phase of our meeting, so I said, "It's a project that I'm doing that requires me to talk to people relative to Central. "Now, you have to stop asking me these questions." He finally relented but couldn't let it go without the last word. He looked at me and said, "Okay but I want to tell you that you're being very vague here. I still don't think you've told me what this is all about." Without trying to explain further I opened my notebook of questions. Upon seeing them I think he remembered why he was there and said "okay you can go on with your questions." At last we could get started, but only because he had given the okay. It wasn't personal. Once again, he was just being the principal.

Who Is Gaylord Moller?

My first question to the man who tried to make me better was, "Who is Gaylord E. Moller and what is his philosophy as a principal?" The question took him immediately out of principal mode. "No one has ever asked me that," he said. I could see by the look on his face that now he knew that this was a serious interview, with me being the interviewer and he the interviewee. He looked to the ceiling as if to ask from where the question had derived, then he repeated it as if asking someone inside himself. "Who am I?" He said out loud more than once and then it started. He immediately scurried back to his childhood and chronicled the life of his father. Now, I heard the distinct voice of that principal I'd met back in 1979. At first he had been sort of talking in a voice that mirrored his age, but now I heard the voice of the Central High principal of decades past, strong, wise and very serious.

He began describing his dad with some big word that he knew I had never heard. But it meant his dad traveled around a lot from place to place, doing a variety of jobs. He said his childhood from elementary to high school consisted of about 13 different schools, in 5 different states, through numerous cities. "Who is Gaylord Moller?" he looked to the ceiling and again asked himself. According to him, he was that kid throughout those migrating years that never had a friend too long in one place. The kid that went from school to school where he was either way behind or way in front of his new classmates and neither situation was very comfortable. He said the life of moving around being a different kid at each different stop gave him a love and respect for kids in school striving to hold together and complete their education. For awhile he was almost his dad, moving in Nebraska from Alliance to Valentine then to Gering. However, that would all end the first time he walked into the west doors of Central High School in 1963. He was 34 years old.

The Omaha Public Schools had called him personally to offer him an assistant principal's position in Omaha, Nebraska at Central High School. Being the loyalist that he was, he wasn't comfortable leaving Gering, a school in western Nebraska that had embraced him in the best of ways. It had been a big move up for him after his seven years in Valentine, Nebraska. It was August 1st and he worried about leaving them on short notice. However, when they graciously announced that they'd be fine without him, he didn't know whether to be pleased or disappointed, but he said they really made it easy for him. Now, as he stood on the **3side** of Omaha Central High he saw a world of education that was like nothing that he had seen in his budding career as an administrator. He never thought it was going to be easy but he indeed felt that he was up to the challenge!

His dad had moved around throughout the school days of young Gaylord's life, never really settling in anywhere. The son had been somewhat similar as an educator, but for a couple of extra thousand dollars and a shorter drive to the University of Nebraska to further his education, it was now time to deviate and settle in once and for all. So he did, and for the next 32 years he would spend them all as a Central High administrator, 27 of which were as principal.

Who is Gaylord E. Moller? He is just a man who earned his doctorate, became a principal then tried to make a difference in every life that matriculated through the hallways of Omaha Central High School.

Before he ever set foot within the four sides a countdown had already begun. It was a countdown to his inevitable position as the Omaha Central High School Principal. He had been invited to the public school's annual nine month party by the highest ranking official in the crowd. Five years later the countdown was over. He had completed his education, his orientation and his internship... it was 1968. It was a year when all sorts of different things happened and a lot of things had begun to change and the times were topsy-turvy. Doc Moller would spend the topsy part of the year in his last semester as assistant principal and then spend the turvy part as principal. Up, down, over, under, around and through; 1968 was all those things and more.

The Topsy Turvy
Wonderful, Tragic, Bizarre,

Movie Ticket $1.50 each

New Car $2,822.00

New House $14,975.00

Average Rent $130.00 per month

Eggs 38¢ per dozen

Granulated Sugar 60¢ for 5 lbs.

Ground Coffee 93¢ per lb.

Gasoline 34¢ per gallon

Average Income $7,844.0 per year

Bacon 75¢ per lb.

Vitamin D Milk $1.21 per gallon

Tuition to Harvard University $2,000.00 per year

1st Class Postage Stamp 6¢ each

Fresh Baked Bread 22¢ a loaf

World Series Champion Detroit Tigers

Fresh Ground Hamburger 50¢ a lb.

U.S. Open Golf Winner Lee Trevino

Pro Football Champion Green Bay Packers

Indianapolis 500 Winner Bobby Unser/152.882 MPH

Stanley Cup Winner Montreal Canadiens

NCAA Basketball Champ UCLA

College Football Champion Ohio State

Canadian Grey Cup Winner Ottawa Rough Riders

*New Omaha Central High School

Happenings of 1968
Creative and Entertaining

President,
Lyndon Johnson

Life Expectancy
70.2 years

Harper Valley P.T.A.
–by Jeannie C. Riley

Hey Jude
-by The Beatles

I Heard It Through the
Grapevine
-by Marvin Gaye

People Got to Be Free –by
The Rascals

Hello, I Love You
-by The Doors

Mrs. Robinson
-by Simon & Garfunkel

Green Tambourine
–by The Lemon Pipers

Grazing in the Grass
–by Hugh Masekela

Honey
– by Bobby Goldsboro

2001: A Space Odyssey

Academy Award Winner-
Oliver

Romeo and Juliet

Yellow Submarine

Planet of the Apes

Here's Lucy

Rowan & Martin's
Laugh-In

Mayberry R.F.D.

Rosemary's Baby

Principal Doctor G.E. Moller

Chapter 2

1968
A time when we were worlds apart

OB

The Year of Laughter and Tears. A Tough Time to Start A Principalship

Nineteen sixty-eight was a leap year. Some said it came with one extra day, others would say later that it brought three too many. The year started promising enough with the introduction of the outrageously entertaining show, Rowan and Martin's "Laugh In". Then it gave us our first look at the raw innocence of Mr. Roger's Neighborhood before teaching us a new way to follow the news, with a show called "60 Minutes". That year the Packers won the Super Bowl and the Tigers won the World Series. It was a bold time, complete with a thirty-three year advanced look into the future, through a movie called "A Space Odyssey 2001." Speaking of movies, the year also introduced the movie that seemed to be a novelty in Central High lore, Clint Eastwood's "Where Eagles Dare". Yes, 1968 brought all those things in the beginning but then riots, war protests and high profile assassinations took over the calendar. March 4th, April 4th, June 6th – indeed three days too many! These would be the last few months of Dr. J Arthur Nelson's 24 year reign as principal of Omaha Central High and a three month unspecified interim trial for his successor, Mr. Gaylord E. Moller.

So you want to be an urban high school principal, huh? Well, if it happens then be prepared for a diverse student body with a wide range of economic differences. The top priority for a principal in such a situation is to monitor and nurture student relations. Ignore it or neglect it and you will spend all your days sitting on a time bomb, while the explosion is eminent! Central High offered this type of diverse setting and with a lame duck principal making plans for the summer, Mr. Moller found himself as one of the leaders sitting on that powder keg.

He was charged with maintaining stability while keeping the avenues of education open during an extreme transitional period. Urban schools across the country were finding themselves touched in different ways by new laws that centered on racial equality. Though Omaha Central had been practicing these new laws for decades, it still found itself having to deal with a different kind of diverse student body, one that was beginning to be more and more influenced by what was happening in their neighborhoods and driven by what they saw daily on national TV. The mid to late nineteen sixties was definitely a very challenging period in any number of venues in our country, but within the educational venue known as Omaha Central, Mr. Moller met the challenges head on!

Changing Times

Although he had a genuine respect for the changing times, Mr. Moller consistently avoided dealing with any one group based on ethnicity. He said he never liked categorizing students in that way. To him, there was no black or white within the four sides, it was all about the purple! He saw all students and teachers as Central High and steered clear of the racial divide that mostly framed life elsewhere during those tumultuous years. His promise to himself was to treat all manner of life inside the school with the same interest and respect. He never allowed anyone to operate or promote a set of standards different than that within the school setting. Because of that, he seems uncomfortable speaking about the racial divide that made every administrative school job, wherever it was, a lot more complex.

I certainly respect his approach, concur in his beliefs and will never bring into question his judgment. However, I did feel that there was an inherent need to expand upon the subject. Mostly because during the days of the 60's it seemed every real life situation eventually ended up being defined in some way that led back to racial equality or the lack thereof. Simply put, in the 1960's there was not a place in the world where race relations were more magnified then the public schools of the United States of America, thus validating its relevance to parts of this book. It is my belief that one could hardly navigate the ten year minefield that was the 60's while omitting this giant elephant in the room.

There's no doubt that the 60's brought on revolutionary change in America and diverse high school settings were ground zero in the interim. For most minorities there was an origin to this quiet revolution. It seemed some promises had been made in 1964 that, according to some, were not being lived up to. It was no secret that black students in a lot of places were being denied those so-called inalienable rights that were said to be out there somewhere for everyone. In 1968, based on a chain of events, things came to a head all across the country and eventually found its way within the cavernous walls of Omaha Central High School. That year Omaha Central Assistant Principal Mr. Gaylord E. Moller was on the verge of wrapping up his doctorate degree at the University of Nebraska, while long time Central Principal, Dr. J. Arthur Nelson, was gradually taking home his belongings after 24 years at the helm. Since Mr. Moller had been handpicked and personally recruited by then Superintendent Owen Knutzen five years before, it was almost a foregone conclusion that he was soon to be the next principal at Central High.

As an assistant principal, Gaylord E. Moller had handled the lines of discipline problems at Omaha Central since 1963. That amounted to, in his words, five years of seeing education in ways he never imagined! As a hands on administrator during the last three years of Dr. Nelson's reign, he had been even more visible than the principal himself. When I spoke with Steve Marantz, author of the Central High book The Rhythm Boys and a 1969 Central grad, he said that Dr. Moller was the administrator that was more involved in the daily routine of the school than anyone else. Lindberg White (now Dr. Khalid Kamal) also a '69 grad said, "There are two things I remembered about Dr. Moller, he was fair and when things got hot, he was there." As far as these two Central alumni were concerned Mr. Moller had become principal long before his first official days were ever consummated.

With the changing of the guard in clear sight, the year of 1968 took on a turn for the worst and left Mr. Moller and his administrative siblings on the front lines of the war of changing times. Governmental laws had been enacted to bring students together. However, the political system and freedom to take flight basically left schools far less diverse than the new laws had intended, as many headed to the suburbs. Central however, maintained a balance that more closely resembled the look of the country. With that in mind, the school along with its assistant principals including Mr. Moller, was one of those left on the frontlines when public schools, old tradition and raw politics intermingled with changing times.

Chaos and Tragedy in '68

Nineteen sixty-eight was one of those chaotic and tumultuous years that served up one tragedy after the other on a day by day clip. "Danny The Red", as a war protester, kept Central hopping as the war in Vietnam was in full bloom and more intense than ever. This all while no one could answer his question of its purpose nor justify its cause. There was also a war in the states. One that centered on racial equality, a madness that seemed to divide the country and threaten the ancient rules that bordered public education. There was poison in the atmosphere that year, and though it was more abundant in the states down south, a lot of its residue had filtered its way up north. Now, just two months into the new year, a bitter dose of that poison was about to spew out just across the street from the east lawn at 124 North 20th Street, in Omaha, Nebraska.

You won't find a record of it in the almanac, nor any mention in the weather section of past local newspapers, it won't be in the archives of the local TV newsrooms either. No, you will never see a record of it, but on March 4, 1968 a "hell storm" hit downtown Omaha! Not a hail storm! I mean a "hell storm" and on that day, all "hell" broke loose!

It was a day when the most visibly, outspoken racist of the day, George Wallace of Alabama, was making a stop in Omaha, Nebraska. Ironically, that stop just happened to be across the street from Omaha Central High. His purpose for the visit was to officially add his name to the Nebraska ballot for president of the United States. On the surface it was a fair and simple process, a right offered to any natural born citizen that was in good standing. However, here in the good old USA this added name to the ballot was different, because in 1968 to many George Wallace was the face of segregation and racial hatred across the country. Now to add fuel to the fire, when he finally touched down in Omaha, he landed at the Civic Auditorium just a stones throw from 20th and Dodge Street and practically on the lush green grass of Central High's east side lawn. This invasion of what many saw as Omaha Central territory, by the highest ranking bigot in the land, instantly placed the school at the epicenter of what was to follow. Simply put, it dropped the issue of race relations figuratively on Omaha Central's doorsteps.

It was no secret that African American students in the Midwest, particularly Omaha, had certainly experienced some biased neglect throughout the years, but not nearly to the degree of what they saw playing out every day on TV in the Jim Crow South. Despite the rumblings and a few minor tremors, things had been okay in Centralville but on March 4th the dam broke! The national face of segregation, racial prejudice and social denial had come out of the TV screen and was now setting up shop across the street. That visit, in weather terms, was the cold air of George Wallace, an open segregationist, colliding with the warm front that had been percolating in the hearts and minds of the young African American students at Central High for years. The results as stated was a major "hell storm" of humanity. A riot ensued culminating in several arrests.

When the pot of hot coffee boiled over across the street at the Civic Auditorium, it eventually seeped into the hallways of Omaha Central High School, causing the administration to do what Mr. Moller never liked, having to react and become involved in outside social and political wars! In this case, however, there was no choice. The politics had virtually made its way into the four sides by association. There was a clash with police that night and some Central students were involved. Some of them were detained by law enforcement, including one Dwayne Dillard, who was perhaps the most talented basketball player in Nebraska state history. It just so happened that all this took place as the state basketball playoffs were right around the corner and Central, being led by Dillard, was the odds on favorite to win it all. But now it seemed that there was a good chance that the Senior Super Star's basket days at Central were over. At this point there was not a doubt, Central High School was now infected with the virus that was, George Wallace's visit.

The arrest of Dillard and others from Omaha Central forced involvement from its understaffed and overworked administrators. In our interview Dr. Moller couldn't quite recall the details of the times but Dan Daly, the English department head, remembered it well. "It was a tough, tough time for everyone" he said. Yes, it was indeed a "hell" night. Despite the riots and chaotic clashes when the smoke finally cleared and the heated rhetoric subsided, the Wallace visit did pass on. He got his votes and was placed on the ballot. Dillard got to play basketball and like always everyone was eventually back at school.

Through it all the Central administration just kept to doing their job. The students rediscovered their niches, old habits were restored and Central slowly began to go back to being what it always was, Nebraska's best high school. As things calmed, Mr. Moller was wrapping up his doctorate degree at the University of Nebraska, while still maintaining the order of passage at Central High every day. The Wallace rally had certainly been disruptive but administratively was dealt with professionally.

It seemed Mr. Moller without being principal had passed his first major test as leader. Now, it was about finishing the school year and beginning his official tenure as the next Omaha Central Principal. However, on his way to his inaugural debut as the Central high leader "1968" struck again, exactly one month after the Wallace saga.

This time on April 4th the most visibly, outspoken voice for peace, freedom and racial equality was gunned down in Memphis, Tennessee. Two months later, as moms and dads had decided that it was safe to allow the kids to go back outside, "1968" happened yet again. Someone shot a would-be president whose brother had been killed while being the president, just five years before. All the while these things were happening, there were huge protests all around, as young kids barely old enough to vote were being killed and maimed by the hundreds, in a war that no one could explain and every teenager seemed to hate.

This tumultuous time marked the fiery Omaha Central beginning of Mr. G.E. Moller, one of Omaha's great principals and as I would learn later, an even better man. When he officially took over as the 14th principal at Omaha

Central High School he was just five years removed from the rural panhandle of western Nebraska. As stated, schools that were basically comprised of a few hundred white students, all economically similar. Now, he was charged to govern over 2,000 of mixed cultures, with vast ethnic differences and a thousand mile economic divide between them. He would spend 27 years at the helm. However, none of those years could begin, until he survived **"1968"**!

Surviving '68

The crazy night that George Wallace dropped in to throw a party across the street from Central's front lawn was March 4, 1968. He had come and gone and the remnants were slowly fading. However, while things were still gradually mending themselves, on that same date one month later in April, the unthinkable happened. When Martin Luther King was assassinated in Memphis, Tennessee it set off riots and violence that gripped urban communities across the country and Omaha was not immune. This meant that in just one short month Omaha had been touched by the man who pushed racial segregation the most and the man who most fought to stop it. Both had ended up figuratively and controversially in the hallways of Central High. It was a culture shock that could not be avoided. "The times they were a changing"!

The spring of '68 was unofficially the interim semester of Mr. Moller's tenure as principal and two of the worst possible local and national societal events of the era were seeping through the walls of all four sides of his school. The year tested his resolve and ruffled the minds of the students permanently. For many of the African American students across the country the death of Martin Luther King became a sort of last straw. A man representing and begging for peace while preaching nonviolence was taken out by the very thing he fought to stop. Thus, a rebellion began from within, and it shouted out "we aren't going to take it anymore."

Out of all the carnage of the spring of 1968 had emerged a new African American student. One who watched carefully as they were dealt with, was suspicious of most authority, daring to be wrongly approached and above all had little tolerance of anything even resembling racism. These students, instead of trying to fit into America, began to claim it as their own. No more colored, Negro nor the big "N". Now, there was a call to dignity and a demand for respect. They wanted people to hear that they were a proud heritage of this country and embraced the new name and moniker of "African American".

Now that these new African American students were walking the halls of Omaha Central there had to be a new recognition and an acknowledgement of their change. So how did Mr. Moller approach this radically changed human being that was filled in many cases with anger and distrust? He felt that to separate and deal with them in some isolated way would be a total disservice to their desire to be educated. He was confident that the dignity and respect they sought, Central had already been giving. His fundamental foundation was predicated on teaching everyone in the school to follow the rules and making it known that they would be treated equally when they did not. It couldn't just be about the dignity and respect of the African American students. It had to be about the dignity and respect for Central High School and its student body... period!

Just Doing His Job

At the end of the school year for the class of 1968 the cover of the yearbook was unlike the lively covers that had adorned others throughout the decade. During the 1960's "O" Book covers (Central Yearbook) ranged from Saturn and the stars in 1961, to the red bricks of 62, from the tuning fork (I think) of 63 to the broken columns of 64, into the flashy powder blue of 65, through the cold black eagle of 66, and who could forget that powerful little straggly tree in 67. All of those yearbooks had an identity, a symbol, a picture. However, in 1968 the annual presented no dynamic symbol or memorable inscription to adorn the cover. No flash, just the words "O Book '68 scribbled toward the bottom in a plain font. It exuded no jubilance and no flamboyant depictions, just dignity, respect and the pride in knowing that the students of the times had survived their half of that transformational year.

By May of that unforgettable year Bob Taylor and Jo Wagner were still homecoming king and queen, Sally Simon headed up the yearbook staff and Paul Lubetken upheld the famed legacy of the Register (the school newspaper). Joe Orduna had made touchdowns in the fall and Dillard made baskets in the spring. Mr. Moller became Dr. Moller amidst the challenges of the year with three too many days. In the end graduation happened just as it always does. Teachers exhaled in a sigh of relief, parents cried, while students laughed. Eventually they all left this expected stop (high school) and headed off to their new lives with the knowledge of having experienced a changing time within the four sides of the forever great Omaha Central High School.

After the closing of the '68 school year, the now Dr. Moller was officially named principal. When I asked him during the interview about handling the turmoil of all the mixed emotions of those young lives during that time, he said he had a hard time remembering specifics. However he did offer this - he said that while life-changing events were happening in 1968 he was going about the business of preparing students for the rest of their lives. He called it "just doing my job". "I don't remember those times too vividly," he said, "They were certainly world events that I followed and kept up with. They were sad and confusing, unimaginable at times, hurtful and deeply disappointing. It made me sick at times but I had to stay in my job, so that's what I did. When I was at work, I worked!" He said he couldn't afford to get into the arenas of the world, he was too busy doing the job he was assigned to do... and I think nearly all would agree, he did it pretty well!

Chapter 3

DOC MOLLER THROUGH THE AGES

Teachers, students and education, how they changed

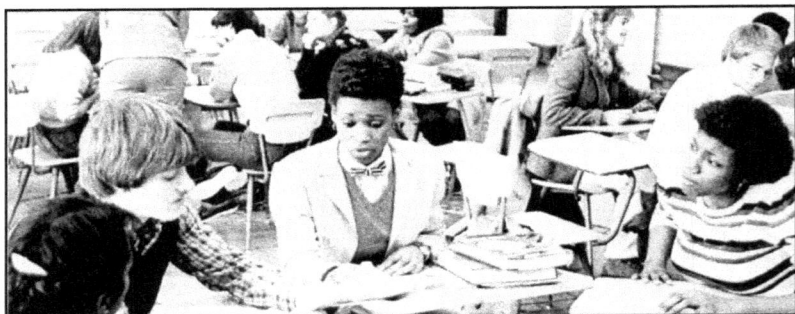

Independence Day!
The Then and The Now

Doc Moller was an Omaha Central administrator from 1963 to 1995. With knowledge of the fact that he wanted to impact the lives of students in positive and challenging ways, I asked him about his challenges in dealing with kids from one generation to another. I asked what changes he might have seen in students at Central from the time he arrived in 1963 to the time he left in 1995. He didn't hesitate. "INDEPENDENCE!" he said, in a tone that suggested no doubt. He said, "Kids of the nineties and even more so since then, have grown up with an independence that was never prevalent in the 60's and 70's."

"I suppose kids today have to become independent, he said, to survive the new times we live in." Toward the end of his career this self serving style of student was beginning to be the norm in high schools everywhere. He said he felt that the independence mostly centered around the change in households, where now both parents work and there are so many more single parent homes. "Today kids are forced to do things and in many cases learn things for themselves, leaving their own adolescent interpretation to decipher the true meaning of it all. The results of such action usually lead to independent thinking." He then began to go deeper and deeper with fortitude. He went into a sort of professor-like lecture mode, as if with intentions to teach. He spoke with conviction, pointing his left index finger in a way that drives home a point. "Kids once came into schools like a glob of clay he said and you could mold them to what you saw was best. However, he said, by the time I left, it seemed the students were trying to mold us!" That's when he knew, it was time to go.

> Time travel is real, we travel to the future every second. It's just that you can never go back !
> *(w. R.o.)*

Doc always had a good sense of recognizing the "then" that would help in the "now". For example, he was walking several miles a week before it was popular, driving economy cars when big luxury cars were a status symbol and gas was less than a dollar a gallon! He would embrace the math department's early recognition of the first computer lab at a time when most administrators hardly knew what they were. But his best foresight in detecting what became the now, was recognizing the change in that glob of clay which were the students of that time. That foresighted detection alerted him that it was a new day and finally time for his exit. Call it foresight, instinct, intuition or just plain seeing the future, for whatever reason Doc Moller always seemed to be ahead of the reality then before it became the inevitable now.

Teachers: According To Doc Moller
The Good, The Bad And The Apathetic

Did you ever meet the kind of leaders who, when you walked past them, you always wondered if you were looking your best and acting with extreme appropriateness? Doc was one of those leaders. The man took the job of principal like it was the last rite of passage to a new life. He was passionate about his duties and confident in his efforts to advance the lives of all students through teachers assigned to his authority. There was no doubt that he was very successful at his job, yet he was smart enough to realize that he could only be as good as his worst teacher and that a school's reputation was often based on its worst students. That meant that he was always working to strengthen his faculty from the bottom up, while demanding that every student, in his words, "toe the line."

"The greatest attribute that a teacher can possess is energy," Doc said in our interview. He pointed out that teachers by trade were smart people, but what separated them was the energy and the enthusiasm they brought to the school and the classroom on a daily basis. He said he detested teachers that came in with the attitude of no purpose, just time spent; no duty, just money made; no involvement, only time served. To him this attitude only added up to time wasted! It was during this period of the interview that his voice began to reach that pitch I remembered from twenty years before, followed by his all purpose, puzzled looking half smile. Then he blared out strongly, "Some teachers were not good enough to have around but not bad enough to send away. It was sad and very frustrating but that's the way it was."

Doc absolutely loathed apathy. He loved the teachers that were willing to interact with all facets of the educational process. In his assessment, whether they were interacting with a student, parent, administrator or fellow teacher, active and engaging teachers were head and shoulders above the rest and always garnered his highest tribute. He said he could spot the differences in teachers from a mile away. It showed in their walk, talk and everyday demeanor, he said. In his opinion, the non-caring teacher could not be motivated no matter what you did. Nor, could they motivate others or even recognize that there was a need to. You've heard the phrase "learning atmosphere?" That's what Doc Moller was always striving to create at Central and he was darn good at maintaining it. Dan Daly, head of the English department said that Doc's greatest attribute was his ability to listen to the heads of departments. According to Dan, by doing so he made the governing of the school a process instead of a man. Dan said that Doc Moller was the best of any of the four principals that he has worked with over his illustrious career as a teacher. Dan also cited Doc's vast successes as a principal being derived from a gathering of knowledge from a selective process of the ways and means of both students and staff. "Doc was quick to weed out students and teachers that were contaminating the atmosphere," he said. After hearing Mr. Daly and others, for me it seems quite clear that Doc Moller's constant protocol was to celebrate the good, regulate the bad and attempt to motivate the apathetic. In thirty-two years at Omaha Central High, that order of business never changed!

OB

Dan Daly, a man who brought tons of energy to school everyday

Chapter 4

A PRINCIPAL'S PHILOSOPHY

Doc's way: Always thinking •
Always caring • Always working

Exploring his Philosophy

I've never met a person that holds to their philosophy as sternly as Doc Moller held to his. He had a certain way in which he believed that education ought to be presented and he never wavered from it. His philosophy was always clear. Within the four sides it was the system rules and he guarded and enforced the laws of that system as if it was the Ark of the Covenant. You adopted the system as a teacher, lived by it as a student or eventually suffered the consequences. ***Based on Doc's philosophy, teachers were expected to adhere to a level of fair treatment of all students and show a broad knowledge and consistent presentation of the subject matter they taught.*** We were bound by his philosophy to never give a student a grade that was not earned! We were expected as teachers to demand a core of specified disciplines for all students assigned to our care. The students were bound to a series of rules and regulations and made to understand that there were consequences when they weren't followed. That was Doc's philosophy inside. His philosophy outside of school was one of cordialness and respectfulness but made very clear that his job and involvement to issues resided inside the walls of Central High and that's where he kept it. Many individuals and organizations outside of Central recognized Doc's keen savvy and rare ability to move a setting and some sought his involvement on occasion. As the leader of Omaha Central High, one of the most unique urban high schools in the Midwest, everyone knew that he could be a great ally for any cause. However, those who sought his involvement often left frustrated and angry. Mostly because he never used the Omaha Central High principal platform inside situations that were outside the boundaries of his authority. That authority ended at the outer boundaries of the high school campus at 124 N. 20ᵗʰ Street.

> *Your direction in thinking constitutes your philosophy in life..*
> *(W.R.O.)*

In other words, if a political battle was going on, he was Central's principal. If there were racial tensions across the country, he was Central's principal. If there were neighborhood issues, he was Central's principal. Natural disasters, local calamities, heart wrenching tragedies - through it all he always first and foremost simply doing the one thing he always said he would, HIS JOB! Here's where I could claim a few status points by saying that I agreed with his position, but I didn't. I thought that as a school with a strong staff and smart students, we should be out there fighting in some of the societal battles. I thought it was a duty of the school and believed we could perhaps make a difference. But the true reality is that a public school setting is not the place to be involved in such. I was wrong to think it should and so were many more.

I'd thought for a while that Doc just didn't care or wasn't aware of real world situations, but that was never true either. In fact he was just as abreast of those things happening throughout society as anyone. But his job was principal and the description for that job included developing and teaching kids in a designated form of planned education. He never allowed himself to get involved in places he did not belong. He just ran the school, governed the students and reinforced the rules, while guiding teachers in fulfilling his and the system's philosophy. In that scenario the possibilities are good that young people will be educated and prepared in ways that would allow them to reach their fullest potential.

Looking back at Doc Moller's overall philosophy I saw him as brilliant in his approach, valiant in holding to his beliefs, staunch in his leadership and unrelenting in his quest to help teachers and students in reaching heights they never thought possible. Some say you couldn't ask for more. I say you could, but where would you find it?

It's Personal!
Doc's Philosophy on Personal Intervention

Once upon a time my life was a Rubik's cube. I couldn't solve it and no one else was willing to try. Any good leader could see the disarray, so I know that Doc certainly did! However, he had a strict policy about one's own personal business that seemed to emphasize the overused phrase of *"mind your own business."* He always realized that delving into one's personal life within the structured world of high school teaching was a scrambled discord that should never be connected. If there were two thousand souls on board the cruise ship Omaha Central, then it meant that there were two thousand personal stories making the trip as well. His rule seemed to be that to engage in such a smorgasbord of personal humanity is risky at best, and could water down true leadership, thereby weakening the leader.

I surmised that this obvious observation is why Doc never once infused himself into my or anyone else's personal life; nor did he ever subject himself to the complex embodiment of social dysfunction as it related to broad scope societal problems outside of school. As mentioned, a public school is not equipped to deal in such things, nor is its staff, primarily because there are always two sides lurking inside any controversial issue. This means that within a school the elements of each side of an issue or point of view are sharing space inside the same building, side by side every day. In such a scenario, they must each be offered a set of the same rules and regulations to play by. While they may be divided outside, it is imperative that they be treated as one inside.

Doc Moller was a master at presenting, enforcing and carrying out this philosophy. It was a philosophy that was made clear to me many times. I would like to believe that Doc saw me as one of those energetic and enthusiastic teachers he spoke of, I think he could have. However, there were many traces of undisciplined actions within my trail of duty that he knew needed repair. One of the largest and most frequent of which was me sometimes trying to be so much the crusader. Meaning delving into the lives of students that I deemed to have had bigger and more serious personal problems outside of school. Doc recognized the practice and made it clear that he did not share my philosophy.

He contended that I had so many personal and school responsibilities that trying to save the world outside of that was virtually impossible. I was quick to explain to him that I didn't agree with his philosophy. What did he mean? That I should ignore the fact that a kid was being mistreated at home? Even when you could see it was interfering with their function at school? Later he sat me down and focused the lens on his microscope at a more defined setting, giving me a clearer view of what he was saying. *He pointed out that the teacher had a definite role in such situations, but that role involved reporting to the proper entities whose job it was to handle such things, not engaging one's self personally.*

Still I wasn't all the way sold on accepting that type attitude. I don't think I really got it until after I had left Central in 1991. That year I saw the movie "Ghost." When Sam, (Patrick Swayze) borrowed Ola Mae's (Whoopi Goldberg) body to touch Molly (Demi Moore), he was zapped when he came out of it. I thought wow! While I was jumping in and out of lives at Central in an effort to help, could I have been zapping myself every time? It finally hit me! The process, that I thought to be helping, was a constant drain that few survived. Why it took the fantasy in a made up movie to finally make me see real life, I do not know, but it surely did.

What I learned from Doc in this battle of uncommon philosophies was that, as a teacher you must care and it is your duty to help. It's just that you have to know how to help while remaining within the parameters of teaching school. All the while you must stay away from the jobs of trying to be social worker, psychiatrist and police detective, and so on. What Doc preached to me over and over again was, and I quote "you can have a big heart, most of us do but you must always remember you're here to teach school first." A lesson I did finally learn, the hard way.

Pride or Prejudice

When a leader has finally completed his journey there are always questions about fairness within the bounds of his legacy. Was he partial to this group or sympathetic to that cause? Was he selective, biased, unseeingly prejudiced or just plain didn't care? One of the grayest areas in diverse American societies, particularly back in the 60's through the 80's, was how well those in roles of leadership were able to deal between the races and how beholden were they to the rich, powerful and the malicious opposition to positive and sensible change.

I'd hear people quip that Doc was partial to the Jewish elite, ignoring of the poor, and insensitive to the plight of black America. They would hint of prejudice not pride and point out past examples of unfairness. You'd hear such garbage can trash and wonder why you remembered it. But then you would find yourself in disagreement with him and he just won't budge from his position. All of a sudden the exchange is over and you're left without a satisfactory resolution. It is then that you go back to that garbage can, dig out that old ridiculous trash that you knew was there, and then sacrifice it to yourself as reasoning for your unresolved situation.

Doc Moller was scrutinized from every side and it was tough, because no matter how biased or prejudiced he may have appeared on the surface it didn't matter, he would never back down on anything based on public pressure. I'll be the first to admit that he had a little Napoleon in him when it came to leadership. Most would agree to that! However in decision making he was always consistent and totally fair. There are some who believed him to be non-caring and not interested in things that affected the whole of society. As previously written, once I was announced as the new Central football coach, I was bombarded with all manner of tales of the school and its by-the-book-principal.

I was told that he was unfair, uncaring and relished in pushing extreme agendas. They said these characteristics in him were even more prevalent when it came to servicing African American students and teachers. Some even went as far as to describe him as prejudiced and downright racist and I'm afraid I must admit that a few years into my term at Central I wondered if they might be correct. From the beginning I saw him as cold and deviously calculating, having neither heart nor empathy for anyone who was of a different background than he.

In those days I could have easily been named president of the DMHS (Doc Moller's Haters Society). How dare he try to chastise me for being a few minutes late? What business did he have demanding that I not use "wit" as a slang for the word "with", who is he to tell me how to speak! Why would he not accept my shortcomings or pay attention to my worldly problems? Could he not see that I was a persecuted black man that deserved a break here and there? "I apologize for the sarcasm here, but I need to make sure that it is known where I was at the time, so that one might better understand where I am today and why I'm here."

For the record, if just one thing is taken from this book, please let this be it - *"Dr. G.E. Moller saw students and teachers in their roles at Central High School as being on the same level, no matter their color or status."* This meant not asking any particular one of them to do anything more or less than what is expected of the other. He felt that all students and teachers; black, white, green or yellow must be prepared for an outside world that didn't offer up free handouts or goodie bag gifts! He felt it was a disservice to any student to be presented a value system that tolerated undisciplined behavior and an unchallenged lack of effort. It was his opinion that there was no room for success when such qualities were absent from the equation. To me this all seem aimed at instilling pride, not practicing prejudice.

I, by no means, would ever present myself as an expert at distinguishing within the parameters of social and racial prejudices. However, it has always been a part of my life. In fact while growing up in the 1950's and 60's Jim Crow South, you had to spot it quick or it could cost you your life! I had the unfortunate experience of actually witnessing some in-depth prejudices and some over the top racists while being raised in the boot state and having been surrounded by Texas A&M - that's Texas, Arkansas and Mississippi. From my knowledge and experiences in the deep south I endured much and learned lots. I was born there in the 1940's, ridiculed throughout the 50's, fought through the 60's and finally escaped in the70's. I know the hearts, minds and faces of prejudiced people and it is beneath laughable to try to place Doc Moller in such a category. His only bias was to Central High School and that label goes to many of us.

For the record, nothing is more damaging to young people who want to learn then degrading and unfair treatment by those in authority, particularly in a school. Those prejudiced individuals who garner power and position, then choose to inject racism within its embodiment, are among the coward and the stupid. Doc Moller is neither. He is too involved to be a coward and too intelligent to be stupid. All that being said, before any person or group began to theorize as to some estranged motive I might have, being a black man offering this type of conclusive praise to one that's white, I offer the following:

I solemnly submit, that I was no grand lover of Doc Moller during many of my years at Central. Nor was I ever considered in his circle of friends. I've never seen his house and never met him for a drink. He just happened to touch my life as he did many others and I just happened to be the one to write about it. Sometimes you're chosen to do things and you don't know why. Somewhere in the midst of doing them you get a feeling as to whether it's right or wrong to continue. In that moment of solace if you believe in powers greater than yourself, then you will not only find out ***why*** you're doing it but you will also realize ***who*** asked you to do it. I can say today with pride and confidence...I know the ***why*** and I know the ***who***.

If you know Doc Moller then you've already learned, as I did over the years, that at the end of each day he was only what he was supposed to be. If you're just learning about him, I submit that he is just a man who became a principal. It's a small position to some but one that he took as serious as the presidency of the free world. It took me years to understand why he took it so seriously but once I did my world was changed and life took on a new meaning. He pushed me to a level that I never knew was there and for that I am eternally grateful. ***Show me the man or woman that will challenge us to be our very best and I will show you one that truly cares.*** (WRO)

As simple as it sounds, engaging into any fashion of prejudice to him was unfair and dishonest. He prided himself on being just the opposite of that. His first years as principal were years when downtown urban schools like Central were left in the desert without food or water, "while school boards across the country waited for them to die." He brought Central through those times, vying every step of the way to leave it better and stronger than before he came. His power base was fairness and honesty. It is what helped Omaha Central to survive and thrive, while nearly every other urban downtown high school in the country during that time was either neglected, diminished or closed forever.

To the question of Pride or Prejudice. *Doc Moller took pride in being Central's leader. He was consistent in his practices and showed prejudice to no one.*

Betty Moller… First Lady of Central

For me, there is no doubt that Dr. G.E. Moller was a great principal and continues to show that he is an even better human being. However, one can hardly extrapolate the glorified successes of a man that has been married to the same woman for over 60 years without acknowledging that woman! The woman is Betty Moller. Somewhere I heard that *"a true man of success can only be as strong as his wife is happy."* Betty always seemed very happy, So Doc was indeed very strong. To me, there was a carefulness to his wide range of actions and reactions to his wife, when or wherever they were.

OB

He made sure that everyone saw an acknowledgement and a deep respect transpire between him and Betty no matter what the event or occasion. I saw it 100% of the time, so I'm sure everyone else did too. When I look back on it now, I think that without making a big deal of it he was simply saying in his actions – this is how you treat your wife, here is the time and respect you give her, here is the love you show in all places, at all times, under all circumstances! And where does that get you? Well, in the midst of a 50% divorce rate nationwide they've maintained a marriage for more than 60 years.

Doc's interactions with his wife always spoke loudly to anyone in view and it spoke volumes to how one should be treated. I not only saw those actions I heard them also, but wasn't really listening. *There is a distinct difference between hearing and listening; you hear everything but you only listen to those things deemed important.* (W.R.O.) For me that message was usually broadcast within the confines of his actions then reverberated in all directions and was precisely clear. *It suggested that you must love your wife, you must honor her daily and you must cherish her for life; for she is your eyes in the present, the memories from your past and the key to all your future successes. (W.R.O.).*

Dr. Moller is married to Betty and if you paid close attention you would see how a wife ought to be treated and respected. She always seemed to be an extension of everything that Doc represented. Sort of an "under boss" if you may, to the modest empire if you will! I always saw it as Doc being the *power*, but she was the *glory* and they are *forever… Amen.*

When it came to Betty it was plain to see that although Doc may sometimes have practiced a dictatorship in other areas, their marriage was a true democracy. She projected that she had clout but was fully aware of the tradition that called for the man to take the lead at appropriate times. Of course not the way of our side of the world today, but it was how things worked at the time. Personally, I always felt good when she was around. Doc seemed to have been a little nicer to me and a bit more cordial when Betty Moller was in the house.

I loved it when he and I had just had one of those one-sided confrontations that he would always win and Betty would pop on the scene for some after school chore or event. She was always smiling and changing the atmosphere to something a little brighter. No matter the circumstance, Doc always seemed bound to be a bit more congenial in her presence. I liked her from the beginning, but some teachers seemed a little stand-offish at times, mostly displaying it in their attitudes. For them she had this very special way of making her point and no matter what she said what you heard was, "my husband is your boss and I'm his wife, get over it!" And all the while she never stopped smiling. Inside the nation that was Omaha Central High School from 1968 to 1995 Doc Moller was the president and within the bounds of that scenario, Betty Moller was a great first lady!

In these United States marriage is a sacred thing full of many vows. Still it only works about 50% the time. So whether you are in the 50% that's in or the 50% that's out, relationships will be with most of us forever. So, with that staunch reminder in tow, take this assessment of Doc's "by example" advice and use it wisely. From it I surmised the following and interpreted it this way:

All in The Family
Back: Gene Claxton, Nikki Russ, Ron Hofmeister, Doc
Middle: Betty, Staci Russ, Londa Claxton, Risa Hofmeister
Front: Jackson and Ben Hofmeister

For as much as he loved Central, it dwarfed in comparison to Betty Moller. For as much as he was the glue inside the walls of the school, he was silly putty in the hands of his wife. For as much as he was respected, he respected her more. For as much as he cared about the family of students and faculty at Central he made it clear that his biological family could not be lost in the process. These are values and principles that keep a man with the same woman for over six decades, sharing a love that has matured and evolved in ways that allowed it to endure a lifetime of challenges and withstand the test of time.

During the interview at Panera Bread I asked him about Betty and how she was doing. He paused briefly, steadied himself and then said she wasn't doing so well. He said an old hereditary illness that had followed her family for generations had finally found her. It was the same condition that had taken Katherine Hepburn from stage and screen and now it had moved in with the Mollers.

I had to take a bit of a pause myself when he said she was no longer allowed to drive. This would be a minor disruption of life in years past but in this day and age it constitutes about an 85 percent relinquishment of freedom and independence. With that thought in mind, for such a prideful and independent lady, I was deeply saddened by it all. Betty Moller is a splendid lady of courage and grace. One that seemed to brighten the dullest of days, heighten the lowest of spirits and support the rules of happiness wherever she goes.

Today the Betty's of the world are scarce and nearing extinction, but their passage through this life will leave an indelible imprint in the hearts and souls of those they touched. Indeed, times have changed and eventually the inevitable brings with it great sadness to all. However, the saddest of them all, is when physicality and awareness is diminished while life goes on.

I recall a time when scary movies for those of us from the dime picture show era, were once movies like Frankenstein, Dracula, the Exorcist, Halloween and the Nightmares on Elm Street. But those movies of then hardly frighten our generation anymore. Instead, today we are all terrified at the thought of Gena Rowlands and James Garner, in a movie called The Notebook. In fact, if you ever need to check your vital signs, just grab a cup and sit down to that movie. If you haven't cried a cup of tears by the time the credits roll then check your pulse, for you are probably no longer among the living.

It is sad when we can no longer do simple things for ourselves but it is devastating to all when we can't remember those we love and the ones who love us. Doc and Betty have met life together at every turn, they continue to and yes, she still remembers. One could learn a lot from their dedication to one another over the years. I certainly have. *I submit that the genuine aspects and quality of a man can be easily measured by the love, respect and treatment of his wife.* By that standard Dr. Gaylord E. Moller is nothing short of extraordinary and Betty Moller is truly deserving of it all!

These days you may find Doc driving Betty or sometimes visiting past colleagues in various homes or care units, some of which because of their conditions are not even aware of his visits. You might also catch him doing meticulous jobs at Procare3, a Physical Therapy chain founded and owned by his daughter Risa and his son-in-law Ron Hofmeister. You'd think that he would settle down a little now…NEVER! Because at age 80 plus he's still the head master, checking on the staff, clearing a path for the family, while trying to make things better. The mind and body says stop, but the heart goes on. He's forever the principal and still… "just doing his job."

Knowing Doc, it is at about this point that he would want me to remind all, that he's not perfect nor has his life been such. I'll go along with that, but for me that makes him and his teachings all the more real. Yes, I am certain

he'll find a hundred or more mistakes in this writing and will tell me about every one of them, that's a given. But then he'll smile and perhaps consider from whence I came, and then wonder if he really had anything to do with it. He will look at me with that famous, puzzling, half smile seeking an answer... but I will never tell!

Doc's Legacy... Final Answer!

I can hear him now, saying "William, why are *you* summing up *my* legacy?" To that I'd answer, someone should and if I don't, who will? Some called him mean, some used the words insensitive, picky, partial to certain people, beholding to certain groups and non-caring about certain things. He's been describe as biased and in some cases just downright unfair.

I've chosen to finish this segment with these rambling gossips based on the finish of my interview with Doc. Toward the end of that interview he spoke of people out there that didn't like him very much and some who believed him to be unfair at times. He even saw it necessary to say to me that he had always first and foremost treated everyone the same. I felt bad that he even had to say that to me because I knew it even better than he did. Having been on both sides of the rhetoric my first thoughts were to squelch all the absurd propaganda with an immediate under writing within this book. But should one underwrite his own conclusion? I think not! What I needed was a bold and honest assessment from a strong and impartial personality. One that was familiar with the man and the school, with a knowledge of circumstances that helped to frame and define one's legacy. I asked myself, where do you even began looking for such a person?

Mary Dean Evans

Luckily there was a time in my life when I talked frequently with someone who I could always count on to be honest, frank and to the point. Particularly when it came to opinionated evaluations of people of inferred power. She was always especially critical of those who may not

212

be on the up and up regarding fair treatment. She has always had that rare ability to connect people by what they do and through that connection make accurate assessments of who they are and what they represent.

She is my forever spirited sister-in-law, Mary Evans. She was a Central High teacher back in the early 1970's who was then referred to as Mary Dean Harvey. I'd known her since my high school days back in Louisiana, where a sister and a brother had brought us together. Down there we just called her Dee Dee. She remains one of the most aggressively brilliant people I have ever known, bringing personality and charm to any setting and life to the dullest of parties. She is strong, fearless and opinionated, yet sensitive to those in need. She has always operated at a high tolerance level, meaning she could take the heat of life up to a thousand degrees. However, when it came to unfair barriers offered within prejudiced boundaries, her level of tolerance dropped to 40 below zero. By her standards, ***if you weren't willing to be diversified then prepare to be crucified!*** To her biased, prejudiced people were like alien creatures from another planet. She was quick to spot them, ask from whence they came and didn't mind telling them where to go.

At different times in Nebraska she was principal at Junior Central, (aka) Lewis and Clark Jr. High School, executive director of Girl's Incorporated, executive director of the North Omaha Boy's Club and director of The Nebraska Department of Social Services, (an office of the governor's cabinet). But of all those jobs and the prominence that came with them, she has always first shown a sincere appreciation for her days as an educator at Omaha Central High School. Those days included working and growing with one Dr. G.E. Moller.

Now residing in Atlanta, Georgia. we recently spoke about good times and bad, old times and new. When we spoke of our separate experiences during separate times with Dr. Moller, we found that even though the times were different, our feelings were the same. She said, " In the beginning stages of my career, Doctor Moller was like a father figure for me. I was sort of wild, crazy and out of control at times. He taught me balance, made me focus and eventually gave me purpose. I love Doc!" I've since learned that her lessons of balance, focus and purpose were Doc's premiere gifts to a lot of people and therein lies his legacy.

Maurtice Ivy left Omaha Central in 1984 as the most prolific female basketball player in Nebraska high school history. She went on to The University of Nebraska where she was a three time All Big Eight star. In 2011, some 27 years after her graduation from Central, her number 30 jersey was retired by the University of Nebraska in a ceremony that included Nebraska Head Women's Basketball Coach, Connie Yori and Nebraska Athletic Director Dr. Tom Osborne. And who was there to help honor her in her time of glory? Doc and Betty Moller were there to honor a Central High student from 27 years past. Maurtice said when she saw him she was overjoyed. He had simply come to tell her how proud he was of all her efforts after Central and beyond. Before I ended my talk with her that day, she gave the highest praise that a 45 year old superstar athlete could offer up to an 81 year old ex-principal when she said in a spirited voice, "Doc Moller? Now that's my Bud!"

That's just two of a thousand stories like it. Whether you were big , small, orange, yellow or turquoise blue, if you were serious and willing to better yourself he was always in support. Unlike Maurtice I'm a little too old to make him a "Bud" so I think I'll stick with Mary Dean's assessment, "I love him too." As for his legacy, I will yield to her also and echo her sentiments! Dr. Moller was a great Central High principal and is an even better centralized man.

The Coach And The Principal... Moving On

You've read several accounts about Doc Moller and by all accounts he is interesting to say the least. Now however, it is time to explain the root cause for my writing about him. There's an almost sacred reason for this book and how it derived from my pen. As stated previously, sometimes God asks you to do things and I believe in such cases it is not our place to ask why.

Neither should we think the thoughts of "Oh God, are you sure?" No! You just do the things asked of you to the best of your abilities and hope in the end that it is a job worthy of He who commanded you do it. In these next chapters, a family, a letter and a heartbreak will expose the root of this true story and that which compelled me to tell it.

Doc Moller, Central High and me; this was an unlikely trio that first had

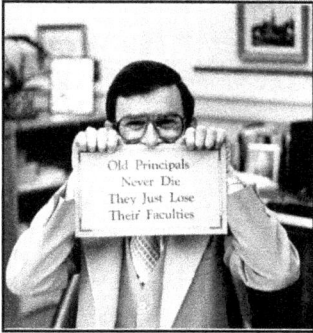

eleven years together and then a lifetime of memories to pass on. In 1990 I left Central and by 1995 so did he. That's how it goes with high school, the characters are ever changing. People come, then they go, but the school remains in all its glory. Omaha Central is all of that statement. The legacy of Dr. G.E. Moller, along with the mark he made and the void he filled for thirty-two years will never die. I am certain that the teachers he served will all agree he will never lose his faculties.

Doc Moller forever the principal

The Remains of The Day

At the end of the day the experience of Omaha Central is one that is uniquely intriguing. It affords you the opportunity to embellish its past, borrow from its tradition while enhancing your future, as you become a living part of its legacy. (W.R.O.) Doc Moller helped me to get that, all the while he was getting it also! After mine and his tenure had ended at Central it would be nine long years before he would bring a grandson for me to teach and I would see him again. That day, it was a reunion of joy and youthful exuberance interrupted by sadness, all followed by a letter of gratitude and tearful acknowledgments. The letter and the golf lessons for his grandsons became the seeds that spawn the verbal roots that grew to become this book.o

Chapter 5

THE LESSONS AND THE LETTER

In all our new ways of communication there is still nothing more personable than reading and writing while teaching and learning

Ben's Lessons

On the surface it looks like just another check. But look again and you will see the small letter "g" that has been given capital letter status; the twisted "E" that more resembles a backwards "B"; and that runaway "r" that leaves all the other letters behind! There's no doubt, it's that macabre signature that signaled authenticity, to every Mollergram written at Omaha Central High School! No, this was not just a check, it was a sanctioning to my new life and though he had forever called me William, on this check for the first time, he wrote Coach Reed!

Had I been a stock that first time Doc Moller brought his grandson to my school, I would have closed at 20,000.25 on the Dow Jones Industrial. At the end of that day I sat alone in my car at 9 p.m. on a day that began at seven that morning. I took a deep breath, paused and thought to myself, that lucky numbers may win you a lottery, number one in the draft in any sport can be worth millions, the first heir to a billionaire"s inheritance gets a fortune. But for me check number 5155 for $117.50, signed by Dr. G.E. Moller... Priceless!

It had been almost nine years since I'd seen Doc, but on the day that he brought his grandson Ben Hofmeister to the Reedway Golf Academy, that all changed. He had retired a few years earlier and I had sort of lost track of him. I remembered being shaken a bit when I heard that someone else was leading Central High School for the first time in 27 years. Somehow it just didn't seem proper. I just couldn't see him doing without Central and I surely couldn't see Central doing without him. The two were made for each other and I always viewed them as inseparable. Yet, time moves and with it so too does people. Doc was no exception and now the extraordinary principal had become simply, Gaylord Moller the grandpa.

However, true to his nature, being grandpa had moved to the top of his importance list and he was going to make darn sure that he was the best one ever. I still remember him in his new role, coming up the steps to the golf school with young Ben that first day. For him it was just giving time to a grandson, for Ben it was just a golf lesson, but for me, it was like a grand reunion that was long, long overdue. Over a six year period I had become deeply entrenched into my golf school. The flood of new young kids every year along with the returnees and the golf team members, always made it an interesting summer. However, the summer of 1999 proved to be more than just interesting.

One day during that year my golf assistant told me that a doctor had called to set up an appointment for his grandson. It was for a private lesson. Golf students not enrolled in group sessions were always listed in one hour slots, by first name only. This particular slot slated for May 1, 1999 at 6 p.m. was simply listed as "Ben". I didn't learn until later that the doctor who had called was one Gaylord E. Moller from Central High School days past. Not wanting to become too preferential, Doc had not made a big deal of the sign-up nor had he revealed any knowledge of our previous involvement. Later that day, as I combed through the next week's schedule I noticed the name Hofmeister and a reference of grandfather, with a telephone number attached. The next day my assistant casually mentioned that the grandfather who was the doctor had made some odd reference to an old Central-something?

She couldn't remember the name so I asked was it a Doctor Moller? She exclaimed, "Yes, that's it!" And at that moment my life of two decades past, flashed before my eyes. The overwhelming notion that Doc Moller's grandson was coming to my school filled me with an honor that I still can't describe. That knowledge was enough in itself to soothe my thoughts, but the next part would prove to do even more. I'd been told that he was sending his grandson but didn't know until they arrived that he would actually bring him personally. The date was May 1st, 1999. A Saturday, fittingly my birthday.

This was déjà vu for me because back in our days at Central no matter the circumstances, the mood or climate, no matter how busy he was or how confrontational we might have been at the time, Doc never once failed in all my eleven years at Central to send me a birthday card on May 1st. I recall getting ripped to pieces by him one May 1st morning, and upon leaving his office I stopped by my mailbox. Inside was this nice birthday card with a personal hand written note wishing me a happy birthday and inviting me to have a nice day. I was literally growling that morning. I could just feel my hands around his neck. But that darn card messed up my mad! Like always, I wanted to strangle him but he had turned the tables on me again. It wasn't out of the ordinary, he always sent teachers birthday cards with a clever little card message offering a bit of advice.

With that history in mind, to my amazement he was now coming to my school on that same special date bringing his grandson for lessons. When I saw Ben and Doc walking up the stairs that sunny day, it was utter delight and silent jubilation. At that moment my emotions seemed to crisscross. I thought I wanted to cry, but instead I burst into laughter. Let me put it in perspective. The person whom I know to have more respect for teaching and education than anyone I've ever met has brought to me one of the people he loves and admires most in life for educational instructions. To put it mildly, I was above honored.

When I started this golf teaching thing back in 1992, Roger Sayers was my first student. The irony here was that Roger is a Central alum also. If you know Roger then you know that he is one of those impeccable reputations from Central, that I mentioned earlier. He's the type that if it's not right, then he's not there. He took eight lessons from me that summer and his satisfaction was the first message to me that this was indeed something I could do. Now, Doc Moller, a man known for his precise judgment and careful calculations was re-enforcing that message from Roger, just by he and Ben's presence. Choosing me to teach the grandson that he loves so dearly was

To: Mr. Gaylord Moller

1999 Golf Lessons for Ben

Date	Cost/Person	#	Total
5/1/99 Private Lesson	$20.00	1	$20.00
5/2/99 Private Lesson	$20.00	1	$20.00
5/8/99 Private Lesson	$20.00	1	$20.00
5/9/99 Private Lesson	$20.00	1	$20.00
5/22/99 Private Lesson	$20.00	1	$20.00
5/23/99 Private Lesson	$20.00	1	$20.00
6/6/99 On-Course Lesson	Green Fees		$10.00
	Cart		$6.00
	Lesson Time		$35.00

1999 Golf Lessons for Mr. Moller

Date	Cost/Person	#	Total
6/25/99 Private Lesson	$35.00	1	$35.00

more than a gesture of faith it was a vivid statement of trust and belief. I was overwhelmed with pride.

The lesson was scheduled for 6 p.m. When Doc walked up to greet me after nearly ten years he took a rather obvious long look at his watch and in amazement he said, "hmmm 5:55" then he looked at me and said, "I can't believe you're on time." and with that we both burst out in uncontrollable laughter. Even though time had separated us for nearly a decade, it was as if it stood still that day and we enjoyed an enthusiastic reunion, like long lost family. Ben was seemingly puzzled, as Doc and I frolicked and teased one another about days passed by. He didn't know the gist of some of our sarcasm so he just stared in wonderment, as if he was observing two slightly off-their-rockers old people.

I had left Doc and Central a long time before. I'd been lost and missing something in my life since then. But when he looked at his watch and spoke about time, it was the best I had felt since he'd asked me not to leave Central all those years before. This was one of those great moments that one never forgets. After our brief reception I was totally energized and ready to go. From the moment I started, every minute I worked with Ben was special. He was just twelve but everything he tried, he made it a mission. I tell you, teaching a young man with the engaging attitude and personality that he possessed at the time was truly a joy. Ben's lessons ended on June 6th, my wife's birthday and I couldn't escape the eerie irony. I hadn't seen Doc for years and it just so happened that the lessons that brought us back together started on my birthday and ended on my wife's! This was all too surreal.

Life was good and this had been one of those unforgettable times that you didn't want to end. Ben and I became instant friends. I taught with passion, he learned with gratitude, and my biggest thrill was that Doc was there to see it all. It was by far the happiest moments of all my golf school days and after Ben's last lesson, I took some expressive advice from the singer "Prince". And I partied that night like it was 1999… because it was!

Being Grandpa

Jackson, Ben and Doc

When I think about those sessions with Ben, and later his younger brother Jackson, I can't help but think about the relationship of a man and his grandsons and how special it was when we were all four there together.

It seemed sometimes that he was trying to make up for every day he ever missed spending with his two girls, during the days when his time was a lot more scarce. Doc seemed to embrace the status of grandpa and like everything else in his life he took it Mount Everest serious! As a new grandpa myself, I was intrigued by the way he interacted with his grandkids, which led to my eventual exploration of this whole grandpa thing.

As parents we can get pretty busy while raising our children. In fact we often miss lots of important events and happenings during that memorable time of them growing up. However, once our children have children, we settle into being grandparents and we get busy with the new kids in ways that are extremely connective, forgiving, understanding and much more open. "I think it is called catch-up time." It's a time that we now can dedicate to our grandkids that we just didn't have 20 or 30 years ago with our own children. It is also a time when we become more reasonable, flexible and we become anointed as "Grand." We don't always feel grand as we find ourselves far less influential in the lives of the children we raised.

We take lots more chances at expressing and sharing affection and we give to the extreme. It's an open contract that allows us to parent like we never knew we could. If the kids become unruly or out of control there's a pause button that wasn't available back in the primary parenting days. In this "grand" business we can simply return them to the custody of their parents and cool our heels until the malfunction is repaired. We can then revisit them a week or so later, check to make sure that all parts have been repaired, press play and pick up right where we left off. This is a fail-safe system that wasn't available on the models 30 years before and it keeps a "grand" motivated indefinitely.

As a grandparent Doc Moller is one of the "Usual Suspects", fitting the description perfectly. He was so patient, so proud and so supportive of young Ben and Jackson. He seemed always willing to give them time and attention wherever possible. And why not, here were two young kids that were vibrant and curiously smart, energetic and full of confidence and both so eager to learn. It became obvious early on that Ben, the oldest, was one of those kids that believed he could learn to do anything and his grandpa was always there in support of his effort.

Young Ben was every bit the new millennium tween, just delightfully impressionable! Watching him and Doc there were two things that stood out. It was obvious that Ben loved and respected his grandfather and absolutely no doubt that his grandfather greatly loved and respected him. At times it seemed that there was a tug of war going on between them. Sort of a war of the ages it seemed. It was a good war! Ben with his curiously engaging smile was seemingly trying to pull his grandpa into the new millennium, while grandpa was trying to teach him the subtle discipline and easy pace offered back in the 1950's. It was clear that Ben was winning, and it was indeed fun to watch.

I loved every minute that Doc was there at the golf school and it was all made possible by Ben's desire to learn the game. Those were the days and I wanted them to last forever. But reaching back to (1968) one last time, I found Mary Hopkin and I think she said it best when she sang "Then the busy years went rushing by us and we lost our starry notions on the way... those were the days my friend, we thought they'd never end." However those days did end and are gone forever and now four years later here we are back together again with at least time to reminisce. For me there's a knowledge that the time we spent together in that short period was more than just golf, it was pure education, regardless the subject matter. It also served as a conduit that brought Doc and I back together. We were able to act, react and interact in ways that were almost magical. I cherished every minute of Ben's lessons and his grandpa never missed one of them.

Later, he would bring a second grandson for me to teach. That time he kind of sneaked up on me. I turned one day and there he was standing right behind me with young Jackson, his second grandson. Jackson was a different type, much more the cool and calm. Nothing seemed to rattle him, he seemed mature beyond his youth and was equally respectful of his grandpa. If you know Doc at all, then you know that bringing a second grandson to

2000 Golf Lessons for Jackson			
Date	Cost/Person	#	Total
6/10/00 Private Youth Lesson	$25.00	1	$25.00
6/24/00 Duo Youth Lesson	$22.50	1	$22.50
7/15/00 Duo Youth Lesson	$22.50	1	$22.50
7/22/00 Duo Youth Lesson	$22.50	1	$22.50
7/29/00 Private Youth Lesson	$25.00	1	$25.00

my school would be his way of saying "you did alright with the first one." I appreciated that magical time and when all was said and done, that sense of accomplishment and satisfaction that I had so dearly sought since starting my own school was finally there. After all those years, he was still a stickler about anything that had to do with instruction. So, as earlier written, to have him bring anyone to me for instruction relative to anything, was simply delightful but bringing his grandsons was over the top! His trust during that time gave me the feeling that allowed me to turn and look forward again, and I haven't looked back since. "<u>Those indeed were the days my friend, those were the days! Oh yes, those were the days!</u>" I will never forget them, for I was reborn in the wake of their happening. That rebirth and the appreciation for it is what drove me to drop everything I was doing in Belize yesterday, to be back with Doc, Ben and Jackson today! It is a gathering that I could not possibly miss.

A Gathering at H-West

It is November 5th 2003, a cold and wintry day in the Cornhusker state. I've been longing all morning for that bright sunshine and 76 degrees that I left twenty-four hours ago in Belize. My body is in a full-blown argument with my brain, demanding that it turn up the temperature in this 1948, homo sapiens body. However the message doesn't seem to be getting through. So, I've dug out my heaviest coat and braved the almost forgotten chill of the Nebraska November.

My first order of business this morning was to head out to church and I made it in good time. It is filled with people young and old. It was a great sermon, solemn, compelling and its message was strong. I remember parts of it and can see several different faces that are standing out. There is a dad that spoke clearly in a letter, and a familiar young face that I thought I recognized in the front row but is much too tall to be him. I see a color here, a painting there and so many things in between. But of all the things I see none prepared me for the sharp clear and melancholy voice that seem to be coming from the heavens above.

It is a mother's voice, I see her sitting in the front row and as Paul Simon sang in 1967, "She was talking without speaking" and the "people are hearing without listening" as the voice "like silent raindrops fell and echoed in the wells of silence."

The voice seemed to come down from the rafters and spread all over the church, through its monotone intercom system. It speaks from above us as if released by the heavens and carried by angels to our ears. Yet, all the while the person to whom it belonged sat quietly in the row across from me, never uttering a word. Her voice flowed majestically across the pews as I watched her clutch her son, still not speaking, yet hearing her own voice. The voice spoke of beautiful things and wonderful times, never missing a syllable, never stumbling on a word. It still rates as one of the purest, most sincere vocal expressions that I have ever heard and I was moved to tears.

The church service has ended and I am among the last to leave, stunned by the strength and fortitude in the messages that I had just witnessed. I was touched, but time isn't waiting and my next stop this morning is one I can't be late to. It's familiar stomping grounds for me and brings back a ton of memories. Years ago, in the early 70's I worked summers for the City of Omaha. Many of our meetings would originate at a place called Pipal Park. Anyone who was ever there for one of those meetings would tell you, that if you'd been to one, then you've seen them all. They were redundant meetings for most of us, mostly about things we'd heard in meetings past.

During that time there were a few of us that were slowly becoming addicted to the most powerful drug in the USA at the time, "golf." So we would always find a way to escape the meetings and slip over to the nearby Cedar Hills Golf Course. The golf those days was so exciting I think mainly because of what it was replacing, those terribly redundant meetings. We had a lot of good times there. Twenty years later it became one of the first courses I used for my trial run of teaching kids the game of golf. Again, "those were the days." Today, I'm following heavy traffic as I head to that same golf course more than 30 years after I first played there.

Doc Moller is waiting there with two of my golf students, his grandsons Ben and Jackson. Just think, yesterday at this time I was in Central America and today I'm navigating the streets of Omaha, Nebraska. It's sort of a re-minder of just how quickly life can change. I'm looking forward to reuniting with them, it has been a while. They brought joy to my life a few short years ago and in a way saved it too. Now, it is time for me to go and acknowledge each of them and to just say thanks for the privilege of past times spent. From the beginning I taught Ben, and then I taught Doc, before that he taught me, next I taught Jackson and in the end Ben taught us all. I am forever proud to be the coach, Doc Moller will always be my principal and Ben and Jackson Hofmeister's desire to learn the game of golf will always be the catalyst that brought us back together.

I had never seen Doc in a display of affection and pride like he showed with his grandsons. He was like a born-again parent and those two kids treated him as such. I felt pride as Doc would watch my every move in my meticulous presentation of instructions to his grandsons. I could see a sort of puzzled pride in him. I think it was some kind of guarded happiness for him to see that I was happy with where I was and good at what I was doing. I could only laugh at his puzzlement when he inquired as to my depth of presentation and its origin. Where did you learn this stuff? He asked and I answered his inquiry definitively. *"**Discipline in the class, respect to the student, knowledge of the subject matter and energy in its presentation; it's teaching 101 and what was demanded me every time I stepped into a Central High classroom. You Doc, I learned it from you!"**

I've only seen him briefly since that time, mostly at golf events, one or two times a year. I haven't seen him at all since my wife's passing in March of 2000, before I moved to Belize. I just keep thinking that it was just twenty-four hours ago that I was in that country. Yesterday, I awoke there to a hot serving of Johnny cakes. Today it's well past mid-morning and I haven't had a bite yet. At last it seems that the line of traffic I've been following has finally dissipated, they're all turning left and I think I'll go straight. Good, it's totally clear this way. After crossing the Caribbean, the Gulf of Mexico and much of Texas, I have finally reached my destination. I've just finished my walk to the top of the hill to find a very peaceful neighborhood at the summit. Whew! That was a pretty steep climb. The sign says H-WEST and I am standing at attention amongst the onlookers. I am definitely standing out, clearly the only African American in the crowd.

As I look to my right I can see the two tall trees that mark the teeing area of the fourth hole at the Cedar Hills Golf Course. This was always a welcome sight back in the day when I worked for the city and played the 9 hole course regularly. Playing that hole meant that I had just finished the tough uphill par four number 3, always a relief. I'm getting lost in the thought of the days I played and taught there. Oh, I can finally see Doc and I'm jarred back to the reality of why I'm here. He is standing with his wife and daughters, son-in-laws, grandkids and other family members in the gathering. I am directly across from him but he's yet to see me.

He is poised, standing majestically and proud. I still don't think he sees me but I can see the strained effort in his face as he is trying to hear every word being spoken through the rustle of the blowing wind. He's squinting; it's that look he always gives when he does not quite understand something, a look of solitude and a stern stare of readiness. I can see the pride for his grandsons bursting out, while a puzzled array of question marks seem to consume him. His mind seems to be drifting back to past days, as mine is also. Doc is a slightly built man but one of the strongest that I have come to know. Yet, right now I'm watching him shiver in the cold damp air, while his face seems to spell unparalleled emotions. In the midst of all this his eyes stand at attention, locked onto the perfectly dressed gentleman that stands before him.

Just now the young lady between us with the really big hair turned to the gentleman next to her and that has opened a line of sight for Doc and I. Okay, we just made eye contact. He seems startled and immediately here he comes! He has broken family rank and is headed toward me, combing through the people gathered. As I watch his anxiousness during his approach, I now truly understand why I'm here. We had first rediscovered one another because of his grandson wanting to learn golf and this special gathering was in honor of that same grandson. So, again at the innocent age of sixteen, young Ben has brought us together once more. Doc has finally reached me and we are embracing for what seems to be an eternity, neither of us seem willing to be the first to let go. Tears are flowing from all four eyes and the crowd has now turned its attention to this weird, yet sincere embrace of what appears to be two very different souls. I can imagine that on the surface we must seem to have nothing even remotely in common. Oh, but if they only knew!

As I look into the faces of the crowd I can see the curiousness of their expressions, all asking the same questions. Who is this man? Why has Doc Moller broken rank to greet him, and why are they both crying so hard? Throughout the embrace I can hear him saying aloud, "You came! You're here! You're here! I can't believe you're here." The humanity of him, that I've always wondered if was there, is now gushing out and I can feel the goodness in this special person. Finally, as the blessings are filtering through our mutually God-sent embrace, and my mind is spinning back a quarter century, back to the days of Central High. I know that I am touching a great friend. A friend who has tried to help develop and teach me in his own unique way, *a friend who has always seen me as a better person then mirrors ever reflected or people ever imagined.*

Thank God my emotions are finally allowing me to speak. "Doc, I wouldn't have missed being here for anything in the world." He's holding my hand and won't let go. He's squeezing and I'm squeezing back. I am so happy to be in his presence and he seems equally as happy to have me here. His grip is tight and sincere, fortunately for me because I am holding on for dear life, feeling as if I might fall far into uncertainty if he ever let go. He's picked me up so many times in life, always there just in the nick of time, never knowing his silent contributions. Now it's my turn to help him up and I've crossed the Caribbean Sea and parts of the Gulf of Mexico to do just that. These are powerful moments, splendor to one's being and the answer to so many prayers.

It seems the wind has finally decided to rest, there's a stillness in the air and a calm resolution to the proceedings, signaling its conclusion. The crowd has begun to stir and at last Doc and I feel safe enough to let go, for this special ceremony in honor of one of his grandsons has come to an end. Doc's quiet now, in fact everyone is, including me. I'm parked down the hill and he's headed in the opposite direction, toward the golf course. We're going our separate ways, slowly and solemnly. He has disappeared over the horizon, while I'm still descending from H-West, the hilltop address that I will never forget. Once down the hill I feel as though I have just visited some place close to the heavens. As someone once said, "it was the best of times and the worst of times."

The Letter

I just climbed into my vehicle and I'm headed out. I've made it about two blocks from the old golf course and I can hardly see through the emotion of the past moments. Man, I can't stop shaking. Wow, I'd better pull over. I've been just sitting here now on the side of the road for what seems like hours, but in reality it has only been a few minutes. At last, I'm somewhat composed.

Looking in my rear view mirror I find myself asking the same questions that all those faces asked back near the course. "Who is this man? Why did Dr. Moller break rank to greet him and why were they both crying so hard?" I'm thinking that I should try to write down those answers. I want to put it all in the form of a letter and let Doc know how much I appreciate all the things he has tried to do in strengthening my life. Okay, if I can just find some paper. Good, I found some. I've gathered all I can and I think it's more than enough to do the job. Let's see, I think I need this to be a letter from me, to Doc, for all time, here we go.

It has been about half an hour now and I'm still writing. The sun is trying to break through and I'm almost finished. Although the letter relates to the happenings of this unforgettable day, it also speaks volumes to lost times and sincere appreciation that echoes through nearly 25 years of memories. It tells of how my life has been impacted by a man that was so passionate and demanding of me and others he led. I'd thought of him as so different. But was he and was I so different from him?

I've paused while writing and I feel a calmness as my mind drifts back to 1979 again, that year we first met. As I travel back I feel that I've missed so much of what he was then and what he tried to do. Man, it is such a gloomy day. Yet, my thoughts and my 11 years at Central High School have just become sunny and crystal clear. I now understand with assuredness that, outside of my parents, this man that I thought to be so different and demanding is actually the greatest soul that ever touched my life! If you asked him, he would never lay claim to bettering anyone, he's not the type to take credit for such things. But on this day I can only reflect on all the things that he has done and how they altered my life for the good.

Once again my thoughts have returned to the pen and paper I am holding and all of a sudden the words I need for this letter are pouring out. All my contact with Doc back in those long lost and sometimes turbulent days are so vividly clear today. I now feel that what began twenty four years ago. The demands and drive for perfection, relative to me, was a powerful push that was meant not to harass but to enhance.

I took his push as over the top ridicule, unnecessary nagging and downright abuse of power every time I was confronted. Stupid observations and careless evaluations lead me to believe that he had an unsustainable biased agenda.

Now I realized that I had simply misinterpreted his message. The problem was the mirror, and the man inside that I had failed to deal with. Before meeting Doc, no one ever in life had asked the reflection within the glass for perfection in real life. Throughout our tenure Doc Moller didn't just ask for it, he consistently demanded it. Many of my positive attributes today can be traced directly back to those demands. The years we spent together always suggested that he thought I could be better. Until I was, he would not stop his relentless push. I never saw it then, but as I delve deeper and deeper into this letter I draw further and further back to our times together within the great Four Sides that is Omaha Central High School.

It would seem that ours had been a chance encounter created by a random assignment of public school officials. I see it as more than that. God was with both of us and only His power could make this chance encounter happen. Today across the street, while Doc held one hand I felt His spirit in the other. As we gripped tighter and squeezed harder I was thinking; to work the gold mines of California back in the day, brought thousands; to dig out the diamonds in Africa, worth millions; the oil wells of Dubai, billions... ***but to work with someone that believed me to be more than I ever thought I could?*** Again that word... ***PRICELESS!***

> I'd like the tears of those who grieve to dry before the sun of happy memories.
> Ben Hofmeister

My thoughts today seem all too dramatic, but believe me they are genuine. Now, as my mind slowly returns to the letter, I am reconnected to the task at hand. Oddly, I see the papers are filled with words, but I hardly remember writing them. A few more strokes of the pen and there, I am done. As I look to the sky, all of a sudden, amazingly the sun has brilliantly taken over. It has broken up some rather ominous clouds that blanketed the entire morning. As that is happening I am proofreading the last lines of the writing, and with that, I've finished my letter to Doc.

With this bright sunshine I remember my golf clubs are in the trunk. Despite the chill in the air I am thinking of the days when I walked the grounds and played the little 9 hole Cedar Hills Golf Course, just across the street behind me. Golf has always relaxed me. Oh, how I wish I could have stayed and played back there this morning. But I couldn't, because you see, the Old Cedar Hills Golf Course was converted in 1992 to the Resurrection Cemetery. Now, on this the fifth day of November 2003, after losing his battle with a rare cancer on October 31st, Doc's eldest grandson and one of my favorite students, young Benjamin Scott Hofmeister was being laid to rest adjacent to it in Evergreen Memorial Park. Sadly, on a plot of land in a section marked H-West a part of his parents, Risa and Ron, brother Jackson and his grandparents Doc and Betty was being laid there with him. These are times when one hardly knows what to say, ponders what to do, with no idea where to go. Today, we all said our goodbyes and went home, while Ben, I am sure, headed on up to heaven.

This day's tomorrow will be Doc's 74th birthday. I know if it was possible his gift this morning would have been to give that birthday to young Ben, while majestically taking his place back there at H-West. But he can't. So, instead for his birthday I sent him a gift. A letter from the heart. One that mourns a life he lost and thanks him for one he helped to save. Like I said, it was the best of times and the worst of times.

This Is That Letter

MAYA MOUNTAINS
RESORTS

William A. Reed, President/CEO
Maya Mountains Resorts
643 N. 98th St; PMB 110
Omaha, NE 68114-2347

November 3, 2005

Dear Doc,

I am stopped here in my car, just leaving Ben's gravesite, not knowing whether to turn right or left, whether to go forward or backwards or whether maybe to just sit still. I decided that to sit still is the very best option.

I need to write this letter to you Doc, not for you, but more for me. I was out of town when in a phone conversation a friend told me she had read about your grandson in the obituaries. Immediately I knew it was Ben. I could only imagine at that moment how much he, his parents and you and Betty had gone through these last few years. I was immediately heartbroken. Heartbroken because I knew a great kid had been denied the chance to become a man, and that a man whom I admire and respect so much must have been devastatingly hurt.

I saw the love, Doc, between you and your grandsons. I saw what you gave them and I saw the love and respect they gave back. You were so good with Ben, so solidly behind him and so good in your support to his activities. I was not surprised at all to learn of his brilliance and his brash and sophisticated demeanor. This child had perhaps the best possible grandparents in the world, and I know for sure the best grandpa.

If I had turned right back there it would have taken me to your daughter's home, had I gone left it would have taken me home. I really wanted to go to your daughter and son-in-law's house, but I knew the crowd would be deep, so I didn't want to encroach upon them and their time with people that I know have been there every minute. Had I gone to their home, I can only think what I might have said to them. I think I would have said that the strength and courage they showed in the service was conducive to a uniqueness I have never before witnessed.

You may remember hearing last year about a 16-year-old child named Ryan Johnston from West Harrison high school in Mondarnin, Iowa. He was a child that I had also given lessons to. He was the star quarterback on the football team, #1 golfer at the school and an honor student. Finishing a summer workout after weight training, he collapsed and died in the gym. Days later, I was called to that same gym by his father to speak to the students and teachers of the school, as well as the citizens of the small town to try to make sense of it all. They said I did well, and later every student who appreciated it signed a huge card and delivered it to me, just to say thanks. It was difficult for me to speak for Ryan, as my relationship had only been as "golf coach".

In the church today, I thought about Ron and Risa and multiplied the hurt that I had felt speaking at Ryan's funeral by 1,000, knowing that as parents, their pain in losing Ben is unimaginable. I am sending them a copy of this letter to say to them that never have I witnessed in such a service the magnificence and sincerity of a father's letter, or the deep love and appreciation in a mother's voice echo throughout a church. I was deeply touched. It was as if Risa was speaking from the heavens. I thought surely Ben was hearing her. I truly wanted to share with them how I need so much for my letter to you to say to them that their participation in this service honoring their son spoke volumes of their dedication and respect for his life. No parents want to ever have to lay their child to rest. If ever I must see again where parents have to, I hope it is with pride, dignity and respect. Like Ron and Risa Hofmeister had to one crisp, cold day in November.

I think Doc that during this time when you have experienced what I know is your greatest loss, that maybe it would be good to hear about a life you saved. In your wildest dreams, Doc, you could not know what it has meant to my life to have you bring your grandsons to me to offer them educational instruction. In my life, which at times has been filled with turmoil, I was given hope and a purpose when this great lover of perfection in education, chose me!!!

You have taught me so much Doc, and in most cases without even knowing or trying. Oh, we all have problems as you have said to me so often. But the point is how we deal with them. Long ago you attempted to teach me how to be a teacher, or at least that's what I thought. I didn't learn until years later that in reality you were teaching me to be a man. You dared to challenge me in mediocre times. Times when you knew I wasn't doing my best. You demanded that I raise myself to a level above. I was too naive during those years to understand, but about five years removed I realized that the greatest life that has ever touched mine is one Gaylord E. Moller. For a long time the lessons you tried to teach me at Central have surfaced in the form of an education in life. I know you won't want to hear all this or take credit for doing so much, but the truth is that you have. "You can't be respected without first being respectable". This was a birthday card you once gave me. I still have it. You taught me how to handle adversity, how to face my problems, how to be efficient, the importance of punctuality, the effectiveness of planning and the total necessity of following through. These are all things that make a man, and today I try to keep things to those standards.

As you brought Ben to me for golf you taught me another lesson. That lesson was how to be a grandpa. Your caring, giving and loving compassion taught me again what a man is supposed to do. My heart is bursting for you, because as the song says — "When grandkids go to heaven, grandpas should be there waiting". There is so much good time you gave Ben, Doc and because of that he was able to get more out of his very short life, a life short in years but so long in accomplishments. You thanked me for coming. Doc, I couldn't possibly not come. There isn't a grandpa alive that deserves more to see his grandson grow up to be a man than you. Today at the church and along the gravesite I wept. I wept first because Ben was gone, next I wept for his parents, brother and Betty for their indescribable loss. But most of all I wept for my friend, a man that helped me and many other lives to be better, a man that saved so many, now having to lose so much. I am so sorry Doc, I'm just numb from head to toe. My heart is with you, Betty, Ron, Risa and Jackson. I have confidence that somehow you will know what to do to help everyone through this, especially Jackson. Until then I pray for your strength, happiness and overall well-being. My heart went down with yours today, Doc. I have never had a more important teacher. I have never learned better lessons than from you. I can only imagine your pain. I love you. I really mean that.

Thanks forever,

William

Afterword

What a great kid you were and what a great man you would have been. On this day when I embraced my friend and life teacher, it was a strong and sincere embrace. We cried together and indeed our tears did dry before the sun of happy memories that were left when life was done. **Just as Ben wanted.**

I've since heard about some of the young men and women that were closest to Ben. Among them there was a strong consensus that as he faced his own mortality, he never allowed any of them to stop to feel sorry for his unfortu- nate plight. Instead he sought to uplift them at every turn by showing happi- ness, spirit and a genuine appreciation for life, no matter how short. Now and then I visit Evergreen Memorial Park to thank Ben for bringing his grandpa back to my life. I've become quite acquainted with the manager out there. We always talk for a bit and then I head on up to H-West. I call it "Ben's place". There's this rare and beautiful pine tree that stands majestically guarding the site. I asked the manager and the caretaker for the name of the tree but neither could define it. It seems that no one knows its identity. He said, "All I know is that it's a very rare breed." And I said "yes, rare indeed, like Ben Hofmeister, Doc's grandson and my golf student." He is sorely missed!

Epilogue

Life comes, people live, people die and all sorts of good and bad things hap- pen along the way. Some are fortunate, as luck and hard work bind themselves to make unimaginable dreams come true. Still sometimes it all seems so cruel- ly unfair. At the funeral of a great person and former Omaha Central assistant principal, Mr. Jim Wilson, one of my closest friends Dr. Jerry Bartee delivered a farewell. In it he said, "I don't always understand what God does, but I trust what He does!" Those are profound words that I think we should all adhere to. Like my wife said, we're all headed for that inevitable end, praying that the journey indeed will take us to a better place. *"I think that heaven is an open gate but it seems you have to go through hell to get there!"* *W.R.O.* I know, because in this life I've visited both places, right here on earth.

So many of us go through life and never get to truly see it for what it is. I got a great view of it from 1979 to 1990, when a great man touched my life during my eleven years within the four sides of one of the great high schools anywhere, Omaha Central. On a dreary cool day in November, I watched that man lose a part of himself alongside a gravesite lined with tears. Since then I've watched him give the rest of that self to the many within his vast circle that may have found themselves in need. I am blessed to be of that circle and it is within those parameters that this strange tale has emerged, a tale of caring, giving, loving, working, respect and discipline. All of it combining to form a system of belief that gave a burned out light a new brilliance. That light is me. To close, I submit that I simply believe in Doc, because although from far different worlds, he always believed that mine could be better.

As someone once said, only in this country is such a bizarre story even pos- sible, let alone true. May my wife always rest in peace; God save these United States and the great state of Nebraska; God bless Dr. Gaylord E. Moller, never forget Ben Hofmeister and long live Omaha Central High School forever.

In Conclusion

I just found out the name of the tree that marks Ben's gravesite, It's called a Blue Juniper! When defined, blue is the color of constancy, while juniper is of Latin derivative from the word Juniperus, meaning young, youth producing or evergreen. Ben was young and constantly produced much as a youth and he is buried in Evergreen Cemetery! What a great statement for an ending... But instead I choose a beginning.

Blue Junipers Forever

Susan A. Buffett, Class of 1971 An avid supporter of her alma mater, as well as an advocate for all children and people in need. Her direct involvement made the extensive land exchange between the Joslyn Art Museum, Creighton University, and the Omaha Public Schools a reality that culminated in the construction of the new Seemann Stadium on Central's campus. It is said that Susan Buffett wakes up every morning with plans to help the deserving wherever possible.

Peter Kiewit, Class of 1918 At 20 years of age, Peter assumed management of the local construction firm founded by his grandfather in 1884 and built it into one of the world's largest construction and mining enterprises. As a civic and philanthropic leader, he created The Kiewit Foundation which continues as the largest private charitable foundation in Nebraska. Peter Kiewit died in 1979.

Edward Zorinsky, Class of 1945 Ed was elected to the United States Senate in 1976 and re-elected in 1982. As chairman of key sub-committees on the Agriculture and Foreign Relations Senate Committees, he received national recognition for sponsoring landmark legislation, and he was also known for his watchdog activity on behalf of the American taxpayer. Ed Zorinksy died in 1987.

Henry Fonda, Class of 1923 Henry J. Fonda appeared in 87 films and 21 plays during his long and distinguished career. Two of his most acclaimed performances were as Tom Joad in the film, "The Grapes of Wrath," and as Mister Roberts in the Broadway play and movie of the same name. In 1981 he received an Academy Award for best actor in the film "On Golden Pond." He died in 1982.

Larry W. Station, Jr., Class of 1982 Larry was a college football player for the University of Iowa. Station, who played linebacker, is Iowa's leader in career tackles and was twice named as a consensus first team All-American. He was inducted into the College Football Hall of Fame in 2009. Larry was one of the three living of the nine initial players to have his name enshrined in the Ring of Honor inside Iowa Hawkeye Stadium.

Alan J. Heeger, Class of 1953 Alan J. Heeger was awarded the Nobel Prize in Chemistry in 2000 for "the discovery and development of conductive polymers." He holds forty patents and has authored over 650 scholarly publications. Heeger is currently professor of Physics at the University of California, Santa Barbara.

Dr. Jack K. Lewis, Class of 1952 Jack K. Lewis, M.D., has served as volunteer physician for Central High's sports programs for over 35 years. After receiving his first degree from Stanford University, he obtained his medical degree from the University of Nebraska College of Medicine where he then served as a professor of internal medicine. Jack Lewis maintains a private medical practice in Omaha.

Ahman Green, Class of 1995 Green is a former American football running back who played twelve seasons in the National Football League (NFL). He is the all-time leading rusher for the Green Bay Packers. Green also played for the Houston Texans, and was a four-time Pro Bowl selection with the Packers. He is now a co-owner of the Green Bay Blizzard of the Indoor Football League.

Susan T. Buffett, Class of 1950 Susan Thompson Buffett's leadership -psychologically and spiritually- in the late 1960's and early 1970's was responsible more than that of any other parent for "keeping Central Central." Susie and her three children made significant civic, artistic, and social contributions to their communities. She served as president of The Buffett Foundation until her death in 2004. Her foundation continues to help and serve deserving individuals and diverse causes across the country and around the world.

Jarvis Offutt, Born and raised in Omaha, NE. Attended Lawrenceville Prep before attending Yale University where he was a member of Battery B of the Yale Batteries. In 1917 he was part of the U.S. Army Aviation Section of the Signal Corps. Transferred to France, he was killed while performing duties as a pilot. One of the great Air Force bases in the United States, Offutt Air Base, in Bellevue, Nebraska is named in his honor.

Roger W. Sayers, Class of 1960 In 1962 and 1963, while competing for UNO, Roger W. Sayers won consecutive NAIA championships in the 100 meters while also winning the 200 meter championship in 1963. In 1962, Roger was selected as a member of the United States Track Team, competing in dual meets against both Poland and the Soviet Union. Roger has been inducted into the University of Nebraska at Omaha Hall of Fame, the Nebraska Black Sports Hall of Fame, the Omaha Sports Hall of Fame, and the Nebraska High School Sports Hall of Fame.

Dr. Jerry Bartee, Class of 1966 Dr. Jerry Bartee's career has included successful positions with Creighton University as its head baseball coach and with the Omaha Public Schools as a teacher at Nathan Hale Middle School, assistant principal and principal at South High School, and as the Assistant Superintendent for Business Services for the district. He has been recognized by his colleagues both for his leadership and for his compassion. Throughout his personal life and in his educational career, Dr. Bartee has been "a decisive leader who inspires distinguished performance and motivates others to do their best." He will always be known as "a person who believed that every child was to be valued and had the right to a quality education."

Dorothy McGuire, Last attended 1932, Dorothy McGuire enjoyed a long and distinguished career as a star of both stage and screen. She received an Academy Award nomination for best actress in 1947 for her role in the film, "Gentleman's Agreement". She got her start on stage in 1930 at the Omaha Community Playhouse opposite Henry Fonda when she was 13. She played summer stock in 1934 and got her break on Broadway in 1938 in "Our Town". She died in 2001.

The Honorary Kenneth C. Stephan, Class of 1964 Kenneth Stephan was appointed to the Nebraska Supreme Court in 1997 by Governor Ben Nelson. Justice Stephan received a B.A. from the University of Nebraska in 1968 and a J.D. with High Distinction from the University of Nebraska College of Law in 1972. He served in Korea with U. S. Army Intelligence and spent 24 years in Lincoln as a private practice attorney. Justice Stephan lives in Lincoln and returns to Central to speak to Law and Justice classes.

Dr. Albert B. Crum, Class of 1949 A world renowned Physician/Research Scientist/Psychiatrist/Forensic expert providing Traumatic Stress Assessment, Court Testimony, Psychiatric Consultations, and Independent Medical/Forensic Evaluations. A Harvard Medical School graduate and a member of Phi Beta Kappa, Dr. Crum has been approved for life full membership in the Sigma Xi, The Scientific Research Society. Dr. Crum is a former Clinical Professor of Behavioral Science, Management Science and Adjunct Professor of Base Science (Biological Science, Medicine and Surgery) at New York University.

Charles Thomas Munger, Class of 1941 is an American business magnate, lawyer, investor, and philanthropist. He is Vice-Chairman of Berkshire Hathaway Corporation, the diversified investment corporation chaired by Warren Buffett; in this capacity, Buffett describes Charlie Munger as "my partner." Munger served as chairman of Wesco Financial Corporation from 1984 through 2011 (Wesco was approximately 80%-owned by Berkshire-Hathaway during that time). He is also the chairman of the Daily Journal Corporation, based in Los Angeles, California, and a director of Costco Wholesale Corporation.

Gale Sayers, Class of 1961 Football player Gale Sayers was the youngest player to join the Pro Football Hall of Fame. He played running back for the Chicago Bears. "I don't care to be remembered as the man who scored six touchdowns in a game. I want to be remembered as a winner in life." He played for the University of Kansas before being drafted by the Chicago Bears in 1965 and being named Rookie of the Year. In 1977, he was the youngest player to be inducted into the Pro Football Hall of Fame.

James W. Fous, Class of 1964 While on reconnaissance mission in Vietnam May 14, 1968, James Fous leaped on a grenade intended for the members of his unit, absorbing the blast with his body, sacrificing his life to save the lives of the three comrades with him on patrol. For this act of gallantry and extraordinary heroism, he was awarded the Congressional Medal of Honor, the nation's highest military honor. While at Central James participated in baseball, football, O-club, and Outdoorsman Club. He attended Omaha University where he majored in business before joining the U.S. Army in 1967.

Richard Holland, Class of 1939 Richard attended UNO, majoring in chemistry; but he returned after his World War II service as an officer in the chemical corps to major in art. After graduation, he followed his father into the advertising firm that the elder Holland had founded. Richard built it into the company that would handle such accounts as the First National Bank, Uniroyal, Valmont Industries. It wasn't long until he discovered that his fortuitous investment with that which was to become Berkshire Hathaway, enabling him to pursue his and his wife's philanthropic interests. The Holland Center for the Performing Arts, Opera Omaha, the Bemis Center for Contemporary Arts, the Child Saving Institute, the Winners Circle, Joslyn Art Museum, and the Omaha Symphony are just a few organizations that have benefited from his generosity.

Brenda J. Council, Class of 1971 Brenda J. Council served on the Omaha School Board a total of 11 years including four terms as President and two as Vice President. Omaha voters then elected her to the city council. Her community service includes membership on boards for banks, private foundations, and theater groups, and she has been the recipient of numerous awards and honors from local, state, and national organizations and universities.

Lawrence R. Klein, Class of 1938 Lawrence R. Klein was awarded the Nobel Prize for economics in 1980 for his work in econometric forecasting. As President Jimmy Carter's economic adviser, he urged more coordinated international efforts to improve overall world economics. He has received 28 honorary degrees from universities in fifteen countries. Lawrence Klein was Professor of Economics (Emeritus) at the University of Pennsylvania before he passed away in 2013.

Keith Jones, Class of 1984 Jones ran for 1,710 yards and 18 TDs as a senior for Coach William Reed at Omaha Central, breaking records set 23 years earlier by Gale Sayers. He ran for a high-school career-high 235 yards against state champion Creighton Prep and 216 yards against runner-up Omaha Gross. Keith received a full ride scholarship to the University of Nebraska, where he starred as a running back. He was drafted by the Dallas Cowboys where he played for 3 years.

Wynonie Harris, Last attended in 1931, Wyononie Harris is gererally recognized as one of the rock 'n' rolls forefathers. He had 15 Top 10 hits on Billboard magazine's rhythm and blue charts from 1946 through 1952. With a fullthroated baritone voice and dynamic stage presence, he eaned the nickname "Mr. Blues. His signature hit was "Good Rockin' Tonight," which was released in 1948 and spent 25 weeks on the R&B's charts peaking at No. 1. A non-graduate of Central, Wynonie was last attended in the school in 1931. He died in 1969.

Inga Swenson Harris, Class of 1950 Regarded as one of her generation's most versatile actresses, Inga Swenson has starred on Broadway, London's West End, at the American Shakespeare Festival, and in regional and stock theatres across the country. Two of her major films are "The Miracle Worker" and "Advise and Consent." In the 60's Inga received Tony nominations for starring in the Broadway musicals, "110 in The Shade" and "Baker Street." Inga is retired and lives in Los Angeles.

Maurtice Ivy, Class of 1984 Maurtice A. Ivy is noteworthy as a high school, college, and professional athlete. She was the highest scoring player for her four years at Central, putting 1,928 points on the board. She started all four seasons in high school, finishing with fifty straight victories and two Class A Championships. In addition to her basketball prowess, she earned six gold medals in track, helping her team win the two state championships. She was an inductee into the Nebraska Black Sports Hall of Fame, the Nebraska High School Sports Hall of Fame in 1998, and the Omaha Public Schools Athletic Hall of Fame in 2006. She went on to play for the University of Nebraska and in 2011 became only the second women's basketball player to have her jersey number (30) retired.

VIRGINIA LEE PRATT

Here is where many books will say, and we all lived happily ever after. But the truth is that in the midst of living we all die. And there's never any happiness in that.

Along with the publishing of this book came the passing of Miss Virginia Lee Pratt. She was crowned Omaha Central Queen in 1937, taught for decades and died with her crown still intact. Her genuineness was witnessed by thousands and like they said back in 1937, she will forever be the ideal Central girl.

Her legacy is that she taught many the disciplines of life through the eyes of mathematics... she was 96 years old. God bless the Queen.

THE
FOUR SIDES

One

Central High

Two

Dr. Gaylord Moller

Three

Coach William Reed

Four

The Letter